The Preacher's Guide to Suicide

The Preacher's Guide to Suicide

A Homiletical Theology of Death

H. C. JOHNSON

RESOURCE *Publications* · Eugene, Oregon

THE PREACHER'S GUIDE TO SUICIDE
A Homiletical Theology of Death

Resource Publications
An Imprint of Wipf and Stock Publishers
199 W. 8th Ave., Suite 3
Eugene, OR 97401

www.wipfandstock.com

PAPERBACK ISBN: 978-1-6667-3460-7
HARDCOVER ISBN: 978-1-6667-9064-1
EBOOK ISBN: 978-1-6667-9065-8

MARCH 17, 2022 10:45 AM

For Aaron

I thank my God every time I remember you . . . . (Phil 1:3)

Contents

Preface

SOMETIMES THE STORIES OF the Gospels are so well-known that many of their details are no longer striking to us. For instance, in Mark 12:41–44, "Jesus sat down opposite the place where the offerings were put and watched the crowd putting their money into the temple treasury. Many rich people threw in large amounts. But a poor widow came and put in two very small copper coins, worth only a few cents. Calling his disciples to him, Jesus said, 'Truly I tell you, this poor widow has put more into the treasury than all the others. They all gave out of their wealth; but she, out of her poverty, put in everything—all she had to live on.'"

This widow has all the signs of someone who is totally hopeless. She is exhibiting the identifying markers that suggest that she is susceptible to suicide. She fits the demographics of someone who is at risk: she is a widow, she is poor, and then, she gave everything away—all that she had to live on. Well, if you give all that you have to live on, how can you live? She gives everything to the Temple.

She gave away her precious life to a tainted institution. Her money, all her money, was given to an establishment that had become corrupt. She had nothing to live on. The widow is not an example of good financial giving! I know, we preachers like to use her as an example of steward-ship for our stewardship Sundays and campaign drives—but really, she's the modern-day equivalent of a senior citizen who has been tricked into giving out her bank account information to a criminal charity that was not a charity at all—just a front for some swindler to line the pockets of the rich Sadducee sell-outs who were obsessed with social standing. She's giving money *to them*? The widow is not an example of good financial giving. No—she is hurting. And what does Jesus do? He points her out to the disciples. He does not praise her for her actions, he simply points her out and describes her actions.

Doesn't Jesus know that she presents many of the signs for active suicide ideation? Why doesn't Jesus do something? Why doesn't Jesus go to her and ask, "Ma'am—are you thinking of killing yourself?" But instead, Jesus turns his attention away to his disciples, to a conversation about the large and massive stones of the temple. And the widow simply walks away. I have felt like the widow before: people comment about me but never step in to connect with me. I have felt—what the heck, it doesn't even matter, my piddly life—not even worth two cents. And the widow simply walks away. Jesus! Don't let her walk away!

Why didn't Jesus do something? He provided food for the five thousand. "The blind receive sight, the lame walk, those who have leprosy are cleansed, the deaf hear, the dead are raised, and the good news is proclaimed to the poor."[1] But this widow is not like the blind, she is not like the lame, she is not like the deaf. No, she is very different. Others were a fulfillment of prophecy, but she—she is not a fulfillment; rather, she is a foreshadow. For in her suicidal giving, she foreshadows God's ultimate generosity.

In a way, it would almost seem that Jesus looks to her as a role model.

Jesus . . . be like her.

Jesus . . . die like her.

Jesus . . . give it all away . . . all away . . . to the church . . . to a corrupted, sin-stained institution. One that would eventually call for the crusades and slaughter countless Muslims, that would call for the inquisition and massacre and persecute thousands of Christians, that would support slavery, that would steal native land, that would drown witches in Salem, and that would turn a blind eye to the sex scandals that continue to ravage the church to this day. Jesus, you are going to cast your life, your precious life, away for *that*? The absurdity of the gospel!

Friends, "very rarely will anyone die for a righteous man, though for a good man someone might possibly dare to die. But God demonstrated his own love for us, that while we were still sinners . . . ,"[2] Christ cast his life as an offering into the coffer.[3]

This book is designed with the preacher in mind. The preacher who deeply cares about God's word and the life-giving power it offers from the Word who died. This book is for the preacher who preaches to

1. Isa 35:5 and Matt 11:5.

2. Rom 5:7.

3. An excerpt from the sermon "Giving Everything Away," delivered by H. Johnson, Lee University, Fall 2018.

a congregation, who has been touched by suicide, and might wonder out loud with Abinadab, "Why my son?"[4] This book is for the preacher who, too, might raise a fist to the sky and ask the question, "How long, Lord? How long?"[5] This book is meant to be an interdisciplinary conversation to empower and equip the preacher in the task of suicide awareness from the pulpit. Ultimately, this book hopes to aid the preacher in his or her daily task of preaching Christ crucified. For the fundamental conviction of this book is that our common responses to suicide should be pruned by a heightened appreciation of the centrality of the death of Christ as a reality and a metaphor for living. Instead of affirming life at all costs and denying death, this book argues that we can only grapple with suicide by learning to die to ourselves and thus die well. It does not labor under the illusion that all readers will quickly be convinced by some of its radical claims; but, if the book breaks up interpretive inertia and prompts a commitment to preaching grounded in the Word then it will be deemed successful.

4. 2 Sam 6:1–7.

5. Ps 13:1.

Acknowledgments

SUICIDE IS ONE OF those topics that touches everyone. Even if some have never known suicide first-hand, they still have a strong opinion about it. The shared voice on the topic of suicide is immense. As one might notice from the extensive footnotes within, this has been a communal project between many friends, family, colleagues, and strangers, even distant strangers over time and place. I am thankful for the many voices who have contributed through the generations to this project. I am grateful to the numerous faculty at Aquinas Institute of Theology, especially Honora Werner and to the colleagues who encouraged my project in the earliest stages. Gratitude goes to the Lilly Foundation who sponsored the Aquinas Institute Delaplane Preaching Scholars and who provided me an opportunity to listen, learn and write. Thank you, Gregory Heille, Deborah Wilhelm, and Martha Brune Rapp for your leadership, critique, and hours of editing suggestions. I want to recognize the pivotal role Paul and Darlia Conn played in their vision for Chapel at Lee University, providing me numerous opportunities to preach suicide awareness. Thank you to the countless faculty at Lee University who stepped in and reassured me, especially David Broersma who read an initial draft and gave me helpful feedback. Likewise, I am grateful for Cleveland Fellowship and those Elders who loved me, cheered me on, and most importantly, called me to preach. I have deep gratitude for Albian Elizabeth and Asher Pascal, for their faithful encouragement. Finally, thank you to Aaron P. Johnson for hours of editing my manuscript and providing a critical sound board for thoughts and ideas. Thank you for not giving up. God has provided me an expansive community, beyond my imagination, all so that this project could become a reality. Overall, I am so very thankful to my Creator, the One who gives life and the One who takes life. Thanks be to God.

1

Moving from Numbers to Words

The Trouble with Suicide Prevention

I HEARD A STORY once of a man who jumped from a forty-second-story apartment window. As he was falling, he thought, he wondered, he considered, and then when approaching the twenty-fourth story he said, "So far so good." When I told this story at the family table, my eighteen-year-old daughter replied with snarky cynicism, "Life, liberty, and the pursuit of happiness." I took her response as interpreting the falling man as one trapped in blind optimism, delusional, as he is headed to utter destruction. I recalled the words of the well-known song by the band R.E.M.,

> Save yourself, serve yourself
> World serves its own needs . . .
> It's the end of the word as we know it and I feel fine.[1]

A rather different response was registered by my eleven-year-old niece. Aghast, she looked at me and asked, "But the man is going to die, how is that good?" My daughter answered, "It's good because he chose it." I had originally misunderstood my daughter. She wasn't being cynical, she was holding up human agency as the defining mark of a "good life," even if that "good life" led to death. Indeed, the good life does lead to

---

1. R.E.M., "It's the End of the World as We Know It."

death; or better formulated, death leads to the good life, because after all, isn't this what we preach? Christ crucified.

I do not know why Sara, my seventeen-year-old neighbor, bright, athletic, and outgoing, decided to die by suicide several years ago. She had friends; she had ambitions; she said she wanted to be a nurse and sail with *Doctors Without Borders*. And she had a family that attended church regularly including many extended relatives who lived in our same town, which made for a very busy and loud Christmas holiday. Sara had a good life, so why did she look towards death? Her mother Amy was haunted by the "text-book" answers that the school counselor provided as to why Sara chose death. There was no note, no red flags. Amy said that she was totally taken by surprise and left in utter shock. A decade later, Amy told me, with an air of embarrassment, that she was so desperate to understand Sara that she had attended multiple suicide prevention training events hosted by the local community college. Amy said she took notes and offered them to me as I wrote this book. But then she said, "My notes have lots of numbers and statistics . . . but . . . they won't tell you anything about Sara."

Like Amy, I too have attended suicide awareness and prevention seminars. But unlike Amy, I wasn't attending specifically to learn about a unique individual. My intent was to learn about suicide in general. And that is what you get when you attend a seminar: suicide in general. Whenever I have participated in a suicide awareness seminar or training event, the instructor always begins with statistics demonstrating numerically just how damaging the situation of suicide is. Then the instructor moves to signs and risks of suicide ideation. Usually, the seminar will then provide phone numbers to call if you should happen to see the telltale signs of someone going beyond just thinking of suicide.[2] Sometimes, after all the formal information is presented, the instructor will open the session up for role-play. These are those awkward moments when students have to partner up and one has to pretend to be suicidal while the other has to talk the suicidal person to the point where they make a promise or a plan not to hurt themselves until they can call that special number and

---

2. Just because someone thinks about or has ideas about suicide does not mean the person is suicidal (see chapter 8). The problem is with the word "idea." Since pondering suicide does not always indicate suicidality, scales have been developed to determine risk. One of the most popular scales is the Columbia Suicide Severity Rating Scale. In response to diverse opinions about suicide, others have developed their own scales such as the Beck Scale, Nurses Global Assessment Scale, or the Suicidal Affect-Behavior-Cognition Scale.

get professional help. This template is typical for how a suicide awareness seminar goes. I have been to dozens and they follow pretty much the same layout, starting with numbers (statistics) and ending with numbers (phone helplines).[3]

After attending so many suicide seminars, I started noticing some discrepancies in the statistical information being presented. Maybe an instructor had older statistics, or maybe they got them from a different source, but it became very obvious that the stats were as varied as the humans who were collecting the data. Anyhow, if someone's friend dies by suicide, no matter how much statistical data is thrown at the grieving, their friend will never be just a statistic to them. The deceased will never be just a number. They will only and ever be a friend, that unique individual who cannot count for just a number. I often wondered what a suicide seminar would be like if we cut out the stats and started with personal stories, with pictures of people, a variety and diversity of people, young and old, employed and unemployed, married and unmarried, healthy and sick, Asian and African, female and male, mothers and sons . . . yet, in suicide awareness seminars we usually start and end with numbers.

Social sciences regularly present statistical evidence as "awareness." Unfortunately, numbers are not adequate "awareness."[4] I have watched educated adults sit through a seminar only to have their eyes glaze over with all the percentage signs and charts feeling a sense of relief when all one has to do is call a crisis information phone number. Seminars are really aimed more at crisis intervention than awareness and prevention. The so-called suicide "awareness" seminars often present statistical facts and then information on who to call when the crisis is in process, relaying the message that one needs to leave "crisis intervention" up to the professionals.

Many suicide "awareness" seminars offer very little or no time for conversation and discourse. And even when there has been time allotted for conversation, the material that was presented was not presented in a manner that solicited deep discussion. The seminar often ended with "Are there any questions?" about the statistical material presented. It

3. Even the QPRT *Suicide Risk Assessment and Management* certification program founded by one of the top suicidologists, Dr. Paul Quinnett, follows a similar outline.

4. Jean Baechler affirms the idea that statistics should not be the base line for understanding suicide (*Suicides*, 5, 6, 26). Raymond Aron rightly states in the foreword, "One must not begin the study of suicide with statistical correlations but with the analysis of individual cases" (xiii).

is very challenging to have questions about statistical information and challenging for the instructor to have answers. For example, if the questions were—"Why is there a discrepancy between that one database and another database? Do these numbers represent only Coroner's reports?[5] How was the statistical information influenced by cultural norms of suicide?" These questions might seem impossible for the instructor to answer since they did not gather the data themselves but are simply reporting it from other sources.

Likewise, in suicide awareness seminars, the lecture usually begins with the behavior of the individual rather than with the collective. I have never attended a suicide awareness seminar where the opening lecture focused on larger cultural and communal issues like the decline of the church, the rise in firearms, the decline in marriage, or the rise of social media addiction. Sadly, "From the outside each death is merely death. It always looks the same and can be defined exactly by medicine and by law. When suicide is a description of behavior and defined as self-destruction . . . all suicides are just suicide. The individual person who has chosen this death has become 'a suicide.'"[6] Thus, suicide awareness seminars fail to give any attention to communal culpability. To do so, of course, would implicate everyone.

Ultimately, the real shortcoming of suicide awareness seminars is the consistent lack of any discussion[7] on the complexity of suicide regarding definitions, contexts, and its place within a communal, biblical and theological framework. Psychology, as a discipline, might say "Suicide is a psychological problem, therefore, leave it to us," while patronizingly patting the pastor on the head. Often pastors will glibly support the authoritative position of psychologists within modern society by offering the excuse that their "gifts" are not within the realm of psychology, they are only "preachers" after all. But psychology is not the definitive field of expertise on human life, whether in terms of research and data or of

5. I recently was made aware of the fact that coroners do not need education beyond a bachelor's degree. The coroner is an elected position. Medical examiners on the other hand need further education and certification. See "Medical Examiners and Coroners," *Suicide Prevention Online Training*.

6. Selden, *The Suicide Solution*, 42.

7. Recognizing the need for open and honest conversation, Dr. Nicole McArthur created *Not One More Vet* after the "world renowned veterinarian" Dr. Sophia Yin died by suicide. See McArthur, *Not One More Vet*.

treatment.[8] Furthermore, suicide is not just a social and psychological matter, but rather it is a spiritual, theological, and ecclesial issue.[9]

The suicide awareness seminars won't say this, but one cannot fully grasp suicide without delving into words. Understanding nuances of the complexity of suicide within a diversity of disciplines includes a multi-dimensional exploration of psychology, sociology, history, literature, medicine, law, and even popular media. Suicide awareness is word-awareness. I have become increasingly cognizant that suicide awareness has a very broad and even contradictory knowledge base that has produced lots of different words. And as a homiletician, I have also learned that defining one's terms is pivotal for sermon preparation. A Christian understanding of suicide is rooted in conversation: a conversation with the Bible, the Christian tradition, the social and behavioral sciences, and our contemporary cultural voices carried on through words.

Clearly, one way to state your case is to present the *need* first; but there are other ways to present the need besides drowning people in numbers. Yearly statistics and phone numbers are not sufficient for awareness because they are designed to pad the listener with facts and a phone number for simple response in the face of a current crisis. Remarkably, with all the suicide prevention workshops, suicide is still increasing. Maybe because awareness is not crisis intervention. Awareness must involve the education that provides a new framework of thinking and preemptive action, ideally avoiding the crisis altogether.

Just on the basis of these brief remarks, there should be a growing recognition that a fundamentally flawed assumption is lurking behind the term "awareness."[10] It is flawed to think that there is a single

8. I have often been asked, "If there are so many suicide prevention and crisis intervention services now, why then is suicide on the rise? Is it because there are more people with more mental health issues than ever before? Or maybe there are just more people in general? Are the intervention services actually working?" Such questions imply that the current set of solutions by "experts" is ineffective. In fact, Frank Selden states, "Psychiatry is not the solution to suicide" (Selden, *The Suicide Solution*, 105).

9. Sometimes people just want to talk about suicide, but they are afraid to even broach the topic for fear that someone will think they are suicidal, perpetuating the lack of honest discussion and furthering the silence.

10. I make a differentiation between the terms "crisis intervention," "prevention" and "awareness." To understand the difference an analogy is helpful. If prevention looked like a motor vehicle passenger wearing a seat belt, awareness would be the prompting bell reminding the passenger to wear the seat belt in the first place. Assuming that the passenger had been educated about the possible risks of driving in a car, the hope is then that the passenger would choose to wear a seat belt in order

unambiguous experience and once we are informed, we will possess the proper "awareness" to respond to it adequately. Suicide is not a singular, monolithic phenomenon about which all people will agree if they are properly trained. Instead, it encompasses a wide range of experiences; and, furthermore it is the church's task to regain a distinctively Christian awareness of suicide within a Christian understanding of death.

Hence, this book is specifically focused on preemptive (and distinctively Christian) awareness, not prevention. A preacher cannot qualify or quantify if the preaching is *actually* preventing suicide within the community. This book, rather, is focused on the meaning and purpose of death in biblical and homiletic exploration within the framework of suicide.

SUICIDE AND THE PULPIT

Suicide is rarely dealt with from the pulpit, although the topic of suicide in pastoral counseling sessions has already received greater attention. The pastoral care that engages suicidal people naturally requires a level of intervention that the Sunday morning homily is not designed to perform. Meanwhile, the counseling session requires extended periods of listening that the preaching event already should have provided as a form of preparation. Preaching as suicide *awareness* is very different from pastoral care for suicide *intervention*. Can preaching provide elements of intervention? Certainly. And pastoral care can provide awareness. But, instead of combining the two, I limit myself to preaching for the purposes of clarity and focus.

Rather than focusing on suicide within the context of pastoral care, this book has set itself the challenge of placing suicide within the framework of the homiletic task. But, in our contemporary church, there are a dizzying number of opinions on what preaching is. One simply has

---

to prevent injury in case of an accident. Crisis intervention is analogous to when the accident happens and first responders, typically professionally-trained individuals, come to intervene during and after the crisis. Medical professionals, police, lawyers, and mental health professionals are those who are trained to be responders during and after a crisis. In this book, I am not focusing my attention on prevention or crisis intervention. I am focusing my attention on awareness (although awareness could lead to prevention or crisis intervention). I digress for just a moment to mention that this seat-belt analogy is one that makes sense only within the culture of the suicide prevention industry littered with nonprofits, seminars, and workshops.

to fill in the blank, "Preaching as _____." "Preaching as Resistance,"[11] Preaching as Celebration,"[12] Preaching as an Outsider"[13] and "Preaching as Reminding."[14] There are also "Preaching as Kindling Art,"[15] "Preaching as Testimony,[16] and "Preaching as Parable."[17] Pretty soon, preaching is applicable to anything one wants. Granted preaching is a difficult mystery to pin down. It is multifaceted and contains both the human element as well as the divine.

Historically, the preacher has often been the community voice that would guide conversations in order to bring about individual and communal changes. Some of the greatest figures who have facilitated major conversations about social justice issues include the Anglican Priest Desmond Tutu, the Baptist preacher Martin Luther King, the city preacher Sloan Coffin, the Roman Catholic Dorothy Day, or the Salvation Army co-founder Catherine Booth. And before the Christian preacher it was the prophets and the elders of ancient Israel. Such preachers are not merely the transmitters of information but the shapers of a people's vision as they speak an ancient word into situations in which the Word may have been forgotten. Preachers who have submitted themselves to the Holy Spirit, seeking to listen to the voices of Scripture, can discern with wisdom the uses or pitfalls of the secular disciplines in order to strategically and faithfully address social issues such as suicide. In this way, they can provide a biblically formed and more well-rounded awareness that can really change the atmosphere of the community's response to an issue.

Preaching is a way of forming healthy suicide awareness and even possibly an (unquantifiable) means of preventing suicide. Of course, awareness is a multi-participant endeavor, which should start with the church and include families, neighbors, friends, and co-workers.[18] Crisis intervention may be suited for the professionally trained individual,

11. See Snider, *Preaching as Resistance.*

12. See Thomas, *Preaching as Celebration.*

13. See Thompson, *Ingenuity: Preaching as an Outsider.*

14. See Arthurs, *Preaching as Reminding.*

15. See Schlafer, *Playing with Fire: Preaching Work as Kindling Art.*

16. See Carter Florence, *Preaching as Testimony.*

17. See Knowles and Wilson, *Of Seeds and the People of God: Preaching as Parable, Crucifixion, and Testimony.*

18. Kastenbaum, *Death, Society, and Human Experiences,* 219.

but as the American Association of Suicidology's logo states, "Suicide Prevention is *Everyone's* Business."[19]

I assume that "everyone" means people who are informed and held accountable since, surely, not everyone has the best intentions to help their fellow humans and not everyone is in the right mental state to be of service to themselves let alone others. For Christians, it is not only being *informed* but being *formed* by the Spirit through the Word proclaimed and the Gospel embodied in the practices of the community of faith. But do preachers really believe in the power of the proclaimed word? Fred Craddock once told a story that gets at what we too often assume about the sermon. After he finished preaching, a young woman told him that his message gave her clarity about what God was calling her to do. She was going to drop out of med school, sleep "under a piece of tin in the back of a pickup truck," and instruct "little children while their parents are out in the field." Craddock's response to her was, "Well, now, I was just preaching, I didn't mean to, you know . . . ."[20]

Do we preachers really believe that what we say can change not only people but the course of history for large groups of people? If we do, then why shy away from topics such as suicide, especially since suicide affects so many?

---

19. See American Association of Suicidology at http://www.suicidology.org/.

20. Craddock, *Craddock Stories*, 53.

2

Suicide, Sickness, and Being Human

"Which raises the critical question: What was meant by suicide? Here, there are difficult and significant problems with words."[1]

SUICIDE IS A THEOLOGICAL and ecclesiological issue. Saying this might give the impression that Christians should dismiss the contributions of psychology and sociology. On the contrary, they are significant interlocutors and should not be disregarded. Because suicide is fundamentally a theological issue, however, any contribution the social sciences might claim to make must be judged by and weighed within a set of biblically informed theological commitments.

Suicide is complex, especially since 90 percent of those who attempt suicide could be or have been diagnosed with a mental illness.[2] That is the statistic at any rate; but the statistic should not be accepted unquestioningly. Mental illness is itself complex—with multi-variable causation involving nature and nurture, subjectivity in diagnosing, and differing conceptualizations drawing on a multifaceted understanding of the brain, mind, behavior, and other people's perceptions of what a mental illness

---

1. Shaw, *Sacred Violence*, 734.

2. 91–96 percent of attempted suicides meet Axis I criteria (that is, substance and mental health diagnosis) according to Paul Quinnett, *QPRT Suicide Risk Assessment and Management*. Thomas Joiner states that it is 95 percent of people (*Myths about Suicide*, 89).

is and what it is not. It is precisely the elusive nature of others and their subjective sensitivities that make people avoid questions like, "Are you thinking about hurting yourself?" The threat of psychiatric incarceration and involuntary treatment is enough for some to pretend that everything is okay. Philosopher Antonin Artaud wrote: "I myself spent nine years in an insane asylum and I never had the obsession of suicide, but I know that each conversation with a psychiatrist, every morning at the time of his visit, made me want to hang myself, realizing that I would not be able to slit his throat."[3]

Along with the clinical assessments in hospitalization, psychotropic medication is considered an important component of effective mental health care. Yet preachers cannot prescribe medicine and are often deemed ineffective in the minds of the "professionals." Similarly, psychotherapy is frequently seen as an essential and empirically validated component of treatment; but these require layers of training and licensure beyond the scope of most preachers. And in any case, such training usually occurs entirely outside of any theological, biblical or ecclesial framework. But preachers should not avoid the topic of mental illness merely because they are not accredited by the academic field or institutional agency, or because they are unable to prescribe pharmaceuticals. If preaching has a direct bearing on the life of the community, should not preachers partner with mental health professionals by providing avenues of discourse?

Of course, preaching cannot treat mental illness the way a therapist or mental health professional can. By no means should preaching usurp and commandeer the culturally accepted specialized role of mental health care professionals. Instead, preachers and mental healthcare professionals can and should work together for the best overall care of the patient and parishioner using different forms of treatment. The collective involvement is a collaborative care method that many health providers are already familiar with. This is especially pertinent to suicide awareness and prevention. Unfortunately, so often, collaboration usually means restricting the preacher to the "religious" sphere while the psychological "expert" does the "real" treatment.[4] I would claim that if anything, the

---

3. Quoted by Thomas Szasz, "Suicide Should Not Be Prevented," in Barbour and Cothran, *Suicide: Opposing Viewpoints*, 155.

4. Larson, Milano, Weaver and McCullough are patronizing to clergy in their article "The Role of Clergy in Mental Health Care." They assert that clergy can "assist" the professionals "by stepping out of their traditional supportive and clerical roles into a more specific educational role." They continue to state that "skilled" clergy could

roles should be reversed, so that life in Christ's body and life lived at the cross become central while modern insights from social and behavioral sciences function to supplement the Christocentric ways of living, thinking, and communing.

Sue Klebold (the mother of one of the most famous school-shooters in American history) sees prevention as a way of growing into habits that originate in awareness. "We teach our kids the importance of good dental care, proper nutrition, and financial responsibility, but how many of us teach our children to monitor their own brain health?"[5] Suicide awareness should be an ongoing discussion in families, and in the family of faith.[6] Not just any type of awareness, but a Christian awareness.

Unfortunately, the discussion is usually seen as unusual, especially from the pulpit. The infrequent and taboo nature of the topic creates even more obscurity and misunderstanding on the subject. The topic of mental health and suicide is often avoided because of the complexity of the issues, certain challenges that seem overwhelming to the preacher, or because there has been a tacit division of labor between preacher and psychological expert. It seems clear that, culturally, the therapist has usurped the priest.[7] Our allegiance to the modern-day priest of medicine became hyper-apparent in our response to the recent pandemic of Covid-19 (not just in our reaction to the virus, but also in how we responded to other people who might put others at risk). Fear of illness and the fear of not conforming to medical authority completely have altered how we do church. And regarding suicide, the church has willingly given over her responsibility by promoting the "separation between 'the couch and the cloth'"[8] and fostering the division of the unity of the self into circumscribed compartments of soul and body, of spirituality and mental health, of religious belief and psychological reality.

Thus, faithful preaching requires the preacher always to be a student, bilingual in multiple disciplines. Education will build confidence. But for

---

be" consultants on cases" regarding" religious content," thus relegating clergy to only "cases involving religious or spiritual issues." See Larson, et al, "The Role of Clergy in Mental Health Care," 135–36.

5. Klebold, *A Mother's Reckoning*, 278.

6. This would include both primary prevention and secondary prevention which would include a partnership between family, non-professionals, and health care professionals.

7. See Foucault, *Madness and Civilization*, 215.

8. Larson, et al, "The Role of Clergy in Mental Health Care," 133.

some preachers, preparation for a sermon addressing mental health or suicide will involve examining their own struggles with personal mental illness. This may require the preacher to seek out spiritual direction and to learn how to talk openly about personal struggles. The French philosopher Gaston Bachelard stated, "What is the source of our first suffering? It lies in the fact that we hesitated to speak."[9] Walter Brueggeman reflects on this by saying, "The silence was first broken, in our tradition, when the slaves in Egypt finally 'groaned under their slavery and cried out'.[10] And their cry initiated a new historical possibility."[11]

The power of the spoken word seems to be at the heart of psychopathology. The therapist asks questions, clarifying and defining, while the patient talks. The patient's words identify how they have been shaped by words and how they shape themselves through the words they speak. As the preacher talks, it doesn't take long for a congregation to realize whether the Scriptures and stories of the ancestors of faith have shaped their imagination and their identity. Anna Carter Florence states that, "Preaching [is] in the tradition of testimony . . . by rooting ourselves so deeply in the text and context that we embody the Word we proclaim— and must testify to what we have seen and believed. Preaching in the testimony tradition calls us to live in and live out the Word of God."[12] Preaching as testimony is keeping a keen eye on the details in Scripture so that the preacher's story can reflect the testimonies within the Bible. Testimony does not mean that the preacher is allowed to be unrestrained in the information one shares from the pulpit. Julia Fast and John Preston caution that, "There is still a lot of shame associated with having a mental illness in our society. Think carefully about how you want to approach this project."[13] This is a warning to the preacher to take the time for prayer and discernment in sermon construction and delivery.

MENTAL ILLNESS AND NORMS

Mental illness is often defined as: "Any of a broad range of medical conditions that are marked primarily by sufficient disorganization of

9. Quoted by Brueggeman, *Preaching the Old Testament*, 74.

10. Exod 2:23.

11. Brueggeman, *Preaching the Old Testament*, 74.

12. Carter Florence, *Preaching as Testimony*, xxvii.

13. Fast and Preston, *Bipolar Disorder*, 33.

personality, mind, or emotions to impair normal psychological functioning . . . ."[14] Symptomology often includes emotional experience and social behavior, varying from mildly to seriously impaired and altered from socially acceptable behavior. Like physical illness when someone is sick it is expected that they will act sick. To expect someone to behave asymptomatically in the presence of an illness would be unreasonable. However, mental illnesses and their presentations lie on a very broad spectrum. In some cases, as with medical illnesses, symptoms are not readily observable and thus the patient does not always *look* sick. Despite not looking sick, illness compromises one's judgments and decisions.

If the patient's behavior violates societal norms or negatively influences others, or sometimes simply if the behavior is different or inadequately understood, the patient's character may be judged as being bad instead of being sick. Illness, whether physical or mental, can impair emotional, and social functions, thus distorting or restricting a person's agency. This might lead to the question: If people are mentally ill, how can they be held responsible to fit into the norm of normalness? The assumed cultural expectation is that the mentally ill person's responsibility lies in reaching out for help and dependency on the other. By doing this, they are thus seeking to be in the norms or normal understanding of what is expected of them. So, if they do not reach out for help and rather, they become isolated and despondent, they defy the social norm and hence are looked upon sometimes with disdain, other times fear, and often confusion by those saying, "What's wrong with that person?" (With a worried thought that "I hope they get help").

Preachers cannot get away from the culture's norms. And preachers should understand that mental illness is culturally considered a deviation from the normal.[15] This is why there are psychiatrists, therapists, and other mental health professionals who devote their whole lives to providing research, medication, therapy, and other efforts to fix those behaving abnormally. "The goal of adaptation to the social order is of the right hand, of conscious counseling."[16] In contrast, the preacher's task is to verbally address social and cultural norms and perceived expectations

---

14. Merriam-Webster Dictionary, *Mental Illness*. It should be noted that, rather than "a medical condition" as such, psychiatry.org defines mental illness more broadly as a "health condition." See "What is Mental Illness?" American Psychiatric Association.

15. For a history of cultural ideas about mental illness, see Porter, *Madness*.

16. Hillman, *Suicide and the Soul*, 15.

of those who behave abnormally by framing the issues in light of Jesus Christ and a "preferential option" for the marginalized.[17]

There is an acute need for familial and community support, and yet those who suffer from many mental illnesses (such as Schizoid Personality Disorder,[18] Dissociative Identity Disorder,[19] Severe Attention-Deficit/ Hyperactivity, Extreme OCD[20], Social Anxiety Disorder,[21] or Antisocial Behavior[22]) are less likely to attend a public worship service. Therefore, the preacher can and should address the perceived expectations and experiences of the family members or friends of those with a mental illness. On the other hand, depression is one of those illnesses that may be very common among the people of any given congregation. Depression is an illness that can be difficult to identify and treat because, "It is very hard to define depression."[23]

Alain Ehrenberg, a historian of psychopharmacology and former director of the Research Center on Mental Health, Psychotropics and Society in Paris, compares definitions from 1966 to 1996 and remarks, "Depressive states are thus lacking in all specificity, and their symptoms are astonishingly diverse. The term 'depression' is vague . . . ."[24] Although most practitioners within the field of psychology find depression to be relatively easy to detect and treat, the *DSM-5*, (the latest version of the diagnostic manual for psychologists) demonstrates the diversity of depressive disorders when it outlines the varying severity, the numerous specifiers, the lengthy diagnostic features, and the differential diagnosis.[25] So many of the symptoms overlap with other possible illnesses. And the causes of depression are identified variously within psychoanalytic, behavioral, environmental, cognitive, interpersonal, neurobiological or

---

17. I borrow the term "preferential option" from liberation theology though not necessarily with the same theological framework.

18. Fuller Torrey, *Surviving Schizophrenia*, 65–66.

19. The *DSM-5* also states that this disorder has a 70 percent suicide attempt rate. See "Suicidal Behavior Disorder: Comorbidity," in *DSM-5*, 295.

20. Hershfield, *When a Family Member Has OCD*, 34, 47.

21. Thieda, *Loving Someone with Anxiety*, 20–22.

22. Fuller Torrey, *Surviving Schizophrenia*, 86–87.

23. Ehrenberg, *The Weariness of the Self*, 71; admittedly, Ehrenberg is a sociologist and not a psychologist or a medical practitioner.

24. Ehrenberg, *The Weariness of the Self*, 73.

25. "Suicidal Behavior Disorder: Comorbidity," in *DSM-5*, 155–87.

genetic theories. The treatments are equally diverse ranging from dietary to somatic changes and pharmaceuticals to electroshock.

Part of the diversity within the field of depression as a mental illness is due to the fact that it is a field that deals with the diversity of what it means to be human.[26] To be human is to be on a spectrum,[27] and so, just like suicide, depression is widely diverse in scope and symptom. Even though authors often do not agree precisely about definitions, causes, and treatments, the consensus, however, is that depression is a real disorder and that depression carries with it a significant suicide risk. Patricia Ainsworth in her book *Understanding Depression* is careful to acknowledge the complexity of both depression and suicide by stating that, "not everyone who commits suicide is depressed . . . ." But speaking for a common understanding of suicide as self-destruction by one's own hand she says, "the majority of people who commit suicide do so during a severe depressive episode."[28] The reason for this is because the person suffering from depression is locked into a challenge-resistant place of thinking and feeling, though the thinking and feeling perspectives vary from person to person. Yet, some research suggests that depressive episodes could be increasing as a result of a special moment in history in which both the self and society are becoming increasingly fractured and restless in the wake of unhealthy technologies of the self, such as social media and excessive consumerism.[29]

26. The study of depression becomes even more complex when social construction becomes part of the conversation. Alain Ehrenberg calls depression a part of "anthropological interest" meaning "that it's medical and social success is linked to a major change in the idea that humanity has of itself" with respect to the history of self-consciousness throughout the romantic period to the enlightenment and modern-day democracy. See Ehrenberg, *The Weariness of the Self*. Another author acknowledges this social element when she states, "Depression as an illness became meaningful to the American public because of the ways in which it addressed preexisting conflicts and issues within American culture, issues that can be traced in changes in popular magazine coverage in the first half of the twentieth century" (Hirshbein, *American Melancholy*, 17).

27. Defining what it means to be human has been a theological enterprise for thousands of years, especially in light of the incarnation.

28. Ainsworth, *Understanding Depression*, 11.

29. Liu, "Social Media and Depression."

WITHDRAWAL

One pervasive reality for the suicidal person is the disgust of oneself. I have heard a variety of seemingly similar comments such as, "I do not like myself. And since I do not like myself, I am not surprised that others do not like me either." These comments are not pitty-pot attention-seeking words. Sometimes, the person legitimately doesn't like themselves, and they have to be with the person they do not like all day long. So, when a student said to me, "I am a burden to everyone," that "everyone" included himself. Thus, the withdrawal process deepens.

When people withdraw, it is natural for others to withdraw. I have witnessed this withdrawal dozens of times in college-aged men and women. When one withdraws others withdraw, like facing the negative ends on a battery. Cynthia Erickson, chair of the psychology department at Fuller Seminary writes that the calling for Christians is to "suffer with."[30] And one way to do this is to combat interior rumination and self-isolation, to "capture every thought" by consciously and unnaturally moving towards those who do not like themselves and act as if they do not like us. Can the congregation be equipped to be not only fishers of men but fishers of thoughts—thoughts about themselves and thoughts about others? Can the sermon be a tool, a net to catch people's thoughts? Can the preacher catch the thought, reshape the thought in light of Christ, and then give a new thought back in such a way that it becomes a building block for change?

History shows us that sermons can and have changed the way people think, especially through story. Martin Luther King Jr.'s preaching is a modern example of how preaching galvanized a movement of people for real communal change. King's preaching equipped the listeners to re-imagine something new and faithful, about themselves, about others, and about God. Inductive Preaching[31] is strong in this regard because it has the structure to show rather than tell. But lest we forget and become arrogant, no sermon is effective without the prompting, moving, and working of the Holy Spirit. Only God softens hearts, opens ears, and

---

30. Eriksson, "Suffering With."

31. Inductive Preaching could be defined as "sermons which reserve the thesis until later in the sermon where the thesis often functions as the result of homiletic exploration . . . ," in contrast to deductive preaching, which could be defined as a sermon that starts with the thesis or the propositional statement up front. See Gore, "Deductive, Inductive . . . And a Third Way."

renews the mind[32] while empowering us to capture every thought that we think.[33]

Sometimes, suicidal thinking is similar to that act of jumping to the end of the book to get it over as fast as possible or it is that feeling of wanting the story to finish when watching a movie with the comment, "I wish it would end already!" Suicidal thinking is that inability to desire or hope for more chapters to their lives. The task of the preacher is to help people re-imagine their lives by making the biblical narrative so vivid that the stories of our lives take on new shape in light of the narratives of the Bible.[34] "The interpretative keys to identifying grace in human experience are located in the biblical story and the basic symbols of the Christian tradition."[35]

I have experienced depressive episodes. I would describe melancholy as being locked into a hypersensitive self-conscious process of reflection on one's purpose (or lack thereof) in the surrounding social systems, "declaring that the dead who had already died are surely happier than the living who are still alive."[36] It is like looking up into a beautiful blue sky with only a few white wisps of a cloud floating by and proceeding to analyze the cloud's purpose: that it is too small to give shade, too white to give rain, too inconsequential for people to notice.[37] And when it is gone from sight, nobody will care or remember because "there is no remembrance of former things, nor will there be any remembrance of later things yet to be among those who come after."[38] The English writer Aldous E. Huxley once said, "Sooner or later, one asks even of Beethoven, even of Shakespeare . . . 'Is this all?'"[39] This self-isolating lack of purpose can be so mind-obsessive and pervasive that hopelessness, fatigue, and seclusion take root, which compounds the situation of social isolation.

Matt Heard in his book *Life with a Capital L* gives an illustration of visiting a little diner in the Upper Peninsula of Michigan. He slid into a

32. Eph 4:23.

33. 2 Cor 10:5.

34. For a significant approach to how the biblical narratives shape the imagination, see Hays, *The Moral Vision of the New Testament*.

35. Hilkert, *Naming Grace*, 49.

36. Eccl 4:2.

37. God's response to Job was, "Who has put wisdom in the clouds, or gives understanding to the mists?" Job 38:36–37.

38. Eccl 1:11.

39. Quoted in Walsh, "Pilgrimage to the Perennial Philosophy," 8.

booth, looked through a sticky menu, and told the waitress in jest that he was so hungry that he was more interested in quantity than quality. She responded, "Well you've come to the right place." He uses that illustration to speak about life. "That it's not only about how long I'm living, but how fully."[40] Quality really matters, and for the Christian, quality beats out quantity. Jack London in his poem Credo says, "The function of man is to live, not to exist. I shall not waste my days in trying to prolong them."[41] Life alone is no life. Social isolation (whether in the mind or body) destroys quality of life. And social isolation feeds the experiences of purposeless existence. As a Christian, one of the loneliest times of my life has been at church. Surrounded by people, happy people, beautifully dressed people, when I suddenly felt terribly alone. And the shallow meet-and-greet moment following the announcements made the isolation worse.

After Jarrid Wilson, a pastor at Harvest Christian Fellowship Church, died by suicide, a woman approached me and asked me, "How could a pastor, who knows that suicide is a sin, who knew all about suicide and prevention, and who was a father and a husband do such a thing?" Her question was not a statement of anger, it was a legitimate question stemming from confusion and she wanted me to answer her right then and there. My off-the-cuff answer was, "Every person is unique and thus every suicide is unique." But what I really wanted to say to her was, "Suicide is not a sin. Suicide is one way people die. Cancer is another, accidents are another. People die. We all have to die. There is nothing wrong with dying! Some die young, some die old. But we all have to do it. Life is but a vapor. Whether you are nine days or ninety years, we appear for only a little while and then we disappear. A better question would be: *Did he die well; did he die in Christ?*" But I didn't say that. Because, we do not talk that way about suicide. In our culture, suicide is bad and people who die by suicide did a bad thing. To speak any other way deviates from what is considered normal healthy thinking and talking.[42] Thus, some just do not talk. We withdraw from the subject. Fred Craddock once said, "The silence is hurtful and harmful, so break it, please."[43] But, I would

---

40. Heard. *Life with a Capital L*, 44.

41. London, *Tales of Adventure*, vii.

42. Just days before Jarrid Wilson died, Gregory Eelss, the head of the counseling and psychological services at the University of Pennsylvania also died by suicide. Dr. Eelss a few years earlier had given a TED talk on the right way to talk in order to build resilience into our lives. See Eells, "Cultivating Resilience."

43. Craddock, et al, *Speaking of Dying*, 133.

caution, there is a risk in speaking on topics that other people withdraw from. The preacher is bound to be faced with cultural resistance. No one wants to be opposed, so silence becomes the safest option. Yet silence is the deadliest option.

The woman who had questioned me regarding Jarrid Wilson was not satisfied with my response. She then asked a rhetorical question, "Did you read what his wife said? She said that he was no longer in pain and was no longer suffering. How could she say that? Doesn't she know that people will read that and be enticed to kill themselves?" When preachers know that their words are being scrutinized, it is hard for preachers to feel confident to speak on such a highly sensitive topic. I understand, I really do. But I also understand what it is like to be a pastor who has never once been asked, "Rev. Johnson, do you ever think about dying by suicide?" I have also never once been asked how I am grappling with my episodes of depression even though many people know my struggles. Likewise, I have never, not one time, been asked how my relationship with God is going. I'm a preacher. Why hasn't anyone ever asked me this? Why do people not ask point-blank personal questions like this? I have been asked a thousand times, "How are you?" But no one has ever said, "No, really, how are you?" Everybody knows that the niceties of "How are you?" do not really mean "How are you?" The words really just mean "Hello." And when one recognizes the impersonal nature of our most common and flippant words, withdrawal becomes the default.

LONELINESS AND PSYCHOPATHOLOGY

Every suicide is unique because every person is unique. Since there are so many types of suicides we should not make a blanket statement about suicide. Yet, loneliness seems to be a widely accepted cause of suicide and often becomes that blanket. It would be useful for the preacher to remember the spectrum in which suicide resides (which I will discuss at length in chapter 4), but it would also be beneficial for the preacher to help the congregation define the terms "lonely" as opposed to "being alone." You can be alone and not be lonely. The two are not the same, yet for suicide they often go together since many lonely people attempt suicide while being alone. The loneliness that researchers most often point to is the loneliness that comes not from being alone but specifically the loneliness that stems from social isolation even in the midst of social settings. Loneliness is that sense of being alone when surrounded by people. The twenty-four-hour watch of a suicidal person is the most effective suicide prevention available right now. But even then, the twenty-four-hour suicide watch rarely defeats loneliness, which causes angst for the one sitting vigil. Christine Pohl sums up the cultural problem when she said, "A steady exposure to distant human need that is beyond our personal response can gradually inoculate us against particular action. It can also delude us into thinking that by simply knowing about it we are somehow sharing in the suffering of the others.[44] But I would add, we frequently show tentative responses not only to strangers, but to those whom we know intimately. The cycle has been described by stating that depression causes isolation and at the same time, isolation causes depression.[45] This cycle is exhausting. Thus, depression is often associated with fatigue. The fatigued person seeks to be alone, to sleep, and slowly becomes further isolated. But that isolation is not the balm required because, in fact, it makes the illness worse. It is like the parched seafaring cast-away surrounded by water. Drinking saltwater will only destroy the health even more. As a child growing up in Colorado, most everyone knew that if you were lost in the snowy mountains, you should not eat the snow. It will more quickly usher in hypothermia. In the same way, if you are depressed, isolation will exacerbate the illness. But when one is sad and tired, the natural inclination of the self is to go lie down in your room. After all, when you are physically sick, you rest and avoid others. It is not only counter-intuitive, but it takes massive resolve to seek community when you are depressed. Therefore, more importantly, it takes the encouragement of the community to help the sick be engaged. This is especially hard when the clinically depressed are unpleasant to be around. Regardless, a theology of hospitality seems paramount when dealing with a theology of suicide.

The *knowledge* of the love of God is not sufficient to combat loneliness. When preachers preach, "All you need is to believe in Jesus," that is incomplete theology. The love to which Jesus calls us never removes the need for each other. Individuals need the community and the community needs the individual. This is a reflection of Trinity—diversity within unity. We humans need to feel that we belong, that we have purpose. When that need is not supplied by the community, hopelessness invades,

44. Pohl, *Making Room*, 91.

45. Putnam, *Bowling Alone*, 265.

and suicide becomes a way out of the loneliness. We not only need to love our neighbor, but we need our neighbor to know that we need them to love us.

One of the things that we as Christians must die to is our false story of rugged individualism. The overstated advice to the struggling to not feel bad because, "God will never leave them" is not helpful instruction apart from the company of other humans. God's presence can only be actualized through the physical body of Christ, his church. God is the one who said that it was not good to be alone. The concept that it is "just me and Jesus" (some spiritual image or feeling of Jesus) is not only detrimental to spiritual health, it is simply bad theology and goes squarely against the social capital that Paul exhorts in 1 Corinthians 12.[46] And yet, pop-Christian culture promotes the notion that all you need is Jesus; a "keep warm and well fed"[47] theology.

Charles Dickens in his renowned *Christmas Carol* subtly promoted the view that change comes from the spiritual realm not the embodied human realm. Bob Cratchit and Fred his nephew, were people who sought out Scrooge, moved towards him in the hopes of eliciting change. But the only real conversion came from ghosts who helped him reflect within himself. And yet, despite that theme, a glaring conflict appears in a modern rendition, the *Muppets Christmas Carol,* where the transformed Scrooge sings, "Life is like a journey. Who knows when it ends? Yes, and if you need to know the measure of a man, you simply count his friends."[48] Ouch. The very idea that you can measure a man by how many friends he has is exactly what you do not want to say to someone who may be lonely, hurt, angry or suicidal. Regardless, the song lyrics seem to contradict the method of change in the original *Christmas Carol,* which came not from his friends, but from ghosts. On the same token, it is not Christian to promote the idea that salvation or transformation comes by looking inward towards the self, to our personal ghost of the past, present, and future.

"Look within yourself to change yourself" is a very popular mantra. But it is not Christian. On the contrary, because of the indwelling of the Holy Spirit, "Thy Kingdom come on earth" is here now. The church is God's body, God's incarnate physical body, so that I am being Jesus to the

---

46. In 1 Cor 12, Paul outlines how the Spirit provides for the common good.

47. Jas 2:16.

48. Williams, "Thankful Heart."

one whom I give a cup of water to, who in turn becomes Christ to me. Salvation and sanctification come from outside of the self. The physical body of believers as God's body reflects Augustine's reasoning when he said, "Without God, we cannot; without us, God will not."[49]

Robert Putnam in *Bowling Alone* states that "Faith communities in which people worship together are arguably the single most important repository of social capital . . . ."[50] But of course, social capital depends on getting the individual connected to the collective. They may have great potential for "social capital," but one wonders when looking at the inactive membership list how well churches are accomplishing the task.

There seems to be something not quite right when the "active" members designate others as "inactive." The "active" have been given special privilege to mark and label others as "inactive" on the basis of activity or lack thereof within a specific group of people. There is a pretentious air about that activity of the active. It is a tunnel-vision approach to the Kingdom of God and how God acts. In all fairness, it can be a challenge to define those who are inactive since many inactive members still *feel* integrally a part of the congregation even though they do not participate in the life of that particular church and may even live in an entirely different community. Thus, some churches base "inactivity" on financial giving or again, the lack thereof. All of a sudden, social capital is based on financial capital.

Counted membership in and of itself might be helpful for the financial well-being of a congregation and her denomination, but I cannot find biblical support for it. Paul may have asked for financial support in order to bring a gift back to Jerusalem, but in no way was the financial support the basis for inclusion, especially in light of the fact that only the Philippian church was reliable in her giving.[51] Baptism is the sign of membership that should defy any denominational walls. And gratitude

49. See Augustine's *Sermon* 169.11 (13): Sed totum ex Deo; non tamen quasi dormientes, non quasi ut non conemur, non quasi ut non velimus. Sine voluntate tua non erit in te iustitia Dei. Voluntas quidem non est nisi tua, iustitia non est nisi Dei. Esse potest iustitia Dei sine voluntate tua, sed in te esse non potest praeter voluntatem tuam. (My translation: "But the whole [is] from God; nevertheless, not as though we are sleeping, nor as if we are not trying, nor as if we are not willing. Without your will the justice of God will not be in you. Indeed, there is no will unless it is yours, there is no justice unless it is God's. The justice of God can exist without your will, but it cannot exist in you apart from your will.").

50. Putnam, *Bowling Alone*, 66.

51. Phil 4:10–20.

for Christ's sacrifice should be the impetus for "social capital" in the church. Henry Ward Beecher's advice on how to feed gratitude was to "multiply picnics."[52] I like this advice. Eugene Lowry once delivered a sermon to his congregation about the parables of the lost sheep, coin and son as a repeated sequence—"Lost, found, party!" Being redeemed from the isolation and brought into the community will lead to gratitude, and gratitude naturally leads to celebration. Isn't that what worship is all about? Ed Loring of the Open Door Community in Atlanta once stated that "justice is important, but supper is essential."[53] A true lunch among believers is after all, an agape meal. And eating is the primal act of the Christian "heritage of hospitality."[54]

But to the ears of someone who prefers to be alone, this sounds sickening. Some people do not like other people. To some, social-death sounds a lot more appealing than social-time. There are many reasons why people are on the "inactive list." One reason is that the inactive people do not want to be around the active people (and certainly wouldn't want to be claimed as mere social capital). It is as simple as that. And many of the active recognize this, which dispels any motivation to check-in and connect with the inactive.

A major factor in this phenomenon is that the active and the inactive have failed to connect in a meaningful and purpose-filled way. Sunday after Sunday there persists a level of civil discourse that is shallow, polite, mundane, and usually revolves around the weather. I experienced this in a profound sense when living in Italy for a summer and as much as I loved the diversity and the novelty of Rome, the isolation that comes from culture-shock is a real thing. The loneliness that comes from being transported into a linguistically isolating terrain makes one long for their mother tongue in a visceral way. Hearing English on arrival to the UK was sweeter than honey. Even that small connection which common language provides can change the feeling of being alone to a sense of belonging. But when one always lives with many commonalities and the niceties of shallow conversation, the active members are forced to go deeper to find the connection that gives a reason for existing as community. Commonalities should not be understated. Being woven from the same cloth makes it much easier to be connected. This makes preaching a

---

52. Beecher, *Yale Lectures in Preaching*, 155.

53. Quoted by Pohl, *Making Room*, 74.

54. Pohl, *Making Room*, 33.

powerful force when proclamation lands on ears that already speak your language. But we must remain intentionally creative to the necessity of deeper communion.

SPEAKING AND PSYCHOPATHOLOGY

Many people think they know what mental illness is as though it were one objective thing. Yet they are not sure how to talk about it, especially with the language of faith. The biblically-formed preacher who has engaged in a study of mental illness provides not only words about illness but the way the words should be spoken. Ephesians 4:15 charges the faithful to "speak the truth" and to do it "in love." While proclaiming the sermon, the preacher is modeling how to speak the truth while doing it in a way that is appropriate.[55] The congregation then, empowered and convicted by the Holy Spirit, will be equipped to think and speak about mental illness in a manner of love to those in their families, places of work, and neighborhoods. This does not mean that people will accept the truth, even if it is spoken in love. Mental illness is not something that can easily be embraced or overcome simply by knowing the truth about it.[56] In fact, it is important to recognize that mental illness might never be overcome; for many it will be a life-long challenge. This challenge requires a new imagination for learning to live with a new normal. "Bipolar Disorder doesn't simply go away one day." It is empowering for the preacher and for the congregation to realize that, "You can never talk to, cajole, or reason with someone who is in a bipolar disorder mood swing."[57] One cannot talk someone out of being ill. Simply reminding others that mental illness is an illness can strengthen the community in their commitment to hospitality and compassion by speaking truth always with an on-going commitment to love.

55. How many people have witnessed the preacher on the street corner or at the pulpit pounding his fist and yelling doctrine? Usually, the doctrine is not bad, rather it is the way that the doctrine is being presented that is unhelpful and misleading.

56. "Compulsive hoarding certainly appears to be a condition of low insight, as are other psychiatric conditions, such as psychotic disorders (particularly schizophrenia), bipolar disorder, and OCD. Because low insight prevents people who hoard from perceiving that they have a problem, they do not believe they need help" (Tomkins and Hartl, *Digging Out*, 5).

57. Fast and Preston, *Bipolar Disorder*, 66.

This is particularly vital in light of the evidence pointing to the positive effects of talking as a suicide prevention measure.[58] First responders such as firefighters or paramedics are trained, social workers are trained, and parishioners can be trained, too, to approach suicide. By building awareness of mental health issues, the preacher is vital within that training. Enriching the vocabulary gives the parishioners opportunities to describe how God is working in their lives. Mary Catherine Hilkert states, "Naming the presence of God in human experience requires pressing to the limits of human existence where both the threat of radical human finitude and the experience of overwhelming meaning and joy raise the fundamentally religious question of the 'ground of our being.'"[59]

Faithful preaching has the power to break taboos and reduce stigma and shame merely by addressing mental illness in healthy and empowering ways. It can be helpful for the congregation to understand what and why there are taboos to begin with. Good preaching is educating. Simply drawing attention to the elephant in the room gives permission to the congregation to reflect on whether the stigma has crippled members of the congregation or not. Good preachers have always been trying to build virtuous community. But moral community only works if it practices the art of acknowledging stigma and if the community is encouraged and equipped to engage and incorporate everyone despite health issues. This claim seems tenuously utopian. Yet, if the church is apathetic to shame within themselves, then truly what does the church have to offer the world? Thomas Reynolds[60] puts it this way, "Wherever Jesus goes the destitute, sick, impaired, and vulnerable in society come to the fore and gather around him. Why? Not simply because they seek Jesus. Rather, because Jesus seeks them." Reynolds continues, "He embraces what is taboo to include it in the kingdom of God. In fact, this practice is part of

---

58. "There is no evidence that talking about suicide (in a respectful, caring fashion, in the context of prevention) increases the risk of suicide. Research does show that talking openly and responsibly about suicide helps people understand that they are not alone and that others care about their situation." See *Ray of Hope*, Mental Health America of Westmoreland County.

59. Hilkert, *Naming Grace*, 49.

60. Thomas Reynold's book *Vulnerable Communion* focuses on people with physical disabilities. It is interesting to note that there seems to exist an unspoken distinction in the Western world regarding those who are "disabled" physically and those who are "crazy" mentally. The preacher should draw attention to this disparity. See Reynolds, *Vulnerable Communion*.

his overall intent to pull the margins to the center: the first shall be last, and the last first."[61]

Thus, to reduce disgrace is to imitate Jesus's grace. A Christian community should want nothing less than to be like Jesus. But before we swing too far on the pendulum, let me be clear that reducing stigma does not mean accepting sinful behavior. Whenever Jesus ate, preached, and healed the broken, he always called people to repentance. Jesus reminded the woman caught in adultery to "go and sin no more."[62] Jesus's concern was not only for the physical well-being but also for the spiritual health of the person—because the body-soul of a person is a united system.

Historically preachers have not been at a loss for words. It is only in our current context where we find ourselves tiptoeing around topics that are "hot-buttons" or "trigger-points," which sadly only solidifies taboos, stigmas, and stereotypes. Suicide is not morose; rather suicide is theologically rich and scientifically studied. Not only is talking about death faithful to the Christian message but talking about suicide can actually prevent suicide.[63] Simply saying the word "suicide" gives the congregation permission to engage in the conversation.

It is important to note here, however, that talking about suicide is not the same as describing suicidal acts. The Center for Disease Control and the National Institute of Mental Health discourage the media from describing particular ways of attempting suicide for good reason. The Werther Effect (copycat suicide attempts) has been proven to be a real phenomenon. Like the media in ethical reporting, preachers should avoid all kinds of speech that describe how a person attempted self-harm.[64] Instead, the preacher should focus on three objectives:

- The wrath and mercy of God[65] (the crucifixion and resurrection of Jesus).

- Biblical literacy (living in the Scriptural texts).

- Ecclesiology (individual dependency on the Holy Spirit in community).

---

61. Reynolds, *Vulnerable Communion*, 223–24.

62. John 8:11.

63. Fuller Torrey, *Surviving Schizophrenia*, 276.

64. Reporting on Suicide.org, 2015.

65. Wrath and mercy are two sides of one coin. See Hab 3:2. We can't have one without the other especially in light of the cross.

Defining our words is imperative. Words are at the core of Christian theology, specifically words expressing God's character of wrath and mercy, words from the biblical narrative, and words that provide calling and belonging. "Speaking of God cannot be reduced to saying things about God; rather, speaking of God will draw us into a relationship with God . . . ."[66] This is the task of the Christian preacher who seeks to include a theology of suicide as an act of advancing the church as life-equipping, life-empowering and life-giving.

BEHAVIOR AND PSYCHOPATHOLOGY

Some maintain that the Bible says that "We will know Christians by their love."[67] This statement claims that people can know the true identity of someone by how that person acts. This idea in psychiatry is known as the "Fundamental Attribution Error." The error is in the act of attributing behavior to true character. The error becomes evident when realizing that some non-Christians can act very loving.[68] On the other side, this "Fundamental Attribution Error"[69] is very pertinent with respect to the negative behavior of people who have an illness. It is not reasonable to call a person lazy when that person is sick. This is the same for those who have an illness of the mind. It is not reasonable to judge someone's character based on their behavior when their behavior is caused by an illness. This is an extremely difficult concept for preachers and congregations to understand because the notion of *orthopraxis* (right living) as a byproduct of *orthodoxia* (right teaching) is deeply ingrained in Christian theology.

---

66. Pasquarello, *We Speak*, 148.

67 Actually, the Bible never says, "You will know them by their love." Rather, Matt 7:16 states, "You will know them by their fruit," and John 13:35 says, "By this all men will know that you are my disciples, if you love one another." The hermeneutical error persists in misquoting, proof-texting, and simple illiteracy.

68. The most glaring problem with this theory is that the word "love" has not be defined. If love is defined as the *essence of God's nature represented through a spiritual gift demonstrated through sacrifice*, then one could say that we can in fact know a Christian by their love, that is if that love represents the very actions of Jesus and does not in any way contradict Jesus. Unfortunately, the interpretation of Jesus's actions is dependent on individual hermeneutics. Regardless, this argument can be rebuked, because according to the Reformed tradition God can act through all of God's creation, Christian or non-Christian. See Calvin, *Institutes*, I. 18. 1, 228–37.

69. Bell, "Fundamental Attribution Error."

Consider the example of people with the illness of Alzheimer's who no longer "believe" in Jesus. Despite their inability to believe, according to the Christian tradition, it is not what we do but what Jesus did on the cross that provides for salvation. "Even the demons believe . . . " says James.[70] The demons believe yet their actions do not correspond with their belief.[71] A recognition of the human's total dependency on God's grace through Jesus should provoke a commitment by the community to not abandon or neglect people with Alzheimer's disease or other mental illnesses and disorders.[72] The fact that mental illness or a disease could cause a rupture between belief and action ought to lead the community of faith toward a disposition of patience and a persistence of care.

Behavior is a difficult and messy subject for the thoughtful Christian. D. A. Carson in his sermon "The Sweep of Praise" states that, "conduct establishes who we are."[73] Likewise, the Bible also demonstrates that true identity is based on paternity. For example, Barnabas's true identity is manifested in the fact that he is "the son of encouragement."[74] Jesus is the rightful heir to the throne because Jesus is the "Son of David" even though he is identified as a carpenter because he is also a son of Joseph.[75] The biblical term "son of" is an identity marker and becomes the basis of orthodox theology regarding Jesus's true identity as God, since the text states that Jesus is not only the "Son of Man" but also the "Son of God."[76] Carson thus concludes that paternity determines behavior. As adopted sons of God we then act like God.[77] To act any other way, shows that we are not sons of God. The paradox is that we humans are both, at the same time, redeemed from sin and yet sinful, both adopted and yet still in our fallen flesh, both saved and awaiting the redemption of our bodies[78] because we are in the now and the not yet.

---

70. Jas 2:19.

71. Mark 6:13 implies that demons have bad behavior and thus should be driven out.

72. A simple question to ask in the sermon might be, "How are we as the church living out what we believe about God (our theology)?"

73. Carson, "Sweep of Praise."

74. Acts 4:36.

75. John 1:45.

76. John 20:31.

77. Eph 1:5.

78. Rom 8:23.

We are at the same time spiritual and physical. And the physical brain controls the self even when the human falsely thinks that their spirits are the ones in control. Consider an alcoholic. Instead of reasoning that the alcoholic drinks too much because they lack self-control, a more helpful logic is that the alcoholic drinks too much because their brain is sick. To say to the alcoholic, "just stop drinking" is not helpful. Our brains and bodies don't work that way.

Behavior should not be seen, therefore, as an individual responsibility nor a divine responsibility alone. For the community is also responsible in individual behavior.[79] Norms of individual behavior are only judged by the collective because it is the collective that is ultimately accountable for behavior (for "judgement begins with the house of God").[80] Therefore, the error in the Fundamental Attribution Error is the myth of individualism.

There once was a young Japanese woman name Kiyoko Matsumoto. The story goes that she was distressed about her sexual feelings for another female classmate named Masako Tomita. Feeling the strain of cultural conflict, Matsumoto decided to escape the frustration and die by suicide. Considering this romantic, Tomita apparently chose Mount Mihara for Matsumoto's departure. Tomita even accompanied Matsumoto to the volcano where Matsumoto leaped to her death in the wintery February of 1933. Tomita then went back to school to share the romantic tale of love and loss which spread to the media and catapulted the region of Mount Mihara into a tourist destination providing economic growth to the local community. Recognizing the financial potential, the president of the Tokyo Bay Steamship Company began advertising trips to the mountain and directing tourists to the newly-named destination "Suicide Point." It didn't take long for Mount Mihara to become the desired destination of copy-cat suicides. Within one year 310 people died by suicide just like Matsumoto had done.[81]

---

79. Just as Apoptosis is cellular suicide, on a large corporate scale the military can be used as an example of "institutionalized death." J. Harold Ellens asks the potentially offensive query, wondering, "Who is willing to ask the question: Why do we send our children [to war]?" A death of a soldier or that which is "necessary for the common good," is defined by Ellens as national "child sacrifice." But what if it really is national suicide? In other words, are we killing ourselves by endorsing, idealizing, and honoring war and the "fallen" of each new generation. See Ellens, "Inequality or Singularity of Institutionalized Death."

80. 1 Pet 4:17.

81. See "The Volcano Suicides," in *Providentia*.

The collateral damage within this story is painfully and obviously collective. Matsumoto is guilty for the numerous copy-cat deaths that followed her. Tomita is also responsible, along with the entire community that benefited financially and the media that needed a tantalizing tale. The whole point of sharing this sorrowful story is to bring attention to the collective nature of individual behavior. Behavior is an issue of communal culpability. This shared responsibility is demonstrated in 1 Corinthians 7:12–14 when Paul reveals that believers can sanctify unbelievers. "For the unbelieving husband has been sanctified through his wife, and the unbelieving wife has been sanctified through her believing husband."[82]

To say that behavior is determined by paternity, that who you are and how you act determines whether you have been adopted into the family of faith or not, requires too tidy of a view of what is really a spectrum of causation of behavior. Human identity is seated in both paternity and community. We are citizens of heaven,[83] we are adopted as children of God,[84] and from the sunspots on my hands to the way I snort when I laugh, I can't get away from the biology of my parents. Thus, suicide, by its very nature is a physical, social and spiritual stew,[85] not an individual sickness.

SUFFERING AND PSYCHOPATHOLOGY

It is a challenge for the preacher to know how to preach about suffering. The word "suffering" is often associated with mental illness, especially since *pathos* in psycho*patho*logy literally means "suffering." When people describe their ailment, they might say something like, "I am suffering from depression" or "I suffer from anxiety." The Bible is not a manual on today's contemporary cultural understanding of mental health; but it has much to offer when it comes to suffering, especially since Christ's suffering is the means by which salvation has come to humanity.

History has shown that humans are incredibly resilient in the face of great misery. This hopeful news should be spoken from the pulpit, couched in God's victory *over* suffering *through* Christ's suffering on the cross. Humans are not fragile. Humans are buoyant and durable. And yet

---

82. 1 Cor 7:4.

83. Phil 3:20.

84. Gal 3:26.

85. Hillman, *Suicide and the Soul*, 26.

we often want to remove all suffering and difficulty from our lives and the lives of those we love. To the contrary, Sandra Gilbert states, "to protest suffering is to earn or even merit suffering. Or perhaps the suffering itself is and always was a sign that suffering was warranted."[86]

For the Christian, in fact, suffering is required. Reflecting on Christ's travail, Kathryn Greene-McCreight asserts, "Suffering is not eliminated by the resurrection but transformed by it."[87] It is precisely the cross and the empty tomb that gives the Christian a personal vocation. The Christian calling is to suffer and to die. The church is built up by the sacrificial suffering of its members reflecting God's power which is "made perfect in weakness."[88] In the encounter with Christ, Paul receives a revelation of "how much he must suffer for the sake of my name."[89] This goes for all God's elect because we are "heirs of God and co-heirs with Christ—if in fact, we suffer with him so that we may also be glorified with him."[90] It is uncommon to hear Christians announce that their calling is to suffer let alone to rejoice in suffering.[91] I've heard students say that their calling is to do ministry or to preach, but never "to suffer." Yet, the truth is, that Christ did not come to bring peace, but a sword . . . a sword[92] that pierced Mary's heart[93] and one that will pierce our own.[94]

Within the liturgical calendar Lent is that time when the Christian church consciously journeys through Christ's suffering by participating in fasting, lamenting, and repenting. Amy Plantinga Pauw states that "Christ ends up on the cross because that is where humanity is, trapped in webs of violence, oppression, and enmity."[95] Lent is when the church embraces suffering only to recognize that we are already suffering, or better yet, that Christ is suffering with us and for us. Our life and death reside in the Friday and Saturday of the Triduum while getting a taste of Easter through worship and true communion while we pray, "Come,

86. Gilbert, *Death's Door*, 95.

87. Greene-McCreight, *Darkness Is My Only Companion*, 59.

88. 2 Cor 12:9.

89. Acts 9:16.

90. Rom 8:17.

91. Col 1:24.

92. Matt 10:34, 39.

93. Luke 2:35.

94. John 17:14.

95. Plantinga Pauw, *Church in Ordinary Time*, 134.

Lord Jesus come."[96] It is when anamnesis and prolepsis (active remembering and anticipation) are present, when birth is not merely an event of the distant past, but given in the present tense:

> O holy child of Bethlehem,
> Descend to us, we pray;
> Cast out our sin and enter in,
> Be born in us today.[97]

In the theological realm, suffering is most often treated as part of the issue of theodicy, or the problem of evil, as if it was somehow caused by the Fall. On a close reading of Scripture, however, we see that suffering was already part of the narrative before the Fall. God created Eve because it was *not good* for man to be alone.[98] Even before the willful act of disobedience, something was not good. That which was not good was loneliness. Suffering is an *outcome* of loneliness.[99]

First, it is important to note that suffering was the outcome and not the source. The source of suffering is often viewed as morally bad. Suffering, however, in its own right, is neither good nor bad. The Apostle Peter states that it is better to suffer for doing good than for doing bad, implying that suffering is an experience of both.[100] Suffering is simply a part of human existence and experience. On the positive side, suffering is a creative force that contributes to how humans develop and change throughout their lifetimes. Humans suffer at all times and at all different levels. In fact, for the Christian, acknowledging our sin and dying to ourselves actually requires suffering.

Opponents to the theory that suffering is neither good nor bad might state that it could cause a sense of fatalism. This fatalism could be understood through the theory of Learned Helplessness developed by Martin Seligman.[101] Learned Helplessness is when someone has come to believe that they are powerless to change their circumstances. A proper approach to suffering should not lead to such a fatalistic view. Recognizing that suffering is morally neutral does not necessitate that one should

---

96. Rev 22:20.

97. Brooks, "O Little Town of Bethlehem."

98. Gen 2:18.

99. "It is an understatement to say that suicidal people are lonely at the time of death" (Joiner, *Myths about Suicide*, 123).

100. See 1 Pet 3:14–18.

101. Kowalski and Westen, *Psychology*, 184–85.

accept such suffering (for example, a person suffering domestic abuse ought to call for swift intervening action). One of the integral roles of a pastor and preacher is to help the congregation to grapple with suffering in a healthy and truthful manner. This involves taking seriously a person's sense of being trapped[102] or on the other side, the denial of that which enslaves them. In fact, denial of one's own suffering can be a symptom of some mental illnesses. For example, a "disturbing hallmark of anorexia nervosa is the persistent denial that anything is wrong. As a result, the progression of anorexia nervosa can be tragic."[103] Thus, the preacher should aim to provide strength and encourage fortitude for the suffering that cannot be avoided (such as aging, illness, or death) while questioning the suffering that could be avoided, actively resisted, and called to task (such as human sinful actions).[104]

Suffering is defined by cultural context, and thus the culture (or subculture) of a Christian community has an opportunity to shape and train how the community will respond to the ever-present suffering. A well-trained response is imperative since part of the Christian vocation is actually to go into places of suffering and to be with people who are suffering. Christian training has a vision to equip people who are themselves suffering to be with others who are suffering. Stanley Hauerwas once declared, that "our willingness to be ill and to ask for help as well as our willingness to be present with the ill is no special or extraordinary activity, but a form of the Christian obligation to be present to one another in and out of pain."[105] This requires the church to invest in the training of living: living while dying and living within suffering. This training can come from a variety of places, but most importantly the pulpit, and can be preached through the narrative of the human experience in the Bible.[106] The recognition that one cannot escape suffering may help the congregation come to peaceful terms with the presence of suffering and recognize that seeking death as an escape from suffering is actually only causing more suffering.[107]

---

102. I use the word "trapped" because that is the word used by the QPR Institute for Suicide Risk Assessment and Management Training Program when describing suicidal people.

103. Siegel, Brisman and Weinshel, *Surviving an Eating Disorder*, 16.

104. This might be considered *learned helpfulness* rather than learned helplessness.

105. Hauerwas, *Suffering Presence*, 80.

106. Hilkert, *Naming Grace*, 50.

107. This is to imply that those who attempt suicide would care about the wellbeing

In addition, the preacher has the challenge to teach suffering as a biological purpose not only to shape human character but to strengthen and influence motivation (we are, after all, embodied creatures). Biologically speaking, if the level of suffering is too low, the motivation to act in that situation will be low. For example, if someone has a drippy faucet, the slow drip may not be providing enough suffering to motivate action. On the opposite extreme, if suffering is too high, motivation can be paralyzed by shock or lack of resources. For example, if the drippy faucet bursts and floods the entire house destroying life and limb in the process, the level of motivation may be paralyzed, and outside help is required. It is between the extreme low and extreme high that suffering plays an important purpose of influencing motivation and shaping the character of people.[108] Because, "the simple fact of the matter is this: people do not see that there's a problem unless they feel distressed by it."[109] Suffering can then be seen as a positive tool for growth and opportunity, thus empowering the congregation.[110]

All suffering feels personal and is often experienced in isolation, heightening the impression that the sufferer is alone. But if the community invites that suffering to be visible it can then become collective suffering and not individual suffering.[111] And if the preacher recognizes that suffering is neither good nor bad (even if its causes, contexts, or attempted alleviations may have sinful elements), but rather views it as an opportunity for growth in faith[112] and dependency on God through

---

of the community who loves them. Some with mental illness do not have the capacity to exhibit empathy or to realize that what they do affects others. Consequently, the preacher may find that their target audience is primarily the family and friends of those living with mental illness.

108. This idea is similar but not the same as the Yerkes-Dodson theory (optimal arousal for peak performance) but rather works in conjunction with Yerkes-Dodson in the optimal suffering for peak motivation.

109. "Low insight prevents people from perceiving that they have a problem." Low insight is often associated with "psychiatric conditions, such as psychotic disorders (particularly schizophrenia, bipolar disorder, and OCD)." This also includes compulsive hoarding. See Tompkins and Hartl, *Digging Out*, 5.

110. In any respect, suffering should never be preached as punishment from God. Christ's death should be proclaimed as the atonement for sin, once and for all. See Rom 6:10.

111. Michael Hecht, *Stay*, 214.

112. To grow to the point where we can "Rejoice in our sufferings, because we know that suffering produces perseverance; perseverance, character; and character, hope. And hope does not disappoint us . . . ," Rom 5:3–5. Note that this suffering that

the community of faith, then the preacher can find hope in preaching on the issues of mental illness and other types of suffering. Luke Powery states it like this, "Real hope is discovered in the midst of death, created on the anvil of adversity."[113]

Suffering is frequently questioned with, "Why me?" People often ascribe meaning to the suffering and desperately want there to be some sort of purpose to the pain. There is always a cause, and that cause will be seen through a subjective lens, which will assign it a meaning or purpose. For the preacher, a goal might be to help the congregation recognize that suffering is due to good or bad causes, while emphasizing that this does not mean that the person suffering is a good or bad person (i.e., deserves it more or less). Of course, we are all sinful, but what I want to say is that judgment should be reserved on whether people are intentionally *trying* to be bad or whether they are simply sick. For example, my grandmother who suffers from Alzheimer's isn't trying to provoke the nursing staff by stealing and eating office supplies. Rather she is relentlessly obsessed with putting everything in her mouth because she is sick. With that said, there is a deeply theological lesson here regarding how one chooses to talk about "good" versus "bad." Of course, this puts us back into the conversation of the Fundamental Attribution Error.

I have mentioned human moral virtue above, and I recognize how easy it is to get caught up in the language of the world rather than the language of Scripture and depart from the voice of my Christian ancestors. For those of you who have "Let the word of Christ dwell in you richly"[114] and thus recognize that "there is no one righteous, no not one,"[115] then you will recognize the dilemma with basic words such as "good" or "bad." Jesus responds to the human moral status with "Why do you call me good, only God is good."[116] Ephesians 2:3 reminds the preacher that "All of us also lived gratifying the cravings of our sinful nature and following its desires and thoughts. Like the rest, we were by nature objects of wrath." This verse states that humans by nature are not good even if we had *originally* been made good. After the fall, by our very nature, we deserve the wrath of God. By our very nature it is then natural

---

the Bible speaks of is a communal suffering.

113. Powery, *Dem Dry Bones*, 6.

114. Col 2:16.

115. Rom 3:10.

116. Mark 10:18.

to suffer. Alister Begg, in a brilliant sermon entitled *The Way We Were*, proclaims to his congregation that the human condition is weakened by sin.

> "The gospel comes and says, you are a dead man sir."[117]
>
> "The difficulty that many of us will face with this, is because we have such a superficial view of what has happened to us when we came to trust in Christ. Until we get some kind of modicum of an understanding of the fact that the way we were was dead, drifting, disobedient, debased and destined for the wrath of God, until that begins to dawn upon our hearts, then we will neither praise him as we should nor will we explain to our friends and neighbors why it is so important for them to know the love of God in Jesus, because in the back of our minds, we will be saying of them what we are tempted to say about ourselves, 'Well ya know, I'm not a bad guy after all'. . . . "[118]

The Scriptures consistently reiterate that "without faith it is impossible to please God."[119] And without the grace of God, we cannot have faith because faith is a gift from God.[120] This leads to the logical conclusion that no one can be good apart from God. Begg continues, "The only way to do evangelization ultimately is to do it under that shadow of the wrath of God, thereby reminding us of the wonder of the love of God."[121] In other words, for the Christian preacher, the cross stands behind us, above us, and before us when we remind ourselves and our people that we are all broken in heart and mind and thus, we all have mental illness. We are all ill in the spiritual and physical unity[122] of what it means to be human.

Thus, suicide is a theological and an ecclesial issue requiring the preacher to step into the messiness of what it means to be human from a Scriptural lens using Christian language in contrast to the language of the world. And it is with Christian language that we speak about suffering. To be a disciple is to take up one's cross and follow Jesus.[123] The Christian life

117. Begg, "The Way We Were."

118. Begg, "The Way We Were."

119. Heb 11:6.

120. Eph 2:8.

121. Begg, "The Way We Were."

122. Nancy Murphy calls this unity "psychophysical unities". See Murphy, *Bodies and Souls*, 22.

123. Matt 10:38.

is littered with suffering because sacrifice requires suffering and sacrifice is at the core of our faith.[124] When Christians regard injustice, when we see bloated children lacking food, war-torn villages (or entire regions) used as pawns in political exploits, or the day-in-day-out shootings in cities, schools and homes, we should suffer deep anguish. For if we are not brought to tears then one might ask if even our God grieves. Suffering is what Christians do.

Some would say that the issue is not to find the meaning, purpose or answers to the age-old problem of suffering, but rather to find friends in the midst of suffering.[125] It should be shared corporately. A kindergartener might say it like this, "You need to share that suffering or I'm going to go tell!" Preaching is a way of sharing suffering. We preachers share stories from history, from Scripture, and from our very lives to point to the suffering of Christ. We shape our imagination to suffer with each other. Suffering is not a topic that can be explored in one sermon or even a sermon series. It needs to be incorporated throughout the weekly and yearly preaching. After all, the liturgy is always connected to the passion of Christ through community.[126]

Ultimately, the congregation does not need to fully understand suicidal behavior to engage in Christian suicide awareness through proclamation. It is the same way that the congregation does not need to fully understand God to engage God. Calvin reminds the church that God is a mystery, that we cannot fully understand God, which "critiques those who would try to give a single answer to the question of the cause of suffering."[127] For the Christian tradition, simple answers do not cut it. Life together as a church is complicated and cluttered. Preaching should reflect that messiness and complexity—not in sermon delivery (messy sermons only add to the confusion), but with an attitude of humility. Suicide awareness and "prevention does not require prediction,"[128] but rather it requires building habits day after day that are life-affirming. This

124. I have often wondered how in the world Billy Graham garnered so much love, affection and admiration from royalty, presidents and dictators when Jesus says, "If they hated me, they will hate you." (John 15:18). No one seemed to hate Billy Graham. This is a mystery.

125. Isolation is a serious problem with those who have OCD represented through Obsessive Hoarding; see Tompkins and Hartl, *Digging Out*, 25, 153–54.

126. Commonly known as "mystagogical preaching."

127. Creamer, "John Calvin and Disability," 223.

128. Klebold, *A Mother's Reckoning*, 275.

book is for those preachers who recognize the paradox that acknowledging illness is actually a healthy thing to do. This book is for those who desire to understand and talk about suicide from a different perspective, a perspective "from below" as Dietrich Bonhoeffer once penned: "We have for once learned to see the great events of world history from below, from the perspective of the outcast, the suspects, the maltreated, the powerless, the oppressed, the reviled—in short, from the perspective of those who suffer."[129]

NEUROTHEOLOGY: AN INVITATION

Assuming that behavior is intrinsically linked to the human brain, the preacher should consider an exploration into neuroscience especially in the particular area that has come to be called "neurotheology." Neurotheology is the engagement of scientific research using brain scans to record the brain activity of religious pursuits.[130] In other words, brain scans are performed while the subject is engaged in a religious activity (prayer, singing, etc.). The interpretation of these particular brain scan results is what Andrew Newberg calls neurotheology.[131] From the context of preaching, I define neurotheology more expansively—the insight brought about by the intersection of neuroscientific discoveries with Christian theological principles.[132]

Neuroscience is the most progressive and cutting-edge scientific discipline for the current young generation. Carl Zimmer in his book *Soul Made Flesh* calls it "the Neurocentric Age—in which the brain is central not only to the body but to our conception of ourselves."[133] Since preaching is often prescriptive and focused on behavior modifications, it is vital for the homiletician to be aware of how the scientific community understands behavior as an indication of brain health. Engaging both the

---

129. Bonhoeffer, *Letters and Papers from Prison*, cited in D'Ambrosio, "The Reform and the Perspective from Below," 77.

130. The term "Neurotheology" was coined by Eugene d'Aquili and Andrew Newberg. See D'Aquili and Newberg, *The Mystical Mind*.

131. Newberg, *Principles of Neurotheology*.

132. Gregory R. Peterson engages neurology with theology on a philosophical level, but like Newberg, only uses the word "neurotheology" in regards to religious experiences recorded through brain scans. See Peterson, *Minding God*, 109–10.

133. Zimmer, *Soul Made Flesh*, 7.

scientific findings and the historical theological principles of the church can develop a richness to our homiletical preparation.

Neurotheology as a theological discipline is a highly underdeveloped area in theological discourse and, in fact, most preachers probably have never even considered thinking about the intersection of neuroscience and theology. The challenge is to bring neuroscientific research into conversation with fundamental areas of theology for the purposes of Christian, Christ-centered, proclamation.

There are many brain illnesses that seemingly create a false sense of reality such as Cotard, Capgras, and Palinopsia syndromes. Cotard Syndrome is a rare mental disorder in which the patient believes they are dead. Capgras Syndrome is a disorder in which a person holds to a delusion that a friend, spouse, parent, or other close family member has been replaced by an identical-looking impostor causing intense distress. Palinopsia is a visual disturbance that causes images to persist to some extent even after their corresponding stimulus has left (sometimes these images are of people). The more well-known schizophrenia also causes other forms of perceptions that are not perceived as real to other people. Most congregations will not have members suffering from one of these rare disorders. But consideration of such disorders opens up our awareness of how the brain can warp someone's sense of reality. The brain has been shown to trick us (by having sensory, auditory, or visual disturbances) but it is equally true that humans can trick the brain (through mirrors, therapy, meditation, pharmaceuticals, and placebos). Disorders in the brain have a variety of causes, from viruses to physical trauma, from epileptic seizures to drug abuse, and even to family neglect.[134] It is a good reminder that the brain is the predictor of reality for the human being. It is not the eyes that see, but rather it is the brain that sees. It is not the ears that hear but, as many have experienced from cochlear implants, it is the brain that hears. Like eyes and ears, behavior has also been shown to be dependent on brain health.[135]

134. ACE or Adverse Childhood Experience has also been shown to be a predictor of whether a child will grow up with mental illness. See Seder, "Adverse Childhood Experience."

135. Dr. V.S. Ramachandran showed how malleable the brain can be and how we can trick the brain back by his demonstration of a brilliant, simple, and inexpensive solution to phantom limb pain by using mirrors. Phantom limb pain is the neurological sensation of pain in an extremity that has at some point been removed. Many amputees experience this pain on a daily basis. Imagine having an itch in the middle of the night on the bottom of your foot only to realize you do not have a foot to itch.

A good illustration of this point is the story of the railroad construction worker named Phineas Gage. Gage was in a terrible accident in 1848 and his behavior changed due to his brain trauma. His behavior induced by brain trauma led doctors to examine the idea that behavior was not, therefore, solely a matter of moral choice. Eliezer J. Sternberg, in his book *My Brain Made Me Do It*, states, "Our belief in moral responsibility, derived from the assumption that we consciously wield control over our thoughts and actions, seems to form the underpinning of nearly every facet of human life."[136] He goes on to question that, if brain health determines human behavior, then how can an individual be held responsible for their actions? This echoes for me the question "Who then can be saved?" Jesus answers, "What is impossible with man is possible with God."[137] This is one of the clearest texts of grace reiterating the truth that salvation is not up to humankind. The intersection of science with theology in asking questions pertaining to free-will and moral agency is not a fringe issue when it comes to suicide and hence not a peripheral topic to our congregations either.

Alzheimer's disease is a good disease to study and include in one's sermon preparation and delivery since many in our congregations may be very familiar with the ailment. Describing behavioral changes that accompany mental decline is a symptom in Alzheimer's disease that countless people have witnessed and experienced in their own families. Just as it is helpful to define one's terms, it is equally helpful to ask the question: If brain trauma affects our personality, then can brain trauma and illness also be affecting the spiritual essence of a person? This question can lead us to other theological questions revolving around soteriology and personal eschatology.

If all one has to *do* to be saved is believe than how is the *doing* vitally affected by brain health? How is grace (that which is not deserved) part of the equation for those who struggle with believing (and behaving like believers) because of brain illnesses? Can the church believe on behalf of those who no longer can believe due to brain trauma or illnesses? Can

---

An itch is one thing, extreme chronic pain is another. Dr. Ramachandran uses mirrors to visually trick the brain into thinking that the missing limb is stretching and moving, thus delivering visual cues to the brain to stop phantom pain. The brain is what produces the pain. See Ramachandran and Blakeslee, *Phantoms in the Brain*, 44–55.

136. Sternberg, *My Brain Made Me Do It*, 26.

137. Luke 18:26.

verses such as 1 Corinthians 7:14[138] or 12:12[139] aid in our understanding of the church as a saved community rather than an assortment of saved individuals? These questions could continue: Can a person who used to profess Jesus, but (due to illness) no longer knows/remembers Jesus or may even deny Jesus, be saved? Is salvation an issue of right doctrine and beliefs? Is salvation an issue of right behavior or could salvation be an issue of belonging to the saved community regardless of one's behavior or beliefs? These are very challenging questions for young theologians and even seasoned preachers, but I promise, your congregation wants to hear you speak to these issues. Questions such as these throw the preacher into the field of neurotheology.

Jill Bolte Taylor, the author of *My Stroke of Insight,* describes a moment when she was dying due to bleeding in the brain. The bleeding in her brain produced a near-death experience or hallucination. Bolte Taylor describes her near-death experience as being "one with the universe" or "Nirvana."[140] These sensations, according to Bolte Taylor, were not spiritual but neurological. Reflecting on out-of-body experiences, Dr. Sherwin B. Nuland, in his book *How We Die: A Reflection on Life's Final Chapter,* does not take issue with the Christian belief of an afterlife. But he does question the so-called "Lazarus Syndrome" explaining that "biochemical mechanisms" such as hormones or endorphins along with "insufficient cerebral oxygenation" and psychedelic drugs have caused similar "out-of-body experiences" in people.[141]

Just as hormones flood our bodies when we are born to insulate us from the trauma of the birth canal, so too hormones flood us with chemicals to grant us peacefulness as we die. For some, this is evidence of a godless-evolutionary process. But for the believer, this is a testimony to God's good creation. Theist and atheist aside, the issue here is between those that grant the possibility that consciousness can exist apart from the biological brain and "the epiphenomenalists" who state, "the mind cannot exist in the absence of the brain."[142] For the Christian, however, it is usually not so much a concern of consciousness as it is an issue of

---

138. 1 Cor 7:14 states, "For the unbelieving husband has been sanctified through his wife, and the unbelieving wife has been sanctified through her believing husband."

139. 1 Cor 12:12 states, "The body is a unit, though it is made up of many parts; and though all its parts are many, they form one body."

140. Bolte Taylor, *My Stroke of Insight,* 135–36.

141. Nuland, *How We Die,* 138.

142. Carter, *Science and the Near-Death Experience,* 7, 12.

the immortality of the individual and personal soul.[143] Using qualitative research and scientific interests, Elisabeth Kübler-Ross[144] collected data regarding near-death experiences, including blind individuals who were able to "see" and recall images during out-of-body and near-death experiences.[145] But even Kübler-Ross identifies the tension between physical and metaphysical when she recognizes that out-of-body or near-death experiences can be replicated in a lab.[146] The intersection between theology and neurobiology can be a difficult map to navigate but because neurotheology is now a part of the cultural landscape it becomes an important journey for the preacher to take.[147] Especially if that preacher is going to engage the intellectual terrain of mental health and suicide.

Inevitably, this voyage requires a dip into the world of pharmaceuticals since nearly 70 percent of Americans take a prescription drug and 50 percent take two prescription drugs.[148] These statistics do not include over-the-counter medication, vitamins, and herbal supplements that support a billion-dollar industry in America as well as the growing cannabis market. It is an understatement to say that the worshiping Christian congregations in America are highly medicated people. It is naïve to think that the intake of other substances isn't somehow affecting behavior. Any time chemicals of different natures collide, change occurs. This is sometimes good, as with table salt. Sodium is highly flammable when it encounters water, while chloride is toxic to the human when digested. But when you put the two together, they become NaCl (table salt), an element that is not only safe, but one that our bodies require for health. Sometimes chemical reaction is positive, but sometimes chemical reaction can be so foreign and so challenging to the preacher's own experiences and education that the preacher feels paralyzed to address the concern.

143. Kübler-Ross, *On Life After Death*, 43.

144. Lucy Bregman states, "Significantly, Kübler-Ross is astonishingly weak in discussing death due to suicide, or the suicidal impulses of terminally ill patients" (Bregman, *Death in the Midst of Life*, 42).

145. Bregman, *Death in the Midst of Life*, 50.

146. Kübler-Ross, *Death is of Vital Importance*, 86, 88.

147. Other resources for the instructor include: Brown et. al., *Whatever Happened to the Soul*; Crisp et. al., *Neuroscience and the Soul*.

148. See "Nearly 7 in 10 Americans."

Just as chemicals can elicit a near-death-experience,[149] chemical reactions have been described as a gateway to spiritual experiences. In Michael Pollan's book *How to Change Your Mind*, he describes his own drug-induced "spiritual experiences" and states, "But the extraordinary promise on offer in the Church of Psychedelics is that anyone at any time may gain access to the primary religious experience by means of the sacrament, which happens to be a psychoactive molecule. Faith is rendered superfluous."[150] By basing the spiritual reality on neurological feed-back one can either dismiss the Divine (as Pollan's approach allows), or one can rejoice in how the Divine has created the ability to experience the Divine through the physical means of the brain (requiring a union of body and "soul" as will be discussed later). A common response to the neurological phenomenon in chemical reaction is the worship of self as the Divine in which the self is the one who governs the spiritual experiences. Some call psychedelic therapy a form of "applied mysticism"[151] as if "Psychedelic therapy is the wedding of chemistry and the meaning of life."[152] Pollan continues to describe how those who use chemicals to have control over their own spirituality can even conquer the fear of death.[153] Is this the reason that over a quarter of all suicides in the US (approximately 7,500 per year) occur while drugged or intoxicated?[154]

But for those who are suicidal and those who have defeated the fear of death, they still cannot defeat the stigma that goes with suicide. According to Thomas Joiner, 44 percent of family members who have lost a loved one to suicide have lied about the actual cause of death.[155] Even in the light of a thousand "spiritual" experiences, people would rather lie about suicide than speak the truth. Individual physical behavior may be

---

149. Esketamine (which is related to the party drug "Special K," also known as the anesthetic Ketamine expected to induce out of body experiences) was approved by the FDA for Depression. See Hamilton "FDA Expected to Approve Esketmine Nasal Spray for Depression."

150. Pollan, *How to Change Your Mind*, 26.

151. Pollan, *How to Change Your Mind*, 334.

152. Pollan, *How to Change Your Mind*, 335.

153. How does the preacher deal with this in light of Heb 2:15? How does the preacher speak in a tangible way to a highly medicated culture that it is not drugs but Jesus who delivers us from the fear of death? How does Jesus deliver us from this fear? Isn't the fear of death a preventative measure for suicide?

154. See "Facts about Alcohol and Suicide."

155. Joiner, *Why People Die By Suicide*, 6.

altered by drugs, but moral behavior on both the individual and collective sphere remains the same.

BEHAVIOR AND HUMAN AGENCY

Adding molasses to an already sticky subject, another vital element of understanding behavior is the recognition and protection of human agency. Agency always presumes choice. Jennifer Michael Hecht states, "Any choices that deprive a person of all further choices must be rejected."[156] If one holds to that statement, then suicide is an unacceptable behavior because suicide is a choice that deprives a person of all further choice. But keep in mind, for some with mental illness, suicide may not involve a rational choice, but a seemingly spontaneous, impulsive[157] action precipitated by the illness or a drug interaction.[158] This begs the question: Is free choice really a choice when humanity is stained and enslaved by sin or the effects of sin?[159]

Volition, agency, human will, whatever you call it, we want it. We want control of our life and the future. But for the preacher, it is imperative that he or she engages in the paradox that our will is damaged in the fallenness and brokenness of our bodies, minds, and spirits and yet thankfully is caught up within the sovereign economy of God's will. In Matthew 23:37, Jesus is "woe-ing" on the teachers of the law and the Pharisees. He says, "Jerusalem, Jerusalem, you who kill the prophets and stone those sent to you, how often I have longed to gather your children together, as a hen gathers her chicks under her wings, and you were not willing." God sent those we call prophets. These individuals were not puppets by any means, but were sent under God's direction. Then the verse implies that Jerusalem had the choice, the freedom, and the agency to will that God gather them lovingly like a mother hen. Here is the catch, if they had only willed for God then God would have heeded their

156. Michael Hecht, *Stay*, 177.

157. Salters-Pedneault, "Suicidality in Borderline Personality Disorder."

158. As mentioned earlier in regard to Saul, Thomas Joiner states that it is a myth that people die impulsively or on a whim. Suicide is always precipitated by actions of self-harm, even if that self-harm is a by-product of mental illness. See Joiner, *Myths About Suicide*, 70.

159. As Augustine stated: "And the free will taken captive does not avail, except for sin; but for righteousness, unless divinely set free and aided, it does not avail" (*Against Two Letters of the Pelagians*, 3.viii.24).

willingness. But because they didn't will, then God removed God's self, leaving their house or their temple in ruins. But of course, the Scriptures tell us that God's will all along was to show us favor by sending a savior.[160] One only needs a savior if one needs saving. If we had willed for our Mother Hen then we wouldn't need that Savior to be sent. We had to be in a place that needed saving for God's redemptive plan through Jesus to be actualized. Thus, Jerusalem didn't will God as Mother Hen because God's will ultimately was for a Savior. Paul sums it up when he says, "It is for freedom that Christ has set us free."[161]

For the preacher, it is more than just defining terms such as "freedom" and "slavery" for the congregation. The congregation needs to recognize the pervasiveness of human slavery especially in light of thousands of years of church history that has attempted to deal with such issues. It is to the preacher's peril to ignore the contributions of our church fathers and mothers who have dug a rich and deep well of biblical and theological reflection on slavery and freedom. It is an immersion in the vast and unending theological investigation that can keep the parishioners hanging on every word of the homily. Do not fool yourself—your congregation wants to hear words that cause them to think, reflect, and ponder. Once they pass the milk stage,[162] do not spoon-feed them and coddle them. Give them something substantial to eat! Behavior is one area of engagement that the parishioner often expects to hear about since behavior modification usually falls under "application" within the sermon outline—especially in prescriptive sermons.[163] It is within the realm of judgment where human agency and the sovereign economy of God could be engaged from the pulpit since the paradox of human agency and God's sovereign economy are both true. Articulating this truth to the congregation is vital and requires work. Behavior does matter, but behavior is difficult sticky stuff.

This chapter has raised more questions than answers and has only sought to gesture in some of the directions preachers ought to take in their studies and pursuit of faithfully bearing witness in the midst of the suffering and sickness within their congregations. Both neuroscience and psychology have tipped off the church that preachers should return to

160. Gen 3:15.

161. Gal 5:1.

162. Heb 5:13.

163. A prescriptive sermon is usually deductive with a "prescription" or instructions for the listener to do something because of what they have heard.

Scripture with more sensitivity, recognizing that suicide is much more complex and messier than first meets the eye. After all, preachers are entrusted to proclaim salvation to communities who are working out their salvation with fear and trembling.[164]

---

164. Phil 2:12.

3

Theology

Speaking Words about the Word

THEOLOGY (*THEOLOGIA*) IS OFTEN mislabeled as the "study of God." But we cannot study God. We cannot put God under a microscope, or swab God's mouth or give God a survey. We cannot objectively study God. But we can subjectively speak (*logos*) about God (*theos*). Muslims talk about God, Jews talk about God, Christians talk about God. There are a variety of words about God shaping a variety of theologies. But which words are the most truthful words about God? Which words are the right words? They say a picture is worth a thousand words; yet Picasso declared "Art is a lie one tells in order to tell the truth,"[1] because one is prompted to imagine what is beyond our sight through a truthful witness. This is faith and it is foundational for theology, which is literally God-talk or words about God.

And for the Christian, these words of God should always point to the Word of God, that is, Jesus.[2] God speaks. In natural revelation, written revelation, and embodied revelation (Jesus), God speaks. God is not silent. God is never silent.[3] Like the Word that goes out and does

---

1. Barr, *Picasso*, 270.

2. John 1:1–3.

3. For a different perspective, see Barbara Brown Taylor's book *When God is Silent*. To my mind, on the contrary, Scripture's very existence reminds us that God is never silent. Romans 11 reminds us that we do not know the mind of the Lord, how then can we know when God is silent or not? The Shema says, listen up! "Hear of

not return void,[4] Revelation 19:13 proclaims, "He is dressed in a robe dipped in blood, and his name is the Word of God." Jesus is the Word. The Word breathed is the One who breathed the universe into existence.[5] If we cannot even describe with our words the color yellow to a man born blind or the smell of coffee to someone olfactorily inhibited, how could we possibly describe the God who created the color yellow and the aroma of coffee? Thomas Aquinas's solution is to speak analogically. God is not a rock, but God *is like* a rock. However, the solution fails at certain points with Jesus, since Jesus is not *like* God. No, Jesus *is* God. Speaking about the true God can only be done through words that are focused on and empowered by the Word Jesus.[6]

As the ever-present and never silent Word, Jesus is of the utmost importance for the issue of suicide—especially in his one moment of silence. It is almost unfathomable to think that the Word could voluntarily be silenced. But that voluntary silence is precisely what the Holy Saturday (when we live through the time between his execution and his resurrection) is all about. I imagine that it might be hard to get one's mind around the voluntary nature of Jesus's death, so difficult that preachers are tempted to tip-toe around the unity of the Trinity when speaking about the cross. For example, Michael Horton in his funeral sermon for a personal friend who died by suicide states, "Although I myself have lost one of my closest friends, I cannot begin to know your suffering, but God knows what this is like. For he, too lost a dear one, his one and only Son."[7] At first glance this type of language seems harmless—it probably seems this way because this language is so widespread, it saturates every pulpit I know, making us immune to the word's inherent division of God's unity. Jesus clearly states that Jesus and the Father are one.[8] Not two. They are one and, like marriage, this is a profound mystery.[9] Horton continues to say, "God committed his Son to dreadful suffering and a

---

Israel." The issue is not with God's word; the issue is with our ears. See also Augustine, *Confessions*, where his repeated statement, "God, you were silent," (*Conf.* 1.xviii.28–29 and 2.ii.2 at Chadwick, 20–21, 24), gives way to "I thought you were silent, but you were speaking. . . . " (*Conf.* 2.iii.7 at Chadwick, 27).

4. Isa 5:11.

5. Col 1:16.

6. 1 Cor 12:3.

7. Horton, "Our Redeemer Lives and So Shall We," 259.

8. John 10:30.

9. Eph 5:32.

cruel death because through it he could save people who hated him and make them his own."[10] I feel confident that his claim is commonplace in Christian circles. But it is statements like this that keep Jesus an unwilling victim. In fact, however, Hebrews states that it was out of obedience that Jesus died,[11] not by being strong-armed, compelled, bullied, and intimidated. The Father did not will the Son to die without the will of the Son, because the Son's will is to do the will of the Father.[12] Jesus voluntarily laid down his life; indeed, he "set his face toward Jerusalem," and this unity of the Son and the Father should change how we view Christ's death. Not coerced, not forced, but voluntary. For God so loved the world that God sent his only Son . . . and by doing so, God sent God's very self. That day on the cross, God died, the Word died, "descended to hell, and on the third day, rose again."[13]

The self-giving Word is both the starting point and the end goal of any words that seek faithfully to engage the Word. The Word is God in the flesh. Speaking about the Word is only empowered by the Word. Keeping this potential and these limitations in mind, we may now consider the proclamation of words about the Word.

I spend an enormous amount of time defining terms within this book. I do this because words are at the core of what the *logos* of *theos* (the Word of God) is. Words are the starting point for any type of awareness. And it is in the fine details of definitions that a Christian understanding of suicide can really take root. *The very act of defining terms* either limits or broadens our awareness of suicide. Not all readers will agree with the definitions set forth here. But they will provide a framework for the rest of my discussion in this book and, at the very least, will prompt the reader to formulate their own definitions. Defining my terms might seem pedantic to some, but it is an act of humility. By defining my terms, I am not expecting you to think just like me and I am not assuming that what I mean by a word you would somehow know by osmosis. Ultimately, defining our words is an essential foundation of the homiletical method of preparation.[14]

10. Horton, "Our Redeemer Lives and So Shall We," 260.

11. Heb 5:8.

12. John 6:38.

13. Christian Reformed Church, *Apostles' Creed*.

14. See McClure, *Preaching Words*. This book has definitions for several forms of preaching, but no entries for "suicide," "death" or "life."

4

The Spectrum of Suicide

DEFINING THE WORD "SUICIDE" is not as easy as one might imagine. "Suicide" is not a very old word; yet, the history of the word reveals that it has significant variations. It was coined or first attested in 1177 in a work by Gauthier de Saint-Victor entitled *Against France's Four Labyrinths (Contra Quattuor Labyrinthos Franciae).*[1] The first English usage occured in 1643 in Sir Thomas Browne's *The Doctor's Religion (Religio Medici).*[2] It would seem that Sir Thomas Browne may have coined the word independently of Saint-Victor from Latin *sui,* meaning "of one self," and *–cide* (from *cidere)* meaning "kill." It is important to note that in antiquity these two words were never combined. Augustine, one of the most important early writers on suicide, used *ad mortem festinans* meaning to "hasten towards death," *mors sontanea* meaning "voluntary death," and *se ipsum occidere* or *ipsum necare* meaning "to kill oneself."[3] With Augustine, the concept quickly took on a rather negative connotation and in the modern period this development went to an extreme when it was alleged that the term derived from "swine" since *sui* was similar in appearance to a very different Latin word: *sus, suis, sui* (forms of "pig"). Edward Phillips in his 1662 dictionary, *A New World in Words,* stated that the act of suicide was so barbarous it "should be derived from a sow."[4] Thus, to kill oneself

1. Shneidman, *Definition of Suicide,* 12.
2. Brown, *Religio Medici.*
3. Shaw, *Sacred Violence,* 735.
4. Shneidman, *Definition of Suicide,* 10.

was to kill a pig. Jesus's casting of the "legion" of demons into the swine takes on a new level of meaning, especially since those pigs then drowned themselves.[5]

The word "suicide" has become so negative that some advocates of assisted suicide prefer to use words like "death with dignity,"[6] "aid in dying," [7] "hastening,"[8] or "self-deliverance"[9] in place of the phrase "assisted suicide." One should recognize that picking one word or phrase over another implies a moral framework.[10]

This is true not just of one word, but of collections of words joined in phrases. Lindsay Tollefson, a University of Colorado University Academic Advisor, states that even the word "committed" attached to the word "suicide" heightens stigma and should be replaced with the words "died by" (since the word "commits" is used in conjunction with murder and other crimes).[11]

When it comes to the word "suicide," judgment usually arises from a narrow understanding of the definition of the word. And this can be exacerbated by *interpretive inertia*. Inertia is when an object stays in motion or at rest unless acted upon by an outside source. Interpretive inertia then is our inability to see all aspects of a phenomenon because of our routine way of looking at and making sense of it. Interpretive inertia, in other words, is interpreting a text or any phenomenon in our world the way one has always interpreted it. It takes an outside force to bump up against long-seated beliefs, to push them in another direction, for a new way of thinking to develop. Seeing suicide on a spectrum helps to stop the long-held trajectory of inertia. There already exists a wide range of ways that people have understood the basics of suicidal ideation with designations such as active suicidal ideation or passive suicidal ideation

5. See Mark 5:11–13.

6. See *Death with Dignity*.

7. See *Compassion and Choices*.

8. Seligman, "Hastening the End."

9. See Humphry, *Final Exit*.

10. "When 'euthanasia' didn't arouse people to march in the streets demanding a right to be killed if they get cancer, activists began using the terms 'deliverance' and, more recently, 'physician-assisted suicide' to assure a wary public that they would only be dispatched upon request. But apparently these terms do not poll well, especially any term containing the word 'suicide'. So, activists dropped 'assisted suicide' and re-placed it with the currently favored euphemism, 'aid-in-dying'" (from "Euthanasia Terminology").

11. Tollefson, "Letters," 62.

(from fleeting thoughts to preoccupation to detailed planning).[12] Within this broad scope of suicide ideation are contained the differential definitions in diagnosis for non-suicidal self-injury (NSSI) involving difference in causation, motivation, and treatment response.

Rather than opting for a euphemistic expression, I choose to use the word "suicide" over the alternatives to remind readers of the vast diversity of death in which the self is willing, aware, intentional, or even uncertainly moving towards one's own death. Some would prefer to have a very narrow definition of suicide, one that is usually based on intention alone. For this study, intent remains a part of the definition while at the same time allowing there to be a wide range of how that intent might be accomplished and interpreted.

In fact, the very notion of intent is problematic, and a person's intent is not always easy to determine. Sometimes intent can be seen as noble (Thích Quảng Đức, who performed self-immolation as a political protest) or forced (Socrates, who drank hemlock as a state-enforced execution). And in some instances of mental illness in which there is impaired ability to rationally intend or logically predict the consequences, the individual can hardly be held responsible for the outcome.[13] With the difficulty of pinning down intent, the definition of suicide must always be fluid and dependent on context.

Every suicide is unique because every person is unique.[14] Therefore, the definition of suicide should have a very wide spectrum.[15] Importantly, this also allows space for complexity within the preaching event. The diversity of the biblical witness can be opened up to speak to the diversity of motivational, psychological, and social contexts of individuals. Thus, there are "suicide-bombers,"[16] and there are "physician-assisted

---

12. Pedersen, "Suicidal Ideation."

13. "Occasionally persons with schizophrenia will commit suicide accidentally in a stage of acute psychosis (e.g., they may jump off a building because they think they can fly or because voices tell them to do so)" (Fuller Torrey, *Surviving Schizophrenia*, 275).

14. Nicholas Wolterstorff says it like this, "Each death is as unique as each life" (Wolterstorff, *Lament for A Son*, 24).

15. Emile Durkheim defines suicide in four different categories: egoistic, altruistic, anomic, and fatalistic. See Durkheim, *Suicide*.

16. Depending on the culture a suicide-bomber might be defined instead as "martyr" and a "terrorist" as "freedom-fighter."

suicides."[17] Other types include "social-suicide"[18] (also known as "social death" or "fatalistic suicide"). Some even describe self-death as "suicide by lifestyle,"[19] or yet again "murder-suicide," or even "suicide-murder."[20] Suicide ranges from "honorable suicide"[21] such as "protest-suicide"[22] or "altruistic suicide,"[23] to the ambiguous "suicide-by-cop,"[24] "accidental

17. "Euthanasia" or "death with dignity" might also be common terms used. Interestingly, the word "euthanasia" originally meant "good-death."

18. Social-suicide is what some might term "social-death." This happens when a person does something on purpose that ostracizes them from the social group. I have actually witnessed social-suicide, it was highly effective. The person actually intended to die or be cut off from the group. I only assume this because the person said publicly, "Do not call me, do not contact me, I never want to see any of you ever again!" However, with every suicide, intent can be difficult to gauge, and assumptions are never helpful.

19. Long term smoking or excessive alcoholic or drug consumption could be considered a slow suicide by lifestyle. Karl Menninger coined the term "chronic suicide" (Shneidman, *The Suicidal Mind*, 87). The atheist author Barbara Ehrenreich in her book *Natural Causes: An Epidemic of Wellness, the Certainty of Dying, And Killing Ourselves to Live Longer*, states, "We can or think we can, understand the causes of disease in cellular and chemical terms, so we should be able to avoid it by following the rules laid down by medical science . . . anyone who fails to do so is inviting an early death. Or to put it another way, every death can now be understood as a suicide" (*Natural Causes*, 97).

20. Suicide-murder can be best described by the "Werther Effect" or "copycat suicides." This refers to the idea that when a person kills themselves, they are essentially setting an example for others to kill themselves. The "Werther Effect" was coined by sociologist David Phillips after the main character in Goethe's novel *The Sorrows of Young Werther*.

21. An example might be when a captain goes down with his or her ship.

22. Protest suicide is also known as political suicide or self-immolation. It is interesting to note that "immolation" literally means "sacrifice." Since 1963 when the Buddhist monk Thich Quang Duc protested via immolation the meaning of the word became understood as "self-death by fire." The Roman Catholic author Simone Weil may be a good example of protest-suicide involving self-starvation. These types of suicide verge on honor-suicides.

23. Like a soldier who dies by leaping in front of a comrade to protect fellow soldiers from the blast.

24. Suicide by cop complicates the concept of intent because it would seem that the intent is to die all the while refusing to do the act oneself.

suicide,"[25] "suicide-as-revenge,"[26] "ascetic-suicide,"[27] "bullied-suicide," "anomic suicide," or "suicide-as-escape."[28] Many of these labels could overlap to varying degrees. And for all of them, intent can seem either straightforward or ambiguous.[29]

In a book entitled *Definition of Suicide,* Edwin Shneidman articulates the difficulty of the task and then offers his own definition: "Currently in the Western world, suicide is a conscious act of self-induced annihilation, best understood as a multidimensional malaise in a needful individual who defines an issue for which the suicide is perceived as the best solution."[30] Shneidman then exegetes his definition "by clarifying the meaning of each word."[31] Meanwhile, the book *Suicide: Opposing Viewpoints* edited by David Bender and Bruno Leone is a collection of essays that chooses not to assign a particular definition to the word "suicide" but rather allows the word greater fluidity.[32]

The *Diagnostic and Statistical Manual of Mental Disorders* (*DSM-5*) contributes to our conceptualization by defining "suicide attempt" as "a self-initiated sequence of behaviors by an individual who, at the time of initiation, expected that the set of actions would lead to his or her own death."[33] Notice that it avoids the concept of intent and only refers to one's expectation of death. The *DSM-5* appears to suggest that a suicide attempt may be sufficient behavior on its own to constitute a

---

25. This is most commonly inflicted by drug overdose or pharmaceutically related substances. In these cases, the intent might be difficult to assess.

26. Sigmund Freud's primary theory is that the person is in fact (possibly unconsciously) attacking a second party when he or she inflicts self-harm. See Michael Hecht, *Stay,* 188.

27. Severe asceticism or self-discipline (usually for religious purposes) sometimes leads to death.

28. This conveys the thought that suicide is a way out of a person's current situation. There are many different people with many different situations who attempt suicide. It is interesting to note that all those who leaped to their deaths from the burning Twin Towers have been labeled as homicides rather than suicides. The intent was to escape, at all costs.

29. Frank Selden in his book *The Suicide Solution* defines "Ethical Suicide" as one that seems like an "oxymoron" but is simply and directly defined as when one "relieves suffering and does not multiply it" (*The Suicide Solution,* 38).

30. Shneidman, *Definition of Suicide,* 203.

31. Shneidman, *Definition of Suicide,* 203.

32. See Bender and Leone, *Suicide.*

33. "Suicidal Behavior Disorder: Comorbidity," in *DSM-5,* 801.

diagnosis (Suicidal Behavior Disorder). However, it remains a "proposed disorder" in the "Considerations for Future Study" portion of the diagnostic manual. This proposed diagnosis helps to understand suicidality by delineating between suicide attempt, non-suicidal self-injury, suicidal ideation, and "preparatory acts." It also argues that an act would not be considered "suicidal" if "initiated during a state of delirium or confusion, [or] . . . undertaken solely for a political or religious objective." The definition presented by the *DSM-5* would eliminate suicide-bombers (religious), immolation (political), and drug or medically induced (delirium or confusion)[34] suicides.

There is a good reason to have as narrow a definition as possible, specifically for medical and legal professionals, and for insurance purposes. But for the church, a narrow definition actually defeats the goal of fostering greater awareness in the community of faith of the multiplicity of ways in which their members might think about and be affected by self-death (as an act or an idea). Furthermore, despite its carefulness, the *DSM-5*'s understanding of a sequence of behaviors as being "self-initiated" may not be entirely adequate in explaining our experiences and the Bible's witness to those experiences. After all, how many individuals who have engaged in self-initiated suicidal activity were thinking rationally or coherently about the cause-effect relations of their actions or doing cost-benefit analysis apart from cultural, social, or psychological pressures and frameworks?

To truly seek understanding on this topic we must allow for a broad definition, one that extends along a spectrum that includes full intentionality towards one's death, on one side, and a sense that one's life and future are entirely out of one's control, on the other. This wide spectrum provides space for conversation within the community and from the pulpit. I consider it not only a preference but a necessity to see suicide as complex. It is in the complexity that the preacher can be more engaged

---

34. This seems a bit inconsistent since according to the *DSM-5*, "Suicidal behavior is seen in the context of a variety of mental disorders, most commonly bipolar disorder, major depressive disorder, schizophrenia, schizoaffective disorder, anxiety disorders, substance use disorders, borderline personality disorder, antisocial personality disorder, eating disorders and adjustment disorders. It is rarely manifested by individuals with no discernible pathology, unless it is undertaken because of a painful medical condition with the intention of drawing attention to martyrdom for political or religious reasons, or in partners in a suicide pact, both of which are excluded from this diagnosis, or when third-party informants wish to conceal the nature of the behavior" ("Suicidal Behavior Disorder: Comorbidity," in *DSM-5*, 801–03).

and engaging, while at the same time remembering that, because of the complexity, blanket judgments are best withheld. There are many *ways* to bring about self-death and many *reasons* for self-death. Thus, I believe that the definition of suicide should allow for fluidity of individual experiences, psychological dynamics, social conceptions, and (sub-)cultural conversations.[35] Having a theology of suicide on a spectrum can be beneficial when it comes to preparing the Sunday public proclamations and contemplating individual cases. And if we look at the individual case of the voluntary nature of Jesus's death, it falls under what might be termed a "sacrificial-suicide." It becomes apparent that to understand the idea of Jesus's death as a suicide one needs to define the word "suicide" with more deliberate and wide-ranging diversity.[36] This is especially true if one includes martyrdom on that spectrum of suicide.

MARTYRDOM

Many would deny that Jesus's death was a suicide (a sacrificial-suicide). They argue that Jesus was murdered and therefore his death should be categorized as that of a martyr. But while some martyrdoms might not lie on the spectrum of suicide, others should. Today the word "martyr" designates: "a person who voluntarily suffers death as the penalty of witnessing to and refusing to renounce a religion" or "a person who sacrifices something of great value and especially life itself for the sake of principle."[37] The *voluntary* nature of martyrdom provides that essential element that allows martyrdom to possibly fall on the spectrum of suicide.

Suicide as martyrdom can be found among some historical Jewish narratives.[38] But a few early church fathers were worried about intention

35. I acknowledge that having a wider definition of suicide does create problems for law enforcement and mental health practitioners. Having a looser definition of suicide, however, can be beneficial for the preacher and the congregation by eliminating stereotypes and recognizing the unique vulnerability of each individual.

36. Recognizing and even maintaining such diversity should not be taken as inconsistency, regarding which it has been stated, "The Institute of Medicine of the United States National Academies . . . identified inconsistency in classification and nomenclature as a major impediment to suicide prevention. . . . " (Nock, *The Oxford Handbook of Suicide and Self Injury*, 7).

37. Merriam-Webster Dictionary, *Martyr*.

38. The people of Masada and Razis (one of the Maccabean martyrs) are the most famous.

and stated that the *voluntary* nature of martyrdom conflicted with their understanding of what it meant to be a martyr. For Clement of Alexandria true martyrdom was not voluntary, but rather had to be against one's will. For those who were willing and *voluntarily* gave up their lives, Clement implies, it was suicide not martyrdom. The counsel to the church from Clement was to flee death rather than be "in haste to give themselves up."[39] It is important to note that his primary motive seems more to have been the legitimizing of flight from persecution than a concern to deny some persons the status of martyr. His position resonates with his own experiences when he fled Alexandria during the persecution of 202. In contrast, other church fathers such as Ignatius and Tertullian,

> . . . stressed the desirability of martyrdom and exhorted Christians to become martyrs. Indeed, some Christians openly flaunted their faith as a way of courting or provoking their own martyrdom. In Clement's view, they are guilty in much the same way as the murderer and the self-killer, the suicide; while martyrdom is to be respected, the true Christian should do everything possible to avoid it, short of betraying one's faith.[40]

The first church historian, Eusebius of Caesarea, like Clement, may have fled martyrdom during the persecution that took his mentor Pamphilus's life. Yet, unlike Clement, Eusebius sees suicide as a possible and honorable deliverance from the persecutions of the enemy. For Eusebius one could imply that suicide is a type of martyrdom. That suicide is an "escape to the Lord."[41] In addition there are clear suicides that are counted as martyrdoms, such as Agathonice who upon witnessing the horrors of others being killed, "without any explicit profession of faith, without arrest, trial or condemnation," leaped from a high place to her death. "And she thus gave up her spirit and died together with the saints. And the Christians secretly collected the remains and protected them for the glory of Christ and the praise of his martyrs." [42] Other popular examples include Apollonia, Perpetua, Carpus, Polycarp or Papylus. "Where martyrs neither kill themselves nor hand themselves over, the voluntary nature of the martyr's death is often stressed. Even in the arena

39. Clement of Alexandria, *Stromata or Miscellanies,* 4.4 (in ANF Series vol. 2.412).

40. Pabst Battin, *The Ethics of Suicide.*

41. Eusebius, *The Ecclesiastical History,* 8.12.3 (at vol. 2.291).

42. Middleton, *Martyrdom,* 53.

when facing execution, in many cases it is the martyrs who bring about or choose their moment of death."[43]

The history of martyrdom highlights the challenges and opposing viewpoints of the early and contemporary church regarding the distinction between suicide and genuine martyrdom: between Christians who engaged in self death, ironically, to avoid violence and those who sought out persecution as an act of "taking up one's cross and following Christ."[44] It becomes apparent that even among the early church leaders there was ambiguity about how to distinguish suicide and martyrdom. And this ambiguity would continue throughout Christian history.

For this reason, the studies of martyrology are complex. And the complexity continues in terms of how one understands the word "witness" (the original meaning of the Greek *martys, martyros*). For example, even though Stephen is usually considered the first martyr, Karl Barth observes that Stephen was not a martyr because he dies, but he dies because he is a witness (*martys*). The idea is that living witnesses are also *martyres*. In his exposition of Psalm 34, Barth said that it is the cause for which the martyr dies that makes the martyr, not the circumstances of the death, the punishment, or the outcome.[45]

The word "martyr" is itself certainly on a spectrum and has been shown to have a diverse set of meanings. The many meanings of martyrdom have ranged from a physical death to a spiritual discipline (asceticism as dying to oneself).[46] It can mean dying for one's own religion or dying for the community's beliefs and thus becoming a symbol of social justice (such are the cases of Matthew Shepard, now a symbol of gay pride who was murdered in a hate crime; Neda Soltan, now a symbol of Iranian democracy who was accidentally shot; Dietrich Bonhoeffer, now a symbol of anti-Nazism who was executed for the crime of seeking to commit murder; or Thích Quảng Đức, now a symbol of religious equality who died by immolation during a political protest). Paul Middleton states, "While saints require a life, martyrs simply need a death."[47] Middleton later adds that martyrs also need a narrative, a narrative created *for* them

---

43. Middleton, *Martyrdom*, 54.

44. See Matt 16:24–26.

45. Barth, *Church Dogmatics*, 4/3.2, 611.

46. For the representation of ascetic individuals as martyrs, see Athanasius, *Life of St. Antony* 46 and 47 translated in White, *Early Christian Lives*, 37 and 38; Gregory of Nyssa, *Life of Macrina* 19 translated in Cox Miller, *Women in Early Christianity*, 200.

47. Middleton, *Martyrdom*, 26.

by the community so as to represent the community.[48] A martyr isn't a martyr without the collective memory of a group.

Regarding the early Christians, G.E.M. de Ste. Croix describes a volunteer martyr as " . . . a Christian who deliberately and unnecessarily provoked persecution and thus sought a death which he might have avoided without any sacrifice of Christian principle."[49] De Ste. Croix later claimed voluntary martyrdom as encompassing "acts of suicide" or "religious suicide."[50] Likewise, Craig Hovey, in his book *To Share in the Body* emphatically states that martyrdom does not derive from just any kind of death. Hovey says that martyrdom is especially different from suicide for the main reason that suicide is enacted as an individual event. "Just as it is not possible to become a member of the church by baptizing oneself, so also it is not possible to become a martyr by directly seeking it or in some way killing oneself."[51] Unfortunately, in this statement, Hovey is not recognizing the community's role in defining individual deaths and their culpability and the often collective nature even of what seems to be "individualistic" acts of suicide.[52] What Hovey wants is a clear-cut definition of martyrdom distinguishable from suicide. Still, he recognizes the challenges when he states in the very same chapter that he is sympathetic to viewing "martyrdom as a discourse rather than a single thing," and that he has "found that martyrdom itself is not a simple concept."[53]

The complexity of martyrdom intensified with the historical tension between "real" martyrs and inauthentic ones. This becomes even more apparent from the historical study of the martyrs of the Protestant Reformation and the Roman Catholic Counter-Reformation. From the Roman Catholic point of view, the protesters were criminals and heretics. From the protesters' viewpoint, the Protestants were the true church and the persecution heaped upon them by the Roman Catholic Church was the

48. Middleton, *Martyrdom*, 30.

49. De Ste. Croix, *Christian Persecution, Martyrdom, and Orthodoxy*, 153.

50. De Ste. Croix, *Christian Persecution, Martyrdom, and Orthodoxy*, 154.

51. Hovey, *To Share in the Body*, 50–51.

52. This could include the Jewish martyrs who died in a mass suicide at Masada or the contemporary phenomenon of physician-assisted suicide or even the well-known copy-cat Werther Effect that requires community.

53. Hovey, *To Share in the Body*, 52.

proof of their authenticity and credibility.[54] "The difference between a martyr and a heretic was a matter of perspective."[55]

It is the claim of this book that the current attempts to limit the word suicide should be expanded, nuanced, and recontextualized for the preacher and for Christian communities. I hesitate to lock in the term too rigidly and would rather allow the terms "suicide" and "martyrdom" to cover two spectrums that partially overlap.

I believe that this flexibility is actually a positive quality for the preacher. It forces the preacher to accept the ambiguities of Christian language and think about the variety of ways that a person might relate to their own death. The concern then becomes not classifying a person's death but rather attending to the particularities of each individual. This applies to individuals today as well as individuals in the past and even our ancestors within the story of faith. The complexity of the word "suicide" comes to light only after examining the many diverse perspectives that can be presented through communication and can be drawn from different disciplines. Without the many voices from a diversity of approaches, suicide would remain constrained in a box of monochrome objectivity. That box is false and misleading, and even worse, that box reinforces taboos, stigmas, and an unhealthy and even unchristian way of thinking and preaching about suicide. When the complexities of suicide are revealed through diverse perspectives and then incorporated into productive preaching regarding the topic of suicide, communal compassion can be realized.

54. Middleton *Martyrdom*, 101.
55. Middleton *Martyrdom*, 94.

5

Ecclesiology and Suicide

"It's against the law to commit suicide around here."
"Yeah, it's against the law where I come from too."
"Where do you come from?"
"Heaven."[1]

THE CHURCH AND HER POLITY have always been engaged in life and death issues. Historically, the condemnation and ultimate criminalization of suicide might have been a tangible way for people to enforce a narrower definition of suicide for state and legal purposes.[2] Likewise, it was a way of drawing a firm line between what was right and what was wrong so that the church could enforce culturally expected behavior.

Clement of Alexandria criticizes those who sought out martyrdom, stating, "If he who kills a man of God sins against God, he also who presents himself before the judgment-seat [to be martyred] becomes guilty of his death. And such is the case with him who does not avoid persecution."[3] In other words, if someone was willingly persecuted or

---

1. Capra, *It's a Wonderful Life*.

2. For an exhaustive study on ecclesiastical and state law, see Murray *Suicide in the Middle Ages*, 396–425.

3. Clement of Alexandria, *Stromata or Miscellanies*, 4.10 (in ANF Series vol. 2.423).

sought martyrdom, they were in turn sinning against God, which of course, was unacceptable behavior.

Augustine, however, was the most influential thinker in how future generations of clergy and laypeople would understand suicide. Like others, Augustine was an early opponent to suicide as martyrdom. Some propose that at the core and "inception" of his great work *The City of God* is the "contemplation" of suicide.[4] He made the argument that if people were being persecuted they should run to the hills (just as Matthew 10:23 said). The following generations of Christian theologians were highly influenced by Augustine when he said, "For to kill oneself is to kill a human being."[5] Like Clement of Alexandria, in Augustine's mind suicide was equal to the sin of murder.[6] For Augustine however, there were exceptions to this rule: Jesus's death, Samson's death, even the impending death of Isaac by the hand of his own father were acceptable deaths on the grounds that they were deaths commissioned by God.[7] Those deaths were acts of obedience to God's will.[8] In theology, this came to be known as vicarious atonement.[9]

For those early Christians who had died in the same manner as Christ's death their names were recorded in a literal book representing the *Book of Life* referenced in Daniel 12:1. These names would be read during worship or recorded in the registers known as *the obituary.*[10] There seems to be a consensus among historians that within early Christianity there was an expression of hope regarding death, confirmed by the historical fact that the church did not start legislating against suicide

4. Shaw, *Sacred Violence*, 727.

5. Augustine, *City of God* 1.20 (in Bettenson, 32).

6. A small exception to the rule was for women who sought to preserve their virginity in the face of sexual violation. Some considered suicide a virtuous option for women facing rape. Augustine, however, did not view suicide as a noble endeavor to avoid sexual violence. See Augustine, *City of God* 1.19. For other resources, see Ambrose of Milan, *On Virgins* or John Chrysostom's sermon *On the Virgin-Martyr Pelagia* in Christo, *Martyrdom According to John Chrysostom*, 179–83.

7. Augustine, *City of God* 1.21 (in Bettenson, 32).

8. Origen of Alexandria held that Jesus's death was voluntary or laid down *before* it was taken from him as an act of obedience to the Father. Thus, voluntary deaths or martyrdoms were suicides, but they were also sacrificial. See Origen, *Against Celsus* 2.11, 22; Tertullian, *Apology* 21.19. Augustine saw this type of voluntary death not as sinful but as faithful; see Augustine, *The City of God*, 1.26 and *On the Trinity* 4.16.

9. Bushnell, *The Vicarious Sacrifice*, 130–31.

10. Aries, *The Hour of Our Death*, 161.

(or martyrdom seen as voluntary death) until the fourth century. Despite the strong arguments against suicide and voluntary death during persecution, Christians were still having to be reminded by a fifth century historian of Constantinople (Sozomen) of "the divine precepts which command us not to expose ourselves to persecution."[11] The early church fathers did not unanimously condemn suicide. Suicide as a sin, as I have stated earlier, was promoted by Clement of Alexandria, but did not gain strength until Augustine in the early 400's.[12]

By the mid-300's (in the generation following the last persecution of Christians by the Roman state), martyrdom as suicide would no longer be considered the will of God since Christ's suicide, being the eighth suicide, relegates it to be the last acceptable suicide. It was generally believed that Christ's death accomplished the will of God once and for all. The logic followed that God, therefore, would no longer will for anyone to take their life. Hence, if someone died by suicide, it was not God's will.

In 305 the Council of Guadix sought to deter suicide and voluntary martyrdom by publicly deleting names post-mortem of those who voluntarily died during the persecutions.[13] By 348 the Council of Carthage condemned all those who had chosen voluntary death under the ruse of righteousness. The first legislation in canon law came in 452 at the Council of Arles where voluntary death or any type of self-death was proclaimed "theft from God."[14] The councils are a small example of how theological leaders heavily engaged in the conversation of virtue and ethics regarding what constituted a good death. For the Christian church the ethics of dying became a vital discussion in regard to Christian identity and what it meant to be a part of the Christian communion.

This was so important that by 533 the Council of Orleans actually denied funeral rites to those who had died by suicide.[15] By 693 the Council of Toledo (influenced heavily by Augustinian theology) would officially declare all those who had died by suicide to be excommunicated; suicide after all (according to Augustine) had become the unforgivable sin because one could not repent after one was already dead.[16] "It was the

---

11. Cited by Fedden, *Suicide*, 123.

12. Aries, *The Hour of Our Death*, 59.

13. Philippe Aries states, "what had originally been the book of the elect became the book of the damned" (*The Hour of Our Death*, 104).

14. Norris, "Suicide," 1094–95.

15. Norris, "Suicide," 1094–95.

16. Augustine, *City of God*, 1.26 (in Bettenson, 38).

church, if anyone, who insisted on the heinousness of suicide." Yet, "the church rarely punished the attempt, and when it did, the punishments were egregiously mild and of a conspicuously penitential character. The church's reaction to an attempt can amount to no punishment at all, but the opposite, in the form of intensified care for the person who has made the attempt."[17]

By 1150, Peter Lombard, a French bishop and professor, completed his *Four Books of the Sentences*, which became the most influential book for the next five-hundred years on sacramental theology.[18] Within the development of the sacraments, Extreme Unction was established as a pastoral act implemented before death. It became very important to receive this sacrament before one died because the church began to understand that how one dies determines one's ultimate identity. This is because of the belief that how one dies reflects how one lived. The inquiry of what is a good death is an essential question because death ultimately symbolizes one's life.[19] A good death represents a good life.[20] Thus, "the idea of a 'good death' presupposes a norm that risks judging as 'inadequate' the death of a person who does not fit the mainstream ideal(-ized) picture."[21]

During the Middle Ages, according to Philippe Aries in his book *The Hour of Our Death*, a good death is first one that is anticipated and that comes as no surprise.[22] Therefore, a good death is one that has had advanced warning. To die suddenly was not a good death. Second, a good death is one that provides the dying with community. Thus, a good death is one in which the dying person is surrounded by others; essentially, it is a corporate event. To die alone is not a good death. Third, a good death is one that has afforded the dying an opportunity to engage in the cultural rituals of confession and the ability by the dying to say their last farewells. To not say goodbye is not a good death. Finally, a good death is one in which the dying can participate in the ritual of Last Rites now known as

---

17. Murray, *Suicide in the Middle Ages*, 425.

18. White, *Introduction to Christian Worship*, 185.

19. Hauerwas, *Truthfulness and Tragedy*, 103.

20. It is interesting to note that for some Christians the interpretation of a good life actually comes from dying to self, also known as "mortification." See Col 3:5 and Rom 8:13.

21. Staudt and Block, *Unequal Before Death*, xliii.

22. Aries, *The Hour of Our Death*, 6–28.

Viaticum.[23] In the Middle Ages, to die by suicide is quite contrary to the view of a good death. Suicide was often, and is still to this day, a private event providing no option for confession, farewells, or last rites. Thus, during the Middle Ages, laws were written against self-death, making suicide a definitively bad death and a criminal act.

One very prominent thinker on the topic of suicide was Thomas Aquinas. In his *Summa Theologiae* he sought to put the dominant prohibition of suicide on a philosophical basis, founding his argument against suicide on nature. He first states that suicide must be wrong because it is contrary to nature, that is, that every living organism naturally desires to preserve its life.[24] Second, it is destructive to the human and social community.[25] And finally, only God should determine when a person will live or die[26] since God created and owns all things.[27]

It is unclear whether such philosophical and theological claims specifically affected state practices. But, when suicide (by one's own hand or by voluntary martyrdom) became seen as a civil crime against the state, the punishment at times was extreme and excessive. People who had died by suicide were used as visual examples to the remaining community. The bodies were sometimes dismembered and displayed. At times, the bodies were exposed to the elements and left to rot. At other times the bodies were thrown in the trash heap or dumped at a crossroads with a large stone placed over the face.[28] Since the church and the State were often intrinsically tied together, this type of corporal punishment

23. Extreme Unction is often confused with Last Rites because at one time it was delayed until the danger of death was immediate. After Vatican II, Extreme Unction became specifically designated for the healing of those who are sick, not only for the terminally ill, and it is now referred to as the sacrament of the Anointing of the Sick. Keeping this in mind, the last sacrament before death is Eucharist as a meal for the journey. See Davies, *The New Westminster Dictionary of Liturgy and Worship*, 512.

24. Through modern biological studies we have learned that many life forms seek self-death from lemurs to beached whales and even to the very small cells in the human body in a process called Apoptosis.

25. Depending on the culture, suicide can bring honor to the society especially when the suicide is seen as a sacrifice *for* the community.

26. This argument is also used by the Christian Science Movement regarding life-saving medical intervention practices such as surgery or even antibiotics. See Vance, *Suggestible You*. Likewise, this is an ongoing conversation regarding The Patient Self-Determination Act of 1990 which allows competent adults to refuse medical care.

27. Thomas Aquinas, *Summa Theologiae*, Question 64.5, "Whether it is Lawful to Kill Oneself."

28. Alvares, "The Background," 10–11.

sadly rendered the church culpable in dehumanizing such people. There was religiously sanctioned violence towards the deceased. The original point of such extreme punishment was to deter other suicides. The good intention to deter suicides, however, soon turned into financial revenue for the State, which at times legalized the foreclosure and seizing of all the deceased's estate, by-passing the family claim.[29] People in authority financially profited from suicide.

The original goal to deter suicide by the threat of punishment, however, was successful. The punishments could be so dishonorable to the person's sense of dignity that suicides were in fact reduced. For example, during the fifteenth century, city and church leaders in Geneva would parade suicide corpses unclothed in the public squares.[30] Some might assume that, for women especially, the thought of having one's body nakedly displayed was enough to deter suicidal behavior.[31] On top of this, the body was excluded from a church funeral or burial. Suicide was seen as a community problem; yet paradoxically, by criminalizing and vilifying the deceased, the community was essentially giving up on the person, exiling the deceased from the community, or in other words *dividing* them from the community and hence making them an in*dividu*al. Capital punishment essentially is when the community abandons the dying to individualism. By forsaking the dying to a segregated death, the community hurts the community, turning the deceased's family into victims of pain, shame, and isolation.

During the rise of modernity in the Age of Enlightenment, the response to death took on a more scientific approach, focusing on medicine and nature and moving away from superstitious myths about the supernatural. During the Enlightenment, suicide gained a positive reputation from people like David Hume[32] or Baron D'Holbach.[33] It was during this time that suicide was seen as a product of sickness, which resulted in the decriminalization of suicide. Because it was increasingly seen as a consequence of mental illness, suicide likewise moved from being an archaic community problem to a modern individual problem,

---

29. Michael Hecht, *Stay*, 54.

30. Mason, *Preventing Suicide*, 60.

31. Mason, *Preventing Suicide*, 60.

32. Hume, *Essays on Suicide*, 10.

33. D'Holbach, *The System of Nature*, 136–38.

seeking solution by social isolation through confinement in an asylum. Michel Foucault mentions that,

> For a long time, certain forms of melancholia were considered specifically English; this was a fact in medicine and a constant in literature. Montesquieu contrasted Roman suicide, which was a form of moral and political behavior, the desired effect of a concerted education, with English suicide, which had to be considered as an illness since the English kill themselves without any apparent reason for doing so; they kill themselves in the very lap of happiness.[34]

For the first time since Augustine, people started to move from the ethics and status of suicide as a corporate blight to suicide as an individual transgression.[35] Within the Roman Catholic tradition, at one point, suicide was an unforgivable sin; but after Vatican II, suicide could be pardoned. The *Catechism of the Catholic Church* states in article 2283, "We should not despair of the eternal salvation of persons who have taken their own lives. By ways known to [God] alone, God can provide the opportunity for salutary repentance."[36]

In the modern day, the Roman Catholic Church has become more empathetic towards those living with or even dying with suicidal ideation. But I cannot say the same thing for Protestants. In the fall of 2021, after a fifty-minute lecture on the blasphemy of the Holy Spirit to sophomore students at a Protestant liberal arts university, 40 percent of the students replied to the written exam question, "What is the unforgivable sin?" by answering "suicide." Suicide wasn't even mentioned in the previous lecture. The unpardonable quality of suicide has become so ingrained in the conscience of Christians that to think otherwise *feels* unlawful, even unnatural. Bumping up against interpretive inertia will always feel uncomfortable. But, can we rewire how our brains think about suicide in a more scriptural and faithful way? I think we can. And I believe we must.

---

34. Foucault, *Madness and Civilization*, 212.

35. This may have been precipitated by John Donne's questioning of the concept that suicide is a sin in his *Biathanatos*. See Donne, *Biathanatos*, 7.

36. *Catechism of the Catholic Church*, 550.

6

Death

*"Homiletics is only theological to the degree
that it is thanatological. . . . "*[1]

I THINK ABOUT DEATH all the time.[2] But I am very cautious in talking about death all the time. People may assume that they know exactly what I mean when I mention "death" and be concerned about my mental state and self-harm. We do not do anyone any favors when we make assumptions about death because death is seriously complicated.

In 2001, I was working as a volunteer hospital chaplain at Boulder Community Hospital in Boulder, Colorado. The attendant at the nurse's station informed me that one of my visits that day was to Ethel who had passed during the night. That is all I was told. I found this odd. If Ethel passed, then why is she still occupying a room? Instead of being smart and asking probing questions, I simply went to Ethel's room where I was greeted by three middle-aged women gathered around the bedside of Ethel. The women were Ethel's daughters, dutifully holding Ethel's hand, stroking her hair and moistening her mouth with a tiny pink sponge on a stick. I introduced myself and noticed immediately that Ethel was breathing. After a few niceties, I excused myself and went back to the nurse's

1. Myers, *Preaching Must Die*, 190.

2. Eccl 7:4 (TLB) states, "Yes, a wise man thinks much of death, while the fool thinks only of having a good time now."

station. "I thought you said she had died," I accused. "She *is* dead," the nurse responded in hushed tones and then explained that her brain was dead and, therefore, she was legally dead by the definitions accepted by Boulder Community Hospital. Yet, her brain stem was still alive, hence the breathing, the flickering of the eyes, and the arm twitching.[3] This was my first experience with the ambiguity of death. Ethel's daughters would sit attentively, singing to mom and brushing her hair until, in due time, her organs would fail. There in that room, those grieving women sat with what many would have considered a dead body, treating it as if it were alive.[4]

Some define death as the point when the brain waves go flat, but others define death when both the brain and the heart cease functioning.[5] In the United States, the Uniform Determination of Death Act of 1981 specified how to determine when someone is legally and medically dead. This legislation concluded that "the entire brain must cease to function, irreversibly. The 'entire brain' includes the brain stem, as well as the neocortex."[6] But in the wider human circle, the definition of death has not been agreed upon. In the *Annals of Medicine*, Rachel Aviv points out that along with "Native Americans, Muslims, and Evangelical Protestants, in addition to Orthodox Jews . . . [the Japanese] never adopted a comprehensive law equating brain death with the death of a human being."[7]

> Declaring "someone dead is an issue that is cosmic and commonplace, personal and civic all at the same time. It involves the laws of a state, the historic identity and mission of a hospital, the writings of medical ethicists, the diverse faiths of the individual on the hospital bed, the friends and family that surround that individual and the health care practitioners seeking to offer treatment and care."

For the Christian, death should always be understood primarily through the Scriptures. The Scriptures describe people who are dead

3. You may remember a similar story regarding Jahi Mcmath; see Aviv, "What Does it Mean to Die?"

4. Saying that a body is dead ignores the thousands of living organisms that make up the body and which provide for the decomposing process. Death is a community activity for the living.

5. Nuland, *How We Die*, 123.

6. See "Uniform Determination of Death Act."

7. Aviv, "What Does it Mean to Die?"

in understanding,[8] dead in their transgressions,[9] and deceased even though their brain and their heart are both perfectly physically operative. The born-again Christian is dead too, that is, dead to sin.[10] In Christ we are both, at the same time, alive and dead. The common and simplified explanation of this seeming contradiction is that the Scriptures are describing people spiritually not physically dead (that is, either dead in sin or dead to sin).

Yet, this explanation does an injustice to the integrated reality of the symbiotic and dependent relationship of the breath and the body. People have been so influenced by non-Christian Platonic conceptions of a soul separate from body that they maintain that the spirit of a person can live apart from the body because they are conceptualizing a person's spirit as something other than what I am imagining. But I am getting way ahead of myself. Part of the difficulty in talking about death is appreciating the systematic nature of death and giving equal consideration to the various parts that make up one's understanding of death.

DEATH AND SOUL

An essential element to constructing a theology of death is developing a theology of "soul." My mother believes that the body has a personal and individual soul. She doesn't know where the soul is located in the body. I do not think she would agree that the soul lives in the liver.[11] She does, however, believe that when she dies her soul (a ghost-like spirit that belongs personally to her), somehow imbued with her personality, her memories, and the shape and look of her physical body, will leave her body and go to heaven. She implies that her "soul" is inherently immortal, that it can never die.[12] After all, my mother would state, "the little boy in *Heaven Is for Real* experienced it this way" so it must be what happens.[13] Ask her about judgment day and she will tell you that it will happen at the

---

8. Eph 4:18.

9. Eph 2:1.

10. Rom 6:11.

11. Plato taught that a part of the soul was located in the liver and thus allowed one to make divinations based upon the shape of the liver; Plato *Timaeus* 70e–71e. Such a notion is referred to at Ezek 21:21.

12. According to 1 Tim 6:16 only God is immortal.

13. Burpo and Vincent, *Heaven Is for Real*.

end of time. Yet, she still asserts that her soul will go to heaven, not hell, before any judgment has taken place.[14]

I also used to believe this, until my grandmother developed Alzheimer's disease. I remember Ruby as gentle, kind with her words, and modest. She was the quiet back-pew person who always smiled and had a purse full of toys for small granddaughters bored with the sermon. I know that she had her moments, like everyone does. But in general, she knew how to behave in public. But then, she got sick. She didn't get bad. She got sick. And by the time my dad put his mom into a lock-down Alzheimer's facility, Ruby had lost that smile. She went from sad to angry and then back again to sad; crying one minute to screaming and cussing the next. She had prayed with me before bed and before meals, reading to me from the Good Book. But in her eleventh hour, she had completely forgotten her name and the name of her Savior. Had she become, as people describe, one of the living dead? Those who are dying while living, or rather, living as dying? Was her soul completely dependent on her physical brain and memory access? Once her memory died, did her soul leave? Had her personalized, individualized soul departed her, leaving behind just the shell with amyloid-clogged brain waves and an active yet oblivious brain stem? Or had her soul gone dormant, sleeping within? Was memory the evidence for a soul? And once we could no longer remember—remember this body broken for you—were we as good as dead? These questions pushed me to re-read the Bible, diligently and consciously resisting that sluggish interpretive inertia and assumptions about "soul" that are so deeply entrenched in modern ways of thinking.

My rejection of the Platonic notion of soul[15] resides in both the biblical revelation and in the symbiotic relationship that undergirds the word for "soul." The main problem with a Christian anthropology is, quite frankly, the word "soul." It is such a problematic word because it carries with it so much baggage.[16] Some folks want to get rid of the

14. Many Christians stubbornly hold on to this teaching even after being presented with passages such as John 3:13, "No one has ever gone into heaven except the one who came from heaven—the Son of Man."

15. In Plato's *Phaedo* the bi-partite soul is more unified than in Plato's *Phaedrus* where the winged soul is tri-partite and always warring against itself. Regardless, in both the *Phaedo* and the *Phaedrus*, the soul is immortal and superior to the flesh (which is bad).

16. Many Christians stubbornly hold on to the teaching that the "soul" is by nature "immortal" and at the same time created and self-possessing (belong to an individual), even after being presented with passages such as 1 Tim 6:15–17, "God,

disembodied, non-physical concept of "soul" altogether (physicalism). Others, like my mom, believe that we are comprised of two parts, the body and the immaterial, immortal "soul" that departs the physical realm upon death (dualism).[17] Still others hold fast to 1 Thessalonians 5:23 visualizing the human to be made up of "spirit, soul and body" (trichotomists). Jesus gives four parts in Mark 12:30, "Love the Lord God with all your heart and with all your soul and with all your mind and with all your strength." In seminary, "soul" was limited to only these possibilities from which to choose. But another option arises when interpreting Scripture by Scripture.

In Genesis, the word *Nephesh* is commonly translated "soul" (*psyche* in the Septuagint's Greek translation of Genesis 2:7). *Nephesh*, that immortal breath, is what sustains the whole person and is essentially what makes one a living person.[18] When *Nephesh* goes away the whole person dies. Watching Ruby descend into a thick fog it became apparent that the human spirit must be material in that it depends on the physical for the ability to express emotions that are related to experiences, whether divine or human experiences. How can the physical be sick and the human spirit unaffected and vice versa? Only if the human spirit is physical as well.

I define the human spirit as physical, represented through emotions, personality, motives behind choices, or objects of choice, all based on the brain function with its hormones, synapses, and millions of other components. Defining "spirit" as physical is a challenge to understand when all our life we have assumed that "spirit" by nature, as the word implies, is spiritual, not physical. To think of "spirt" as physical we have to intentionally reason differently.

And thinking about "soul" differently forces us to "understand resurrection differently: not the re-clothing of a 'naked' soul with a (new)

---

the blessed and only Ruler, the King of kings and Lord of lords, who *alone* is immortal and who lives in unapproachable light, whom no one has seen or can see. To him be honor and might forever. Amen." (Italics mine). The "soul" could be seen as immortal if it was understood to be *Nephesh* but that would require relinquishing beliefs of self-possession of soul as a created thing.

17. In Mary's Magnificat she sings, "My soul glorifies the Lord and my spirit rejoices in God my savior" (Luke 1:46). Reading this from a union perspective of the body and spirit this text could be understood as God glorifying God when the Holy Spirit descends upon Mary equipping her to sing with all her emotions (spirit) to God. God glorifies God in *Nephesh* while Mary sings. It is a partnership of praise.

18. Ps 119:175.

body, but rather restoring the whole person to life—a new transformed kind of life."[19] After all, "soul" defined as a ghost of an individual is a Greek idea not a Hebrew one.[20] This type of thinking divides the New from the Old Testament (with an assumption that the New Testament teaches soul-body dualism) and keeps us from gaining revelation from the whole of the Scriptures.

When God commands God's people to love God with our soul, it is a command to love with all of our physical, emotional, and spiritual energy by the equipping of God's breath. When Hannah prayed, she prayed with all that she had; she prayed with her whole being equipped by the Holy Spirit.[21] The symbiotic relationship of the human body and "soul" fits into the paradoxical nature of the Christian faith: just as God in Christ is both human and divine, seen and unseen, explained and unexplainable, so too the body is dependent on God's breath. From the time God breathed, the two have gone together like a tree and its roots, like a cloud and water, like ants at a picnic.

Let us not forget that Adam was created physical at first. And it was good. But it wasn't complete until God breathed into "them bones, them dry bones."[22] Breathing into us did not somehow create physically-shaped, individualized, personalized, inherently immortal human "souls" or ghosts. Rather, breathing into us was God's act that gave us life and sustained our life. "The Spirit of God has made me; the breath of the Almighty gives me life."[23] But "if it were his intention and he withdrew his Spirit and breath, all mankind would perish together and man would return to the dust."[24] And when we die, that breath (which does not belong to the human individual), that borrowed breath, goes back to God. Ecclesiastes 12:7 says it this way, "The dust returns to the ground it came from, and God's breath returns to God who gave it." And

19. Murphy, *Bodies and Souls*, 23.

20. Modern day *Yahrzeit* (Yiddish), the day of remembrance of the dead (for relatives and others), includes the idea of "soul" as a ghost-like characteristic of an individual. It is difficult to find evidence for this concept of "soul" in ancient Hebrew. Fasting in remembrance of the dead may have developed as early as the Second Temple period while contemporary practices of *yahrzeit* probably began in Germany about the fourteenth century. See https://www.britannica.com/topic/yahrzeit.

21. 1 Sam 1:10.

22. Gen 2:7 and see Ezek 37:5.

23. Job 33:4.

24. Job 34:14.

David sings, "when you take away their breath, they die and return to the dust. When you send your Spirit, they are created."[25] And just as we die, Christ "must necessarily die, yet at no breach or battery . . . he gave up the Ghost and as God breathed a soul into the first Adam, so this second Adam [God incarnate] breathed his soul into God. . . ."[26]

But doesn't the New Testament offer a different view of the soul? After all, it is not written in Hebrew but in Greek and thus instead of *Nephesh* it uses *psyche*, the term used in Greek literature for a "soul" that could be detached from a body and remain self-existent.[27] James Dunn is particularly helpful when he writes,

> . . . in simplified terms, while Greek thought tended to regard the human being as made up of distinct parts, Hebraic thought saw the human being more as a whole person existing on different dimensions. As we might say, it was more characteristically Greek to conceive of the human person 'partitively' whereas it was more characteristically Hebrew to conceive of the human person 'aspectively'. That is to say, we speak of a school having a gym (the gym is part of the school); but we say I am a Scot (my Scottishness is an aspect of my whole being).[28]

In fact, the New Testament, though written in Greek, attempts to maintain the more holistic Hebrew concept. Recognizing this, translators will only sometimes translate *psyche* as "soul." For instance, when Christ claims that anyone seeking "to save their life" will lose it, the word translated as "life" is *psyche*. It may not always be explicit, but the New Testament shares the Hebrew notion of soul, or *Nephesh*, as God's breath. The breath of God gives and sustains life. In regard to this breath, "both the chicken and the egg come second."[29] As God's breath, the "soul" preexisted the human body. Therefore, the "soul" is not mine or somehow the real me. Of course, the question begs to be asked then, what exactly

25. Ps 104:29–30.

26. Donne, "Death's Duel or, a Consolation to the Soul, against the Dying Life, and Living Death of the Body," in Thornton and Washburn, eds., *Tongues of Angels, Tongues of Men*, 286–87.

27. It should be noted that there is more diversity in Greek literature about the nature of the soul (even in Plato's own corpus). See Long, *Greek Models of Mind and Self*.

28. Dunn, *The Theology of the Apostle Paul*, 54.

29. Logan, *Air*, 307.

is me? This was a question that I asked while watching Ruby deteriorate. What really made Ruby "Ruby" and when was she truly Ruby?

Aside from minerals, oxygen, nitrogen, and water, the human body is made up of microbiomes outnumbering human cells by ten to one.[30] From the food that we eat and the language we learn, to the air that we breathe, we humans are ecosystems, communities formed from both dead communities (great-great grandpa's DNA) and living communities of organisms and borrowed materials. "Breath requires an exchange, it requires an inside and outside, and it requires give-and-take."[31] Hence, defining "me" apart from the millions of elements and miniscule bodies that make me "me" is not only narrow-minded, it is detached from the everyday cycles of life. The fact of the matter is that most of what makes me human isn't even human! An appreciation of microbiomes offers a rich and complicated view of the "me" rather than the bi-partite distinction of body and soul. Along with the Bible, the communal, symbiotic reality of what makes me "me," aids in dislodging interpretive inertia from its customary path and offers us opportunities to engage in the hermeneutic of suspicion (suspicion, that is, of the ways our unquestioned assumptions have caused us to find in Scripture things that might not be there—or might not be there in quite the way we thought).

The atheist author Susan Sontag who resisted her personal demise stated that "Death is unbearable unless you can get beyond the 'I.'"[32] But this is not the case for those (like the mythological Narcissus) who are so obsessed with the 'I' that their self-love begins to hate the "I" to the point of destroying the "I." For Christians, we are told that God loves personally and communally and that nothing can separate us from that love.[33] For the Christian it isn't about getting beyond the "I" but rather about being in a personal and a communal relationship with the "Thou" and acknowledging that one's whole existence rests in the "Thou." For the real way to know who you are is not to look inward but to look outward. You cannot know who you are as a spouse without that marital relationship. You cannot know who you are as a teacher without students, a parent without a child, a sister without a sibling. We are who we are because of the relationships we inhabit. This is a reflection of the God who is One

30. National Institutes of Health, *NIH Human Microbiome Project Defines Normal Bacterial Makeup of the Body*.

31. Logan, *Air*, 305.

32. Quoted by Rieff, *Swimming in a Sea of Death*, 167.

33. Rom 8:38–39.

yet Three. The "I" is not an "I" without the "we." Even though thinking about death requires the "I" to do the thinking, we only think the way we think about death because of how our communities and relationships have shaped our thoughts in the first place.

Thus, preaching death, especially death on the cross, is vitally important as it shapes the "I" within the fellowship of the "we" so as to die with Christ. Think of it like the relationship between a woman and a man. One cannot "be" without the other. A woman gives birth to a man, but a man provides the seed. Their existence is integral to and for the other. This is also the case for life and death. Death has no real significance apart from life and vice versa because, "each gains its particular sense and nuanced meaning from the other."[34] Just as the body is dust without the breath of God. We truly become "we" when God breathes into us.

DEATH AS ENEMY

Many of us take for granted certain assumptions about death. The beliefs are usually that death is: 1. Unnatural. 2. Not what God ever intended for God's creation. 3. An intrusion and an undesired rending of relationships. I too thought this way. But now, I no longer think of death as unnatural. Like most Christians, I originally assumed that "natural" meant being included in the original plan and intention. I thought that death was not originally part of the plan and thus, it must be unnatural. Like Augustine's understanding that evil is the absence of good, death was somehow a rip, a hole, an absence of God's good creation. This absence of good is used by God but certainly not created by God, the giver of all life.[35]

In 2010, I was leading a group of seventh graders through confirmation. One very bright boy made the statement, "I wouldn't want to live in the Garden of Eden because they didn't have bread and I love bread." I inquired why he thought the Garden of Eden would not contain bread and he said, "Because bread has yeast and yeast has to die so that the bread can get puffy." He didn't need to say anymore. I understood what he was saying. I had implied that death arrived on the scene because of the disobedience of Adam and Eve, thus, before "the fall" there was no death. But is this true? As the young confirmand pointed out to me, the death of yeast makes something very wonderful. The death of leaves in the fall

34. Davies, *Theology of Death*, 151.
35. Augustine, *City of God* 11.17 (in Bettenson, 448).

turns the high-altitude aspens of my home-state of Colorado into a sea of yellow. The death of organic materials makes hearty, loamy soil, and the daily death of my skin cells sloughed off in the shower makes way for soft supple skin. Are these deaths not natural, pertaining to the natural rhythms of life and even nourishing life? Death can and does sustain life, in so many ways. When I look at the creative order of God's world, death is part of that creation that supports on-going life. The thousands of spores and fungus that scavenge the dead left from our hairbrushes or from fallen trees do us a mighty service. Were spores and fungus not created until after the fall?[36] "The only reason that the world is not awash in the dead is that the fungi return them to the earth."[37] Not only is death natural, but it was included in God's original plan of seasons and cycles before disobedience.[38] Death should not be treated as alien, foreign, or even opposed to life since "death is part both of creation and salvation."[39]

This is significant because Jesus and the cross were not afterthoughts. Jesus's death was not a backup plan in case humans should make a wrong turn.[40] Jesus was not some solvent or household scrubbing agent to clean up and fix the mess Adam and Eve got us into. Really, if we follow the train of thought that Jesus was an addendum, what does this theology say about the very nature of God? That God has no foresight, sovereign wisdom, or even an ultimate design? On the contrary, we should reject the idea that Jesus was an unintended postscript as pitiful theology. Jesus was, from the very beginning of time, the plan. God in his love . . . in his love . . . predestined us.[41] From before the creation of the world we were chosen *in Christ*. In view of God's very Trinitarian and relational nature as Life-giver, God planned for death.[42] Why else would death

36. I have not defined "the fall." The Scriptures never use those words. By using them, I am employing vocabulary from outside theological sources, making the assumption (dependent on my interpretive inertia) that humanity has gone from up to down.

37. Logan, *Air*, 33.

38. The story of Adam and Eve does not include the word "sin." Even though "sin" is used in the story of Cain and Abel, John Behr states that, "The only period which has something in common with the customary picture of the Fall is the period before the Flood" (Behr, *The Mystery of Christ*, 79).

39. Davies, *Theology of Death*, 9.

40. Behr, "Learning Through Experience," 38, 41.

41. Eph 1:4–5.

42. This planning is what orthodox theology has labelled the "economy of God" (from the Greek *oikonomia*).

be an option when God said to Adam, "but you must not eat from the tree of the knowledge of good and evil, for when you eat from it you will certainly die."[43] Death was an option because it was already an element from which true life came. Jesus's death and resurrection are the whole purpose for the entire creation of the universe. And like a stone thrown into a pond, the ripples of the crucifixion move out in all directions. Those who were chosen before the cross look forward to the cross just as after the cross we look back to the cross for our salvation. For there is no other way to be saved,[44] no other way for any person in all of time, but through the name of Jesus.[45]

Death, as God's wage for sin, is ultimately a blessing.[46] The fact that Adam did not cease biological respiration immediately upon disobedience reveals that death can be understood on varied levels, or should I say, on a spectrum. Romans 12:1–2 demonstrates this dynamic when Paul states, "Therefore I urge you brothers and sisters, in view of God's mercy, offer your bodies as living sacrifices, holy and pleasing to God, for this is your spiritual act of worship." Notice that offering our *bodies* as a sacrifice is a *spiritual* act because the (living) sacrifice only truly lives by dying (sacrifice), following in the footsteps of Jesus. In fact, death can only begin to be understood in light of Life, that is, Jesus. The One who destroyed death did so by dying, or in other words: through the Way, the Truth, and the Life's death, Life gave up life so others could live. This is the heart of salvation. Karl Rahner's closing paragraph in his *On the Theology of Death* provides this basic Christian understanding of the paradoxical nature of death when he says, "again and again death is that terrible and blessed event. . . . "[47]

---

43. Gen 2:17.

44. Acts 4:12.

45. John 20:31.

46. R.C. Sproul's explanation for why Adam did not die right away includes, "God does not enact the penalty [physical death] immediately as an indication of his [God's] grace." Claiming God's grace does not make theological sense though, since Adam eventually dies physically. With salvation history in mind, God's penalty had originally been designed for Jesus. The exaltation of Jesus's humiliation on the cross is the moment of saving grace. And even after Jesus Christians continued to die, because the penalty of death was much more than just physical death. See Sproul, *What We Believe*, 127.

47. Rahner, *On the Theology of Death*, 119.

DEATH AS LIFE'S LIFE-PARTNER

If death was part of God's original design, then why, some might ask, does death hurt so badly? Why does it feel like an intruder that rips away relationships? It doesn't just feel like an intruder. It is an intruder. But, an intruder that in its very act of severing relationships, forms new relationships and new ways to relate, to the living and to the dead.[48]

When Kitty Murray died, I said to her four daughters that the eldest was now the matriarch of the family; a new way to relate to each other, without mom. And with every birthday, holiday, anniversary, or All Saints Day, there will be a new way to relate to the dead. The grief in the wake of loss does not "get better." Life doesn't "get better" when someone dies. But it does get different. And different doesn't have to be bad. As Ecclesiastes reminds us, there is a season for everything.[49] A season for death brings a season of new birth. Spring always comes after winter, morning always comes after night, and life comes after death for God's children.

But doesn't Paul call death the last enemy to be defeated?[50] Yes, Paul does say this. And anyone who has lost someone to death can testify to their pain that death stole like a thief, a thief who cared less of the need and value of this loved one. A thief is not for us, a thief is against us, a thief is an enemy. The grief process of a suicide is different than normal grief in death. That there is guilt, remorse, and the nagging, "What if I had locked the door so the thief couldn't have gotten in?" But for the one who died by suicide—did that person see death as an enemy or as a friend?

Regardless, Paul still calls death an enemy. How can anything good come from an enemy? In this train of thought, we who are opposed to death then view those who see death as a friend as being delusional or better yet, sick. In my hospital rounds and sitting with the frail in hospice, some have said to me, "I do not want to live forever," or "Why am I still here?" or "Maybe I will see you again tomorrow, but then again, maybe I won't," (spoken with a cockeyed wink). Sarcastically I used to mutter, are these people non-Christians or something? Don't they know that death is the enemy? Shouldn't we fight and resist it with every breath and every

---

48. This is similar to the Hegelian Dialectic where two things die, in order to make one brand new thing.

49. Eccl 3:1.

50. 1 Cor 15:26.

medical intervention possible? "Do not go gentle into that good night!"[51] Yet, if this is true, then why do so many believers in Jesus have Do Not Resuscitate directives (DNR's)? Shouldn't we be preaching against DNR's? Isn't a DNR active suicidal ideation? Or is a DNR an act of faith?

Yes, Paul says death is an enemy. Therefore, how can we defeat this enemy? The answer is: we don't. We do not defeat death. Only God defeats death and Jesus defeated death—by first dying. For he "has put everything under his feet."[52] A former pastor of the First Lutheran Church of Duluth, Minnesota, Michael Rogness in his sermon entitled *The Last Enemy Defeated*, says it like this: "Life comes not by avoiding or escaping death, *but by dying!*"[53] If this is true, then we cannot avoid the certainty that life depends on death. And if life depends on death, how could death be an enemy to life? After all, it is through the cross that we are saved and receive life. In other words, Jesus, upon encountering the enemy (death) brought forth life. It was death that defeated the enemy death. We usually think it was the resurrection that was the birthplace of salvation. And indeed, the resurrection is the pinnacle, the crest and the crown, the cherry on top, that extra undeserved bonus, and the glimpse into that window of God's glorious, over-flowing, mind-blowing generosity. But the cross is the center, the apex, and the hope. For without death there would be no resurrection. For since death entered the world through sin,[54] it would only be by sin's death that death would die. Jesus, who was without sin, carried our sin to the grave.

Furthermore, "it is only in the light of the Passion that we can even speak of 'Incarnation.'"[55] Both Easter and Christmas are contingent upon Good Friday. The womb foreshadows the tomb. Hebrews 2:14–15 states, "he shared in [our] humanity so that by his death he might destroy him [the devil] who holds the power of death . . . and free those who all their lives were held in slavery by their fear of death." The power of the incarnation was designed with death in mind. And just as Christ, by Pentecost, incarnates us into his body, Easter actually empowers and energizes us to die, as Paul states, "Why do we endanger ourselves every hour? I die every day—I mean that, brothers. . . . If I fought wild beasts in Ephesus

---

for merely human reasons, what have I gained? If the dead are not raised, 'Let us eat and drink, for tomorrow we die.'"[56] Being born again happens at the cross—drowning at the waters of baptism.[57] The deluge of Noah's flood was not only catastrophic, it was, at the very same time, redemptive. This is death for us—devastating yet liberating—a *eu*catastrophe (a "good catastrophe").[58] Death is a necessary enemy, one that has now become subordinate under God[59] because Christ was obedient to the point of death.[60]

Death is no longer our foe because Christ is our victor. We may weep, but we do not weep like those who have no hope.[61] "And we know that in all things God works for the good of those who love him, who have been called according to his purpose."[62] Since death has been made null and void, then, in a way, for the Christian death is now an illusion (certainly, its finality is an illusion). Death, for the ransomed is more like a portal, a door from one way of living to another way of living. Proceeding from time, we move into eternity. This will be a new way of living for sure, one that we cannot even conceive of since our minds currently are limited by time and space. Douglas Davies describes this illusion in the motif of "imaginary partner of covenant." Or in other words, death as a lifelong partner (or a "life partner") with the one who is Life.[63]

Death, Paul says, is an enemy. Jesus spoke many times about enemies, that we should pray for our enemies and even love our enemies. How did Christ defeat his enemy? He did so through love on a cross. This concept "is foolishness to those who are perishing, but to us who are being saved it is the power of God."[64] It is foolishness to those who are dying, but power for those who are called to die to self through Christ's death. This power of God frees us from the "fear of death." We no longer have to fear death because the penalty for sin[65] has been destroyed. In Christ,

56. 1 Cor 15:31–32.

57. John 3:5. "I tell you the truth, no one can enter the kingdom of God unless he is born of water and the Spirit."

58. "Eucatastrophe" was a term coined by Tolkien, in *The Monsters*, 156.

59. 1 Cor 15:26–28.

60. Heb 5:7–9.

61. 1 Thess 4:15.

62. Rom 8:28.

63. Davies, *Theology of Death*, 153.

64. 1 Cor 1:18.

65. Rom 5:12; 6:23.

because of his suffering, salvation has been made perfect and death for the Christian is not to be rejected or feared. Hence, the same Paul who called death an enemy could later proclaim "to die is gain."[66]

But when it comes to suicide, on that broad and lengthy spectrum, the fear of death is sometimes shown to be fearlessly faced, not because of Christ's sufferings alone, but for a varied array of reasons including political protesting, escapism, and/or mental illness. Does this lack of fear stem from a glimmer, a glimpse into what theologians called "common grace"? Do they receive death as a balm?[67] Some die by suicide in fear, others die without fear. Regardless, the Christian has diagnosed that this life doesn't cut it. Christians recognize that this present world is seriously waning. For this is not our home. And many others, find this life meaningless. It is as if "all labor and all achievement springs from man's envy of his neighbor. This too is meaningless, a chasing after the wind."[68] Solomon in all his splendor states, "I hated life."[69] And we Christians know, that "If for *this life only* we have hoped in Christ, we are of all people most to be pitied."[70] Paul reminds us that "the whole creation has been groaning as in the pains of childbirth right up to the present time. Not only so, but we ourselves, who have the first fruits of the Spirit, groan inwardly as we wait eagerly for our adoption as sons, the redemption of our bodies."[71]

DEATH AND IMAGO DEI

As has become clear, one of the tasks of this book is to be distinctively Christian by confronting our interpretive inertia. A very popular contemporary discourse is the invocation of the idea that all humans reflect the image of God (the imago Dei). I would like here to rethink the imago Dei, because even if many affirm this idea for all humans, the concept frequently functions to legitimate a "me-centered" narcissism. A return to Scripture confirms that the current understanding of the idea

---

66. Phil 1:21.

67. The human being, across all cultures, seems to continue to desire and create that which is permanent. For the business-minded man, the future permanence of a company requires planned obsolescence.

68. Eccl 4:4.

69. Eccl 2:17.

70. 1 Cor 15:19.

71. Rom 8:22–23.

is fraught with difficulty and error. While I don't expect every reader to agree with me, I hope at the very least to spark critical self-reflection regarding how interpretive inertia touches all of us in various ways. If we want to tackle suicide and we seek to affirm life this should not come at the cost of elevating the equally sinful idea of self-exaltation. Self-idolatry is not better than suicide. Self-reverence and self-praise is not the solution to suicide. In fact, I would suggest that a better understanding of the "image of God" recognizes the centrality of death and self-emptying in the image itself.

"Despite all the significant technological advances by which the race has invaded the shallow segments of outer space, *man* is still *man's* most frequent subject."[72] So it is no surprise that any account of death (in particular suicide) must grapple with the question: What does it mean to be human? This is philosophical but also very theological. It is theological because many historical and contemporary Christians have stated that to be human means to reflect the image of God. But this raises certain fundamental questions. What does it mean to be human in light of being originally created in the image of God?[73] And, is it possible to be human without the image of God?

To reflect God's image is not the same as *Guernica* reflecting some characteristic of the inner workings of Picasso. Both *Guernica* and Picasso were created from the dust of the earth. God cannot be compared since God is not created. Modern Christians, to the contrary, take the image of God to designate a unique dignity belonging only to humans. Yet, there is immense dignity in all God's creation, from a blade of grass, to a beetle, or a drop of rain, or a ray of sunlight. Furthermore, seeing humans as uniquely dignified fails to recognize that humans are uniquely sinful precisely because they put themselves at the center of creation. Instead of developing theories like this about what the image could possibly be, what if we allowed Christ and the New Testament witnesses to tear down our own false images of the imago Dei? For a human to reflect God is for creation to reflect that which is not created. This can only happen

72. McEwen, "Conversations with a Grave Digger," in Motter, *Preaching About Death*, 56.

73. Wis 2:23 says, "For God created man for incorruption, and made him in the image of his own eternity, but through the devil's envy death entered the world and those who belong to his party experience it." See "Wisdom of Solomon" in *The Apocrypha*, 104. Note that the phrase "the image of his own eternity" seems to be taken directly from Plato's *Timaeus*, 37d.

by the indwelling of the creator *in* the creation. According to Scripture, however, God dwells only *in* those who were chosen before the creation of the world to be adopted according to his pleasure,[74] even while at the same time God sustains all creation.[75]

The New Testament definition of the image of God is this: the Second Person of the Trinity in Jesus the Christ. Jesus "is the image of the invisible God,"[76] and "The Son is the radiance of God's glory and the exact representation of his being, he sustains all things by his powerful word."[77] Or again: "The glory of Christ, who is the Image of God."[78] And upon "seeing" the image of God, the man born blind knelt and "worshiped" Jesus.[79] By faith the man then was conformed to that image.[80] This image is not the human male figure. This image is the Son of God, the second person in the Trinitarian relationship of the One God. We must read the Genesis account of the image in the light of the full revelation of God in Christ.

Death came through one man, Adam.[81] When Adam violated God's precepts, Adam died. His death was the loss of the image of Life. Adam was a dead man walking because he no longer carried the reflection of true Life. Adam lost the imago Dei. The imago Dei withdrew from humanity because of our disobedience. After all, how could a sinful being reflect that which is completely without sin? For the fallen, original sin passed down from father to son, mother to daughter; we are not born sick or broken but rather we are born dead.[82] We are dead on arrival[83]—yet, a dead baby planned, before the creation of the world, for adoption into Life.[84] Who wants to adopt a dead baby? Only a loving (and life-giving) parent would.

74. Eph 1:4–6.

75. Acts 17:24–28.

76. Col 1:15; 3:10.

77. Heb 1:3.

78. 2 Cor 4:4.

79. John 9:38.

80. Rom 8:29.

81. Rom 5:12.

82. Eph 2:1.

83. I take this phrase from Ligonier Ministries(www.ligonier.org/learn/devotionals/dead-arrival).

84. Eph 1:4–5.

Well-meaning preachers make broad platitudes (because of interpretive inertia) and in the name of inclusivity will often say that "all humans reflect the image of God." Adam may have originally been made in the image of God. But he lost that image. Currently, not *all* humans reflect the image of God. Just because all people experience God's goodness[85] does not mean that all humans reflect God's goodness as his image and likeness.[86] Often, the label imago Dei is a feel-good cliché heightened by the idolatry of the self in an already narcissistic culture. And if we are honest with ourselves, the idol of self-centeredness is pervasive in our pulpits.

At the same time, by our very existence, we do reflect our Creator. But as already noted, all creation does this. Imago Dei is something unique and special. Biblically speaking, after the drowning of creation under the chaotic watery deluge,[87] one does not read about the imago Dei (referring to God's reflection in humans) until the New Testament. Neither Moses (after Genesis 9) nor the prophets ever talk about human beings made in the imago Dei. David never sings about humans as the imago Dei. On the contrary, the only images mentioned are idols and the patriarchs and the prophets consistently call for the death of false images. Graven images were strictly forbidden, even those of the human figure. After the apocalyptic flood we see a growing plethora of man-made images of a god (humans and other created things), all of which were and are false and misleading. The death of the image due to Adam's disobedience is akin to looking in a mirror—the image reflected back to us is the fallen image of humans attempting to be like God, apart from God.

The Scriptures declare that the image of the true God is only regained through faith in God's Son Jesus. "For those God foreknew

85. See Matt 5:54, where "He causes the sun to raise and fall on the wicked and the righteous" indicates a sign of "common grace."

86. "Goodness" is a fruit of the Spirit; see Gal 5:22.

87. Gen 9:5–6 is the last mention of imago Dei in the Old Testament. Here it is presented as a chiastic poem harkening back to Cain and Abel accounting "for the life of his fellow man." If we translate "man" as "brother" (both in verse 5 and 6) we can glean a spiritual parallel to "brother" in the New Testament, not of *all* humankind, but only of those who share the faith in Jesus through a spiritual adoption. See 1 John 4:21 in relationship to 1 John 5:2. "Whoever loves God must also love his brother"; and "This is how we know that we love the children of God: by loving God and carrying out his commands." Not all people are children of God. Only those who resemble God through the image of God. See 1 John 4:2 and John 1:11.

he also predestined to be conformed to the likeness[88] of his son . . . "[89] and "we who with unveiled faces[90] all reflect the Lord's glory, are being transformed into his likeness with ever-increasing glory, which comes from the Lord, who is the Spirit."[91] The image of God is not somehow *naturally* imbued in us, since our nature is now defective because of sin; but rather the image of God comes from outside of us. The image of God comes from God. And when the image of Life was taken away from Adam, Adam died. But by the power of Christ's death, Christ's image is restored in us. By the death of God, the imago Dei was born again so that "with regard to your former way of life, [you] put off your old self, which is being corrupted by its deceitful desires; [you are] made new in the attitude of your minds; and [you] put on the new self, created to be like God in true righteousness and holiness."[92] The death of the imago Dei in Adam reflects the death of Jesus. The imago Dei died so that we could be restored unto the Image. The image of sin is covered by the imago Dei like the blood that covered the door posts at Passover. The story of salvation was originally composed with the preordained design of the fall of humanity so that the Son of Man could be lifted up. The image of God died in humankind in order to reveal the resurrection of God's Image.

An analogy might be helpful here. Imagine a pillar of marble, originally with an image, that has been sitting at the bottom of the sea for a thousand years. An underwater archeologist might be able to make out that the pillar at one time had some sort of image despite its decomposed nature. If you can image that then you can understand how John Calvin views the imago Dei—"not totally annihilated and destroyed in him, yet it was so corrupted that whatever remains is frightful deformity."[93] Effectively, then, there are no remains of the image (if the prototype is no longer detectable then the image is no longer an image). Sin has completely destroyed the image. One might ask, "But doesn't all of creation reflect her Creator?" Yes, animals, trees, stars and oceans reflect God's character qualities of order, beauty, diversity within unity. But this is not the same type of reflection that was once imputed to Adam and Eve. The imago

---

88. It should be noted that theologians typically differentiate "likeness" from "image" for many good reasons, including the inclusivity of Jas 3:9.

89. Rom 8:29.

90. 2 Cor 3:13.

91. 2 Cor 3:18.

92. Eph 4:22–24.

93. Calvin, *Institutes*, I. XV. 4.

Dei was specifically unique to humankind. Humans require the Holy Spirit for re-creation of the image and the imputing of righteousness.[94] As Clement of Alexandria says, "As I see it, he himself fashioned man from dust, regenerated him by water, made him grow by the Spirit, and educated him by word, guiding him to adoptive sonship and salvation by holy precepts, with this in view, that, *refashioning the earthborn man into a holy and heavenly man by his coming, he might fulfil to perfection those words of God, "Let us make man to our image and to our likeness."*[95] The imago Dei therefore, does not come by high platitudes of humanistic dignity. It only comes by being in Jesus. One does not bear the image of God if one rejects the Son of God. A mirror that turns away from the sun no longer bears an image of the sun.

I have paused over the imago Dei as a theological principle, in this chapter for two reasons. First is the fact of the stark reality that the paramount image or idol in this world is the love and reverence of the self.[96] The self can easily become the center of one's universe. Our culture encourages self-adoration, even self-glorification and it frequently uses the casual comment that all humans reflect the imago Dei as an unwitting justification for self-love. It is good for the economy after all to be devoted to the self. And as we worship ourselves, we expect to have the most honorable seat at the table. "When Jesus noticed that all who had come to the dinner were trying to sit in the seats of honor near the head of the table, he gave them this advice . . . ," sit on the floor.[97] Because it is on the ground that the kernel of wheat falls and dies.[98] It is, in fact, totally natural to die by suicide. But it is supernatural to die with and *in* Christ.

Therefore, a second reason I have paused over the imago Dei is that, if Christ is the true image and if we only truly bear that image through him, then self-emptying, not self-glorification, is at the heart of being an image-bearer. We are called to follow Christ in his humility. Humility is death. It is death to the self as an idol. Humility cuts down the person.

94. See Cyril of Alexandria, *Responses to Tiberius* 10: " . . . the Holy Spirit makes the divine image gleam in [Christians] through sanctification" (quoted in Burghardt, *The Image of God in Man*, 65).

95. Clement of Alexandria, *Paedagogus* 1.12; quoted by Burghardt, *The Image of God in Man*, 78.

96. Paul states that the end of the world will not be marked by earthquake or famine, but by the love of self. See 2 Tim 3:1–2.

97. Luke 14:7–11.

98. John 12:24.

"Anyone who loves their life will lose it."[99] Voluntary humility, the kind that comes from the realization that we are not the center and we are not worthy, turns to tearful gratitude for what God has done, for who God is, God's character, God's glory. This is the gospel. God in God's honor saves the dishonorable by emptying God's honor on the cross.[100]

Christian primary education often teaches early on that to honor yourself is good stewardship towards God. Unfortunately, the warning tag attached to the mattress is ripped, removed, and forgotten. Caution should be counseled with respect to the fine line between care of the self and the exaltation of self. Good stewardship of self-care frequently turns into self-love, under the guise of self-esteem, to assure self-promotion. What if, instead, we told our children to hate themselves? Because, that is what Jesus tells us to do: "Anyone who hates their life in this world will keep it for eternal life."[101] Paradoxically, the most loving thing to do for yourself is to hate yourself. The Greek mythological Narcissus was the opposite. He loved himself, adored himself, idolized himself to the point of destroying himself. But Christians hate themselves for the sake of loving God and others. That is, we humbly and repentantly recognize what we are, what we really are—dirt in the shadow of God's grandeur. The brave preacher affirms the suicidal person, "Yes, hate yourself." Whoa! What preacher would say such a thing? Only the preacher who knows that loving oneself is not the true path to life and that "true humility and fear of the Lord lead to riches, honor, and long life."[102]

DEATH AS LEGACY

Nicole Nordeman sings, "I want to leave a legacy; How will they remember me?" *Legacy* is a popular Christian song despite Ecclesiastes 9:5, which warns "that even the memory of them will be forgotten." Legacy usually means to leave something behind. We humans desperately want permanency, but to covet permanency without the One who is permanent is a futile deception. First Timothy 6:16 states that only God is

99. John 12:25.

100. "Having instituted a new exodus to the promised land of the new Jerusalem, Jesus leaves in place the tribulation of the exodus whereby the people learn humility—even while he also makes clear that for those who are united to him, death has lost its sting" (Levering, *Dying and the Virtues*, 133).

101. John 12:25.

102. Prov 22:4.

immortal. Everything outside of God someday will be reduced to dust. From the billion-dollar paintings in the Louvre to the jewel-encrusted crowns in the Tower of London to the faces and memories of those on Mount Rushmore to the Andes Mountains harboring Machu Picchu to the vast Mariana Trench and even to the memories of kings and queens of old—all creation groans[103] because death is the great equalizer.[104] "The grass withers and the flowers fade but the Word of our Lord stands forever."[105] We are not God's equal.

According to John 1, the Word is God, the Second Person of the Trinity, the Son who became incarnate as Jesus. And Jesus had no sin. But he who had no sin actually became sin. In fact, God is the One who presented God to be sin for us.[106] And "the wage for sin is death." Death, according to Romans 6:23, is the payment for sin. But, let us not forget that this wage is required by God, who, in God's very nature, is good.[107] Thus, death reflects God's goodness as a wage that we did not earn, but rather a "gift of God [who] is eternal life in Christ Jesus our Lord." Like a loving father who disciplines his daughter for disobeying him, the penalty's purpose is not to destroy but to restore. For the Christian, death is not the end. God in God's patience provided a chastisement that contained within the very nature of the price a nugget that reflected God's goodness, God's redemption, and God's merciful righteous judgment. God's wrath is not separate from God's mercy, the two go together, eternally woven and described thus:

> My life is but a weaving
> Between my Lord and me.
> I cannot choose the colors,
> He weaves so steadily.
>
> Oft times he weaveth sorrow
> And I in foolish pride,
> Forget he sees the upper,

103. Rom 8:22.

104. The first mention of the phrase "death is the great equalizer" is often attributed to Mitch Albom in his popular book *Tuesdays with Morrie*. But this is incorrect. The first mention of this exact phrase goes back to a pioneer woman who may have been influenced by James Shirley's poem *Death the Leveler* in 1646. See Moodie, *Life in the Clearings*, 77; (reprinted by Blackmask Online, 2002; quotation on 36).

105. Isa 40:8.

106. 2 Cor 5:21.

107. Luke 18:19.

And I the underside.

Not till the loom is silent
And the shuttles cease to fly,
Will God roll back the canvas
And explain the reason why.

The dark threads are as needful
In the Weaver's skillful hand
As the threads of gold and silver
In the pattern he has planned.[108]

We do not always understand, but God is not dependent on our understanding. From God's very nature, God's wrath reflects God's goodness. Even in God's wrath of handing us over to ourselves (just as he handed himself over to us),[109] there is always hope in God's character of unrelenting mercy, softening of hearts, unplugging of ears, and God's sending God's voice through the voice of a preacher. For the salvation of one depends on the voice of another. And according to Martin Luther King, Jr., in his sermon *Transformed Non-Conformist*, it isn't just any other, but rather, "Human salvation lies in the hands of the creatively maladjusted."[110] And those prophets who spoke and recorded the words of God, one could argue, were creatively maladjusted. Salvation has been experienced, written, and exposed through the record of the revelation and the life-changing, heart-warming whispers of God. Thus, we "follow the Lamb wherever he goes."[111] We even follow him in death. My point in saying all of this is to encourage the Christian to address suicide not by rejecting death or being afraid of death, but rather by moving towards death. We might be able to kill the body,[112] but we cannot destroy that Word, the breath of God that provides and sustains all of life.

Does this sound as if I am encouraging suicide? What legacy is there in suicide? Saying, "move towards death" sounds perilously dangerous. What preacher says such things? Well, to begin with, John Calvin. He

---

108. Alt, "The Weaver." This poem has also been attributed to John Banister Tabb, Grant Colfax, Benjamin Malachi Franklin, and Corrie Ten Boom. See http://www.theworshipbook.com/blog/lyrics-whodunnit for more information.

109. Rom 1:24.

110. King, "Transformed Non-Conformist," 11.

111. Rev 14:4b.

112. Matt 10:28.

preached, "Above all, when we look to the martyrs of past times, well may we detest our own cowardice!"[113] Or Thomas à Kempis who preached, "the Cross is the right way of living well," and "Follow Christ, Who leads by his Passion and his Cross to eternal rest and light; because if ye are now his companions in tribulation, ye will shortly sit down with him at the heavenly table in perpetual exultation."[114] But of course, we really do not have to look farther than Jesus who proclaimed the short prescriptive sermon when he prayed, "not my will, but thy will be done."[115] The will for what? The will to die.

Death is part of life. And this is reflected in the legacy of our liturgy.[116] The Christian calendar and our sacraments are centered on Good Friday. And it would seem that even revelation itself is contingent on death. Paul states, "I deliver to you as of first importance what I also received, that Christ died for our sins in accordance with the Scriptures, and that he was buried and that he was raised on the third day in accordance with the Scriptures, and that he appeared to Cephas, then to the twelve." John Behr states that what is most germane is the repetition of "in accordance with the Scriptures."[117] For, "Only after his Passion, his crucifixion and exaltation, do [the disciples] begin to understand who Christ is and what he has done, and they did this by turning back to the Scriptures."[118] Jesus's years of ministry, teaching, and fantastic miracles were not enough for belief. It was only in reading the Scriptures in light of the cross that they remembered "what had been written of him and had been done to him."[119] If revelation stems from the cross then so should Christian preaching. The Gospel is no gospel if it is not founded on the cross. For Christians, this is our living and dying legacy.

113. Calvin, "Enduring Persecution For Christ," in *The World's Great Sermons*, 209.

114. Thomas À Kempis, "Taking Up the Cross," in Thornton and Washburn, eds., *Tongues of Angels, Tongues of Men*, 198, 201.

115. Luke 22:42.

116. I define "liturgy" as the work of the people, not only in the order of formal worship but also in the work of informal worship in our daily lives through prayer, service, and acts of loving one's neighbor. Douglas Davies defines "liturgy" as "the formal expression of how, theologically, we make sense of *life*" (italics my own). See Davies, *Theology of Death*, 58.

117. Behr, *The Mystery of Christ*, 22.

118. Behr, *The Mystery of Christ*, 22.

119. John 12:16.

The good news begins with the truth of our needy, reliant, helpless, darkened, pitiful broken state and moves to God's ultimate purpose for us "before the creation of the world, to be holy and blameless in God's sight . . . in Christ Jesus."[120] Isaiah's encounter with God in the temple begins with a call to worship—"Holy, holy, holy." Like a rock next to a diamond, Isaiah recognizes his deplorable status and cries out in confession—"Woe am I, a man of unclean lips."[121] The confession moves to the assurance of pardon which came through red hot coal, not from within himself, but from outside of himself. And then comes the proclamation of the Word, by the Word—"Whom shall I send? And who will go for us?" Isaiah responds to the Word, "Send me!" Isaiah 6 is a snapshot of the liturgy, a window into worship opening with heavenly song while man's posture falls prostrate in the revelation of sin. The result of recognizing God's glory is the self-comprehension of our dull state. The light of God illuminates our darkness. Thus, the proper response to God's restoration of humanity back into God's image is not seeking death but rather demonstrating gratitude by submitting joyfully to God's Word by receiving his death. Like Isaiah, who recognized his near-death rescue into salvation, which overwhelmed him with thanksgiving, we give glory to God in responding to the call—to the point of death. And like Isaiah, the praiseworthy mission for the disciple is to preach death ("Until the cities lie ruined"),[122] while demonstrating what it looks like to die to self. Self-death is freeing, liberating, and empowering to the point that we can say to the violence of the world, "You can't kill me! I've already died! You've lost your power, my fate to decide!"[123] Present-day social justice issues, topical lectures, self-help speeches may be the current accepted norm; but preaching Christ crucified is and has always been at the core of homiletics. Preaching the cross is the Christian response to suicide. God forbid that we should glory in anything other than the cross of Jesus,[124] "by whom the world is crucified unto me, and I unto the world."[125]

---

120. Eph 1:4.

121. Isa 6:5.

122. Isa 6:11.

123. Ylvisaker, "They Can't Kill Me."

124. My paraphrase of Gal 6:14a.

125. Gal 6:14b.

DEATH AND SIN

In a room full of priests, at the Norbertine Community in the high desert of Albuquerque, I nonchalantly stated that "In the Roman Catholic Church suicide used to be considered a sin." A retired priest immediately said, "What do you mean, suicide *used to be* considered a sin. It is a sin." Another participant in the group interjected and said, "Catholics do not view suicide as a sin." A Dominican brother piped in with a shrug, "What is sin?" This was a conversation between three cradle Catholics. If there is this amount of diversity on the word "sin" within the same communion, imagine the vast array of colors in the Protestant world. The biggest problem with speaking about sin (across denominational lines) is that Christians tend to disagree on what sin is. There is no Christian consensus of what constitutes a sin. Another interlocutor added that in just the last thirty years she has witnessed that the sin "goal posts have been moved." Certain sins of thirty years ago are no longer considered sins.

Your congregation deserves your voice regarding what is known as a theology of hamartiology. They want to hear what God says about their lives and sin. On second thought, who really wants to hear about their sin? It is so much more satisfying to talk about the sins of others, is it not? Regardless, an initial step when approaching sin is first recognizing that there are sometimes subtle and complex differences between the words sin,[126] evil,[127] and finitude.[128] For some theologians the differences are vast, for other theologians the differences are a matter of degree. The complexity of sin can be shown in a tangle of discussions on the tension between humanity's basic connection to sin (original sin) and the fact that Jesus was without sin and was at the same time human. Other issues have to do with the source of sin and the results of sin on the individual and communal relationship to God and each other. There is the social dimension or systemic sin and sins of commission and omission. Other discussions have focused on the historical and evolutionary development of sin including the concept of the scapegoat and punishment. The ideals

126. The Greek word *hamartia* literally means "missing the mark," which obviously can have many shades of meaning.

127. Augustine does not believe that evil exists. His theory is commonly known by theologians as the Augustinian Theodicy. See Augustine, *City of God*, 11.17, 22 and 12.2–8.

128. Being finite (versus infinite) means having the inevitable characteristic of making mistakes because one is not all-knowing, at all places, or all good all the time.

of justice and freedom, of course, move the conversation to the theology of grace and mercy (if we never had sin, we would never know grace). The dialogue regarding hamartiology will eventually dive into the questions of providential theology, that is, the theology that deals with God's administration in the world. This includes discussion on God's sovereign economy versus human free-will.[129] The Bible uses a variety of words to describe sin such as "ignorance,"[130] "error,"[131] "negligence,"[132] or what my confirmation teacher illustrated with bow and arrow as "missing the mark."[133] My grandfather explained the different versions of the Lord's Prayer with a joke that Presbyterians were born halfway between the bank and the ice house, and thus "debts" was the Scots' preference while the English cared more about "trespassers." Rebellion, iniquity, perversion, abomination, from thoughts to action[134] to guilt, punishment, consequences, and cure—hamartiology is wide-ranging and there is no end to the theological literature on this topic.

And when it comes to suicide as a sin, at first glance, it would seem that it is either sin or it is not, there is no middle ground. In 2017 I asked twelve senior college students to answer the question: is suicide a sin? Without hesitation or definition all twelve students said "yes" suicide was a sin. In order for interpretive inertia to be shifted in another direction I had to respond with a second question: What do you mean by sin?

One might state: if someone is sick then their freedom may be restricted and therefore it would not be fair to state that suicide (a consequence of illness) is a sin; the person's culpability is no longer clear. An alternative way of looking at the statement is to say that in a fallen world sin is an inevitable element of freedom, that in every "free" choice one makes there is the taint of sin. Suicide then becomes more an issue of finitude because finitude is affected by original sin. In genetics, the line between human freedom of choice and biological determinism can be even more blurry. Eliezer J. Sternberg, in his book *My Brain Made Me Do*

---

129. I reject Pelagianism and the emphasis on moral behavior and the platonic concept of an untainted personalized soul. Arminianism is simply a modern-day version of Pelagianism. For further reading on Pelagius see Evans, *Pelagius*, 82–83.

130. Eph 4:18.

131. Rom 1:27; Titus 3:3.

132. 2 Cor 10:6; Matt 18:17.

133. Smith, *The Bible Doctrine of Sin*, 20. In fact, this is the classical meaning (Liddell, Scott, and Jones, *A Greek-English Lexicon*, entry for *hamartia*, I.1).

134. Niebuhr, *The Self and the Dramas of History*, 35–37.

It: The Rise of Neuroscience and the Threat to Moral Responsibility, states
that "If you believe that mind and body are separate, then you can easily
hold that free will and moral agency exist."[135] But if one believes that the
mind and the body are vitally interconnected, he says, "the correlation
between the dysfunctional brain and the dysfunctional behavior shows
that free-will does not exist."[136] Free-will is the idea that the person has
a choice in how to control their behavior. But with mental illness, this is
not the case.[137]

It is becoming more obvious to me from looking at the current diversity and even fracturing of Christian moral discourse that the notions of
sin, evil, and finitude are subjectively and culturally constructed. In other
words, sin, evil, and finitude are defined more by the society than by a
particular religious book.[138] It is the community that interprets and it is
the interpretation that develops the agreed upon orthodoxy; it is then
those particular communities that create the norms and definitions for
their members.[139]

We can see how certain attitudes or even diagnoses have changed
throughout history from behavior being regarded as sinful to currently
being considered part of one's finitude. For example, at one time in
history certain symptoms of mental illness described in the Bible as
foaming at the mouth or cutting oneself were described as demonic

135. Sternberg, *My Brain Made Me Do It*, 48.

136. Sternberg, *My Brain Made Me Do It*, 55.

137. Tourette's syndrome, Parkinson's disease, Alien Hand syndrome, and Akinetic
Mutism are just a few debilitating diseases that Sternberg mentions.

138. Consider the issue of homosexuality. Even though the Christian religious
book (the Bible) states that homosexuality is "detestable" (Lev 18:22, 20:13; Rom
1:24–27; 1 Cor 6:9–10; and 1 Tim 1:9–11), certain Christian communities choose not
to define homosexuality as a sin. Jack Rogers, states that acceptance of homosexuality
is akin to being like Jesus. See Rogers, *Jesus, the Bible and Homosexuality*, 90. According to him, all those Christians who claim that homosexuality is a sin simply have not
"properly understood" the Bible (126). Yet other well-established biblical scholars have
argued for the opposite interpretation. See Hays, "Awaiting the Redemption of Our
Bodies." The fracturing of Christian ethics also could include issues such as pacifism,
materialism, abortion, infant baptism, closed or open table, and many others.

139. Adopting a stance of relativism is not the answer to the fractured Christian
discourse. The goal should be unity, and unity can come through self-critical reflection, individually and as a community which has an incessant and careful discipline
of prayerfully reading the Scriptures with others. Ultimately, unity can only come
through a gift of the Holy Spirit. This chapter seeks to combine the self-critical and
biblical reflection necessary for moving beyond the dominant societal norms.

possession.[140] Today, many scholars and medical practitioners interpret certain behaviors in the Bible not as demon possession but as evidence of mental illness. Much scholarship has focused on the parallels of demon possession with mental illness.[141] Even paralysis could have been interpreted as due to someone's personal sin.[142] With scientific discoveries the interpretation of the effects of sin has changed and today it is less common to hear Christians interpret behavior associated with mental illness as demonic or sinful. The dense intricacy of the topic allows the preacher and the congregation to embrace a sense of total dependency on one another while humbly reserving judgment for God. This is like a dance in which "man plans his course, but the Lord determines his steps."[143]

I know that there is a fine balancing act between God's judgment in God's self and God's judgment through the Holy Spirit in us.[144] Unfortunately, what I have experienced in Christian congregations is an overwhelming unspoken assumption that sin, evil, and finitude are easily identifiable and in need of inflexible judgment. Unspoken assumptions reinforce taboos and shame.[145] These assumptions often go unchallenged by the clergy. I hope that by demonstrating the complex nature of the theology of suicide in the Scriptures, we can directly affect the way we talk about God which can benefit the congregation by helping them pause before making judgments; not cease in making moral determinations, but slow down a bit and be reflective.

140. An example could be the story of the Gerasene Demoniac in Mark 5:1–20.

141. For interesting discussions on the subject, see Hollenbach, "Jesus, Demoniacs, and Public Authorities"; Ossa-Richardson "Possession or Insanity?"

142. Luke 5:22–24 could be taken to equate the forgiveness of sins with the physical healing of the paralyzed man.

143. Prov 16:9.

144. Eph 1:19.

145. I can empathize with the desire to depart this world *because* the world can be such a shame-inducing and sinful place full of experiences of being abused, lied to, stolen from, slandered and being overlooked and ignored. It can be a unique perspective to see suicide not as a sin but as a way of seeking escape from the sin of others and of the brokenness of the world. The Christian calling to die to self (metaphorically, spiritually, emotionally, and even physically) is one possible way of understanding suicide as a way of rejecting the sin of self and the sin of the world. Dying to self is theologically confusing, however, since the concept of "self" is made up of what it means to be sinful and in need of grace. If we are to die to sin what is left of the understanding of the self and the concept of what it means to be human? Especially since to be human is to be sinful. This is an example of one small element of the complexity of hamartiology.

Let me clarify here. According to Matthew 7:1, God's people are not to judge who is saved or who is damned. We are, however, based on Matthew 7:15–20, called to judge right behavior from wrong behavior. In fact, in the previous sentence I judged that judging others' salvation is not our responsibility but that judging right from wrong is. Of course, the obvious dilemma is that suicide is a behavior. And for many Christians, behavior does not save but indicates whether one is saved or not saved. But then John 20:23 throws a dry log in the fire and reveals the enormous power that Ephesians 1:19 talks about—the power, "like the working of his mighty strength," to forgive sins. "If you forgive anyone his sins, they are forgiven; if you do not forgive them, they are not forgiven."[146] Thus, if someone should be unforgiven for any sin, it is because of the one who withholds forgiveness. We believers, filled with God's Spirit, have an obligation to forgive sins so that sinners can be forgiven and hence, saved. The action of the saved . . . saves. We, as Christ's co-heirs share in his responsibility as Judge. Thus, we should take sin seriously and be very cautious in our words.

The church must seek simultaneously to affirm life in an uncompromising fashion (to not condone or promote self-harm in any way) and to resist condemnation against those who attempt self-harm while harming their families. There are still to this day well-meaning preachers who preach hell as the final destination of a person who died by suicide. This judgment is not based on how they lived, but how they died. And (aside from simplistically avoiding the complex nature of each suicide) this type of judgment fails to recognize forgiveness as lifesaving, for the dead and the living.

REPENTANCE AS DEATH

On the internet there are a variety of videos of children getting glasses for the very first time. Before the glasses are positioned on the nose the little ones are sometimes fussy, and not attentive to their surroundings. But when those glasses are gently placed on the bridge, inevitably the child becomes very still and quiet. Hardly moving, the child moves only their eyes around. Seeing clearly for the very first time has a profound effect on the child's posture and movements. Seeing what was once hidden determines their behavior.

146. John 20:23.

Similarly, upon being diagnosed with presbyopia, at forty-two I finally got glasses. I really didn't see the need until I got home, and I was aghast at how dirty my kitchen counters were. I could see the dirt and immediately I grabbed a rag. I believe this describes Romans 2:1–4. Paul had been describing the dirt in the previous chapter: "wickedness, evil, greed and depravity . . . envy, murder, strife, deceit, and malice. . . . " He can tell me all about this dirt, but until I see it in myself, I fail to receive God's "kindness, tolerance, and patience," which leads to repentance. God's character of leading, calling, opening my eyes inevitably unveils my spiritual sight so as to see the dirt. Humility is the natural first response. God as First Mover moves me to repentance. Because ultimately, a good Christian is one who recognizes that they are not good.

Repentance, true repentance is dying. Death is the beginning of one's relationship with the God of Life. Before one enters into the waters of Baptism, the Living Water in the Baptism of the Holy Spirit washes our corpse as we stand in shock at what we really are. If we do not see the dirt we will never know about the dirt and if we do not know about the dirt we will never feel the *need* for washing. God must come near us, "The word is near you; it is in your mouth and in your heart, that is, the word of faith. . . . "[147] God grants us his Word, like placing Christological glasses on our nose, we can see who we really are and it is in that seeing that we recognize our need. The need to clean. But we can't clean ourselves, thus we call out "Jesus is Lord" and believe that he can raise the dead, and then the scrubbing begins. This is salvation: saved from our dead selves by dying to self. What does the living have in common with the dead? As new living beings we shed the dead. Let the dead bury their own dead.[148] "Everyone who calls on the name of the Lord will be saved."[149] But why would anyone call on the Lord if they can't see the dirt?

True salvation as a response to repentance leads to an overwhelming sense of gratitude.[150] The same gratitude I imagine that Isaiah felt when he was saved by the intercession of the burning hot coal. He was saved from being condemned. He was saved not by anything he did, but what was done for him. His gratitude manifested itself as "Send me." It was in view of God's mercy that he was willing to offer his body as a living

147. Rom 10:8–9.

148. Luke 9:60.

149. Rom 19:13.

150. Tim Keller states, "Rejoicing and repentance must go together. Repentance without rejoicing will lead to despair" (Keller, *Counterfeit Gods*, 191).

sacrifice.[151] In view of God's mercy, Isaiah had no questions to ask about the journey ahead. No questions like, "Where are we going? What should I bring? Do I need a hotel reservation?" But just simply, "Here I am, send me." Isaiah's response is a glimpse into sincere gratitude to the gift of Life.

In repentance we die. A spiritual-suicide,[152] initiated by God, transforming the physical; "crossing over from death to life."[153] It really is a process of being born again, seeing the world differently and hence living differently. And this behavior, this act of committing suicide, is the Christian's daily life with God. It is our duty to die. Dying is what sanctification is all about. Christ's death, as an act of ransom, provided forgiveness of sin. Forgiveness leads to gratitude demonstrated in humility and submission. This is a gratitude that provides our own willingness to die to self. Thus, in the act of being pardoned we die to self, so that we can pardon others.[154]

---

151. Rom 12:1.

152. When I say spiritual what I mean is the emotions, the choice, the will in a unity with the physical. A spiritual-suicide is like breaking an egg. Without breaking the shell the egg has little worth and purpose. Spiritual-suicide is required for the transformation and the renewing of the mind. See Rom 12:1–2.

153. John 5:24.

154. Luke 7:46–48.

7

Suicide in Scripture

"We have been wedded to death by the command of God. . . . "[1]

WHEN WE TAKE THE TIME to really chew on the text, we will find that our contemporary taboos about suicide are surprisingly not found in Scripture.[2] It is important to note here that nowhere in the Bible does it ever state *explicitly* that thinking about, talking about, or even dying by suicide is wrong, that it is a sin, or that it is a crime.[3] Maybe because of this lack of written code, we encounter many people in the Scriptures who take their life in what would seem an honorable way to die. In the following pages I would like to highlight each person who died by suicide in the Bible. While not attempting to offer a complete exegesis of each relevant passage, this chapter offers observations on each in order to emphasize the complexity of motivations before the suicide, the number of other characters involved, and the diversity of evaluations of each suicide.

1. Behr, "Learning Through Experience," 47.

2. I am not including the apocryphal texts in this study.

3. Most discussions of the biblical perspective on suicide appeal to the command against murder in the Decalogue. My point here is that the command does not explicitly state a prohibition of suicide or explicitly include suicide under murder. This is why Augustine had to spend much effort defending his interpretation of applying "Thou shall not kill" to suicide in *City of God* 1.20–21.

ABIMELECH

In the book of Judges, Abimelech, the first king of Israel, out of pride or honor has the will to die. Literally speaking, he does not kill himself with his own hands, but rather he asks someone to kill him.[4] Technically it is murder, but a requested murder, nonetheless. Thus, his suicide raises the difficult question of culpability. In fact, Abimelech shares culpability because of his intentions. His death could be considered a suicide resembling our modern concepts of euthanasia or physician-assisted suicide.[5] This assistance not only comes from his armor-bearer but also from God. Like other biblical suicides, God is an active participant in Abimelech's death.[6] Some, however, gloss over his death with no mention of suicide at all. John C. Yoder, a historian states, "Tragically for Abimelech, the people of Thebez managed to crush his head with a millstone as he was preparing to burn the tower's door."[7] This retelling of the narrative fails to include the Scriptural narrative in which Abimelech's head was not crushed, but was cracked by none other than a woman dropping a stone on him. It was the fact that the assailant was a woman that prompted Abimelech's plea to his servant to end his life. But the text shows us that Abimelech had falsely accused a woman for his demise when actually it was God who orchestrated the events. Judges 9:56 states, "Thus God repaid the wickedness that Abimelech had done." God is the one who controlled the events that led to Abimelech's willful request to die. The story of Abimelech is a sad example of how sometimes people tend to look past the Scriptural narrative and the details that lie therein.

Interpreters don't just make this mistake with Abimelech. The pattern is visible in commentaries on the entire Bible. Rachael A. Keefe in her book *The Life Saving Church: Faith Communities and Suicide Prevention* spends very little space on the Scriptural narratives of suicide and focuses mainly on her own experiences as a pastor who struggled with an eating disorder and sexual identity. Her first words of advice for funeral preparation of a suicide is not to pray or study, but " . . . to list the Suicide Prevention Lifeline number on all printed material."[8] In fact, the only

---

4. Judges 9:52–57.

5. Abimelech wanted to die honorably. See Schneider, *Judges*, 148.

6. Judg 9:56 states, "Thus God repaid the wickedness that Abimelech had done to his father by murdering his seventy brothers."

7. Yoder, *Power and Politics*, 99.

8. Keefe, *The Life Saving Church*, 85.

time she mentions any of the suicides recorded in the Scripture is in a list of Bible references in a footnote.[9] One would think that a book regarding "Faith Communities" would at least spend a little more time on those communities' sacred texts.

I have often wondered why Jude would say, "men whose condemnation was written about long ago have secretly slipped in among you."[10] How is it that false teachers and preachers are able to simply slip in? The answer is right there in the passage. If people do not know the written word, the story of our faith and the testimonies of our ancestors which was "written long ago," then the ignorance of the listener blinds them to those who are "blemishes at your love feast," clouds without rain and uprooted trees, twice dead. Biblical illiteracy renders the church defenseless.[11] The church is called to be a community formed by the Scriptures by living within the Scriptures. If we fail to attend carefully to the words of the Scriptures, we will be formed by other terms, texts, and tones that may have little or no connection to the voice of the true Word.

SAMSON

The second suicide in the Scriptures occurs in the case of a judge named Samson.[12] At the outset, Samson exhibits a lack of self-control, an absence of concern for others, shortage of judgment, and a deficiency in recognizing consequences. After twenty years of leadership, his behavior had hurt animals, people, and ultimately himself. When the Philistines finally capture him, they gouge out his eyes. With a habit of revenge (and, one can only imagine, a deep depression caused by his sudden blindness and betrayal) he kills himself along with thousands of others.[13] Within our present historical context, this suicide might resemble that of a suicide bomber, just without the bomb. In fact, Samson receives martyr-like hero status by being mentioned in the "hall of faith" found in the book of Hebrews.[14]

9. Keefe, *The Life Saving Church*, 71.

10. Jude 1:4.

11. Stetzer, "The Epidemic of Biblical Illiteracy."

12. Judg 13–16.

13. The experience of humiliation or the attempt to avoid humiliation seem to be a red thread in many biblical suicides.

14. Heb 11:32.

One would be remiss to define the events of Samson's suicide exclusively as a consequence of Samson's behavior alone. There are others who make choices within his story. Delilah, being the most vocal partner with Samson, talks with him to discover the source of his power. She talks so much that she finally persuades Samson to betray himself by breaking his vow, and thus to betray God. By her talking, over time she convinced him to bring about self-harm.[15] If self-harm can be elicited by human words, one can imagine that words can be equally powerful when devoted to the affirmation of life and flourishing.

Of course, Samson and Delilah are not the only actors on the stage. In fact, on a close reading, Samson does not seem to be the central figure of the story; rather, God is the central character. From the very beginning when Samson's barren mother had a divine encounter informing her of the upcoming pregnancy, God seems to orchestrate the whole story.[16] The reader becomes aware that it is the power of God that moves Samson to take a fancy for a Philistine woman, and it was the power of God that allows for the imparted strength in Samson's hands to tear apart a lion. It was the power of God that drove Samson to mass murder of thirty men which led to his wife's ultimate demise. It was also the power of God that gave Samson the capacity to kill a thousand men with a donkey's jawbone. At the moment of his death, Samson prays for the same power of God to come down and empower him to ultimately kill others and kill himself.[17] What does one make of this? Did God answer Samson's prayer for death? Within the context of the narrative it would seem so.[18] The story is complicated because Samson's motives are unclear, and his mental state is uncertain. Likewise, the narrator represents Samson's death as a satisfying end with God's silent aid.[19] Jichan Kim in his exhaustive study of Samson notes that, "the conclusion of the narrative is that Samson killed many more Philistines in his death than during his life. Paradoxically, he lived up to his vocation through his death."[20] In other words, suicide

15. For a modern-day Delilah story, see Cappell, "Text Messages Urging Suicide."

16. Judg 13.

17. Judg 16:28–30.

18. Augustine (*City of God* 1.21 and 26) goes so far as to suppose Samson was responding to a divine command.

19. "Despite seeking revenge through suicide, Yahweh is still Samson's God, and his appeal is ultimately what God desires—the death of the Philistines—even if their reasons for desiring this common goal are not the same." See Butler, *Judges*, 354.

20. Kim, *The Structure of the Samson Cycle*, 363.

helped fulfill his calling. "His lifetime achievement was with his performance in dying."[21] Thomas Haynes, an author from the seventeenth
century demonstrates many ways in which Samson is a foreshadow of
Jesus Christ, withholding vocabulary of self-death yet including words
about God's sovereign economy and over-arching control.[22]

The story of Samson is complex which allows for the reader to pause
before making too quick of a judgment regarding suicide. While Samson
does seem to bear some responsibility, his own agency cannot be disen-
tangled from other factors. In addition to the role played by other characters (both human and divine), forces in the areas of culture, gender, and
body all took a significant toll on the path Samson took.

SAUL AND HIS ARMOR BEARER

The next suicide is in the case of another prominent leader, namely the
first anointed king of Israel, King Saul.[23] He took his life when military
defeat seemed imminent.[24] Rather than be taken as a prisoner of war
and be killed by enemy hands, he asks his armor-bearer to kill him. Out
of fear the armor-bearer refused and so Saul was forced to kill himself,
falling on his own sword. "Saul, although rejected by God from the king-
ship, remained 'the Lord's anointed' and under divine protection.[25] Yet
he could not protect himself from himself."[26] At the same time, however,
seeking death was protecting himself from dishonor. And dishonor was
considered worse than death. The armor-bearer, with sudden boldness,
then took his own life, becoming the fourth suicide recorded.[27] The text
continues by narrating that the foreign oppressor then desecrated the
corpses of Saul, his armor-bearer, and Saul's family who also perished in
the battle. Upon the news of the desecration of the bodies, the Israelites
valiantly retrieved the deceased and gave them a proper burial. A proper

21. Kim, *The Structure of the Samson Cycle*, 369.

22. Haynes, *The General View of the Holy Scriptures*, 217–18.

23. 1 Sam 31.

24. Joiner, *Myths About Suicide*, 70.

25. 2 Sam 1:14.

26. Chapman, *1 Samuel as Christian Scripture*, 213.

27. There may have been a societal expectation that the armor-bearer take his life
(like a bride-burning in India) so it may not be entirely voluntary. The question then,
"What does it mean for an action to be *entirely* voluntary?" in a case like this adds to
the complexity of suicide.

burial is no small statement. For to receive such courteous reception by the community gives the reader a clue that the community viewed the king's and armor-bearer's death as being honorable enough to receive proper treatment.[28] Or it could be that to not bury the dead would have been a dishonorable act of the community.

Sometimes, young readers of Scripture fall into the temptation of viewing the characters within the Bible as superheroes, able to withstand seriously traumatic circumstances without physical repercussions. This immature way of envisioning the text has often been fed by well-intentioned books and films such as *Veggie Tales* or *Adventures in Odyssey*. To my naïve surprise, I startled a seventh-grade confirmand one day when I reminded the students that the people in the Bible were actually real people, whose stories were reported by humans with presuppositions and agendas, hopes and hurts. The confirmand honestly reported to the group that, "I kind of only think of them as characters in a play." Real people are complex, messy, and quite fragile, and when we begin to read the stories of the Bible as recording real human events, it then becomes hard to imagine the Bible characters as escaping the human dilemma of mental trauma. Humans are like all others, yet like no others, while being like some others.[29] Since our biblical forebears are like us yet not like us, it is quite realistic to state that our ancestors experienced a variety of disorders due to family neglect, abuse, and long-lasting trauma.

King Saul is most commonly pointed out by biblical scholars as having some sort of mental illness. Post-Traumatic Stress Disorder might be one possible diagnosis for Saul. In 1 Samuel 18 Saul exhibits some of the classic patterns of distress including, but not limited to, episodic remembering (possible flashback), sudden arousal, and excessive fearfulness.[30] Chapter 18 states that Saul was "afraid" three times.[31] In his moment of fear, he suddenly switches from a peaceful state of listening to music (maybe he had fallen asleep) to a sudden arousal in which he becomes defensive, protective, and engages in violent action by throwing a spear twice at the young musician and soon to be king, David. This behavior continues to happen so often that many in Saul's advisory team seem to walk on eggshells around him, waiting for any moment in which

28. See Isa 14:19–21.

29. Kluckhohn and Murray, *Personality in Nature, Society, and Culture.*

30. See "Suicidal Behavior Disorder: Comorbidity," in *DSM-5*, 271–80.

31. Paul Borgman deals at length with the differences between Saul's fear and David's fear and connects fear to suicide. See Borgman, *David, Saul, and God,* 54–77.

Saul might erupt in a violent explosion of military anger. Saul will sometimes have moments of remorse, only to fall back into the impulsive fear
and negative manners. This destructive behavior is exhibited by estrange-
ment from his family and he seems consistently unhappy and unable to
connect with others.

Relying only on the text, one might reasonably conjecture that
the trauma was war-related. Before chapter 18, Saul had already been
in hand-to-hand combat with the Ammonites (which he "slaughtered"),
Amalekites, and Philistines. I would like to add also, however, that there
may be a bit of trauma that was more personal and closer to home.
Samuel, essentially Saul's supervisor, clearly does not want Israel to have
a king while he is still presiding as a judge. Samuel anoints Saul, yet, Saul
can never seem to please Samuel. Samuel finds and points out Saul's faults
very early in their relationship. The human storyteller of the narrative
demonstrates Saul's rejection by Samuel and thus rejection by God, ultimately maligning Saul to the reader and providing evidence of neglect
(or feelings of betrayal) on top of any war-related trauma.

Yet, even though Saul becomes a villain, David, who is clearly the
protagonist, shows pity on Saul. David had many chances to kill Saul,
but at every opportunity David chose mercy, hence choosing life.[32] The
text indicates that David spared Saul's life because David would not kill
"God's anointed."[33] The story of David demonstrates that David did not
have a difficult time killing people. Saul was special to David and it was
more than Saul's being a king. Saul was, after all, family. Could it be so
off-base to say that David loved Saul? David certainly loved Saul's children Michael and Jonathan. To love someone with mental illness naturally moves one to an attitude of putting aside retribution or judgment.[34]

It must be very hard to live with someone who is like Saul. In fact,
David ran away to a safe place. It would be easy to say, an "eye for an eye,"
or "if he gets angry at me, I will get angry at him," or "if he throws a spear,
I will throw a spear," but David did not. The narrator develops David's
character as one of patience—or in other words, *longsuffering* with someone who is unstable and ill. How many in your congregation personally
know that longsuffering firsthand? David became a care provider, in a
way, by keeping himself safe and by keeping Saul safe from David's own

32. 1 Sam 24:4.

33. 1 Sam 24:6.

34. 1 Sam 24:7.

military men. It is an example of the safeguard put in place to prevent one person's trauma from creating another person's trauma. David showed the importance of offering mercy to someone who may have deserved retribution on the face of it, but instead was offered grace as an act of love. The author allows the protagonist to demonstrate a few ways of how one can care for those suffering from mental illness. People with PTSD (Post Traumatic Stress Disorder) struggle with fear and thus can create fear for those they live with, but they should never be retaliated against or dismissed. David recognized that Saul had personal worth and he was committed to caring for him by providing safety for the entirety of Saul's life.

Saul often found himself in chilling suffocation of fear and panic. At one point, Saul saw the Philistine army gathered for war and the text states that "he was afraid, terror filled his heart."[35] Fear is an emotion that should not be underestimated, a powerful mind-altering agent that can have unrestrained control over the human will. It has led people to grab a weapon and shoot their own children in the night.[36] Fear makes people do unthinkable things, because fear muddles our thinking. Unless they have been trained, people normally do not respond well to fear. Fear by its very nature paralyzes us into submission. Instead of turning towards God, fear causes "each to help the other and say to his brother, 'Be strong! No worries!' The craftsman encourages the goldsmith and he who smooths with the hammer spurs on him who strikes the anvil. He says of the welding, 'It is good.' He nails down the idol so it will not topple."[37] Fear leads us to idolatry, even to the point of helping each other to idolatry. The antidote to fear, according to Isaiah, is to turn towards God because God "took" us, "called" us and "chose" us saying, "Do not fear for I am with you."[38] The very presence of God "renews our strength"[39] and "upholds us."[40] If he had only listened to David's singing.

> Where can I go from your Spirit?
> Where can I flee from your presence?
> If I go up to the heavens, you are there;

---

35. 1 Sam 28:5.

36. Flatow, "Father Shoots and Kills 14-year-old Daughter."

37. Isa 41:6–7.

38. Isa 41:10.

39. Isa 40:31.

40. Isa 41:10b.

if I make my bed in the depths, you are there.
If I rise on the wings of the dawn,
    if I settle on the far side of the sea,
even there your hand will guide me,
    your right hand will hold me fast.[41]

In the end, Saul does take his own life. According to *DSM-5*, suicide is sometimes associated with PTSD (Post Traumatic Stress Disorder). Thomas Joiner in his book *Myths about Suicide* states that it is a myth that people attempt suicide impulsively or on a whim. Joiner states that people work their way towards it, little by little, by participating in physically destructive acts, learning fearlessness in order to prepare them to attempt suicide.[42] If Joiner is correct, this could provide information about Saul's life on which the text is otherwise silent.

Saul's suicide is usually not considered a direct behavioral outcome of PTSD. Most view his suicide on the spectrum as an honor-suicide. This approach would assume that Saul did not want to kill himself but viewed it as the moral and honorable thing to do at that moment. If he wanted to die, he certainly did not want to bring death to himself. In desperation, while the enemy's army was closing in around him, knowing that he must do the honorable thing, Saul asks his armor bearer to kill him. The armor bearer refuses. It is only then that Saul realizes that he must to do it himself, to protect his honor.[43]

This particular suicide can be viewed as a cultural outgrowth originating in an honor-shame society (namely a society in which all significant moral decisions are determined by how one's peers in the community will evaluate the person, either with honor or disgrace). Cultural expectations make for some powerful stuff. Thus, this type of suicide is not necessarily the same type of suicide that those with PTSD often experience in our 21st century American culture. Or is it? Honor and shame run deep in modern military communities just as in the days of Saul. Is it possible that some contemporary veterans view their death as

---

41. Ps 139:7–10.

42. Joiner, *Myths about Suicide*, 70.

43. For some, suicide is not viewed on a spectrum which can cause suicide to be regarded as a dishonorable act at all times. Paul Borgman states, "The sorry state of Saul's military leadership ends appropriately in colossal defeat, with his troops fleeing and Saul committing suicide." Without the spectrum, suicide is assumed to be negative in all respects, therefore Borgman views Saul's death as appropriate since it fits with defeat. See Borgman, *David, Saul, and God*, 298.

more honorable than continuing to live their life? How could a community respect the suicide of a veteran despite their loss and grief? How could the weekly sermon speak to the complexity of the nature of what it means to be human in this particular culture in which communal forces collude with individual experiences and trauma? The story of Saul ends on a positive note with King David and the people of Israel gathering up Saul's mutilated body and providing a proper burial.[44] Saul was cared for in life and cared for in death, despite his self-destructive behavior.

The story of Saul also proposes a challenge to the reader in regard to how one should deal with not just a friend or a family member with mental illness (maybe PTSD), but how the community should deal with those who are leaders plagued with mental illness. Saul was a king, Hitler was a dictator, and Jim Jones was a pastor.[45] These seem like extreme examples, but every day there are leaders in businesses, schools, and churches who struggle with experiences in more or less unhealthy ways and may have people walking on egg-shells around them. The stories of Saul, Samuel, and David could be a good starting place for future discussion in the church community about mental illness, accountability, leadership, grace, and suicide. This is also a good place for preachers to reflect on their own leadership. A leadership that moves us to decrease so that Jesus can increase.[46]

AHITHOPHEL

Another biblical suicide is once again a person in a position of leadership. Ahithophel was the advisor to King David. The text indicates that he was a man who was inspired and spoke for God.[47] Ahithophel also advised David's son Absalom, enticing Absalom to treason. It was not only treason he proposed, but he gave barbaric advice to engage in a brutal act of raping ten women who "belonged" to the King. Absalom followed

---

44. Paul Borgman disagrees and sees Saul fully "blameworthy," responsible, and willfully hardening his own heart; thus, Saul did not die honorably because Saul's death came in a hyper-fearful state, because he did not trust in God. See Borgman, *David, Saul, and God,* 71–74.

45. Discussion surrounding Romans 13 often elicits questions about hyper-fearful leaders. Paul calls civil leaders "God's servants" (Rom 13:4), worthy of taxes, revenue, respect, and honor (13:7).

46. John 3:30.

47. 2 Sam 16:23.

through on Ahithophel's initial instructions regarding the rapes, but not the subsequent counsel regarding treason. Instead, Absalom heeded Hushai's advice about military advancement, which brought Ahithophel and Absalom to ruin. Ahithophel realized his counsel would be revealed and he would eventually be arrested as a co-conspirator. With the fear of that dishonor Ahithophel hung himself, thus becoming the fifth biblical suicide.[48]

Craig E. Morrison states that Ahithophel's suicide is not one of impulsive passion, but rather it was a deliberately planned choice, one that required Ahithophel to travel all the way back to his hometown in order to make preparations for his death. "The phrase 'to set one's house in order' . . . reveals his determination to end his life by putting his affairs in order."[49] Dying by his own hands offered a means of escaping the inevitable humiliation of arrest and trial under King David. Therefore, one might conclude that Ahithophel's death was dishonorable as a way to escape judgment; and yet it was shown to be deemed honorable in light of the mention that he had a proper burial. And once again, the question of God's culpability comes to the surface when we read that David had prayed to God and asked God to intervene in the circumstances, "to turn Ahithophel's counsel into foolishness."[50]

Did God answer David's prayer? Did God prompt the advice that Ahithophel gave? Maybe just the secondary advice that led to Ahithophel's downfall? Surely not the first advice of mass rape. I will be honest. I make interpretive decisions based on how I feel and how I want God's character to be. But at the end of the day, who am I to say who God is? I am the pot and God is the potter. Yet, God has called me to preach. One's interpretive decisions need to be dependent on the guidance of the Holy Spirit and accountable, in prayer, to the Scripture and to the worshiping community.

48. 2 Sam 17:23. Once again, it is important to note that God is an active participant in Ahithophel's death. See 2 Sam 17:14b. Some scholars find parallels between Ahithophel and Judas, comparing the betrayal of David and that of Jesus. See Anderson, 2 Samuel, 216.

49. Morrison, 2 Samuel, 232–233.

50. 2 Sam 15:31.

ZIMRI

Zimri, like Saul, was a king of Israel; but he was considered a bad king because he had murdered the previous king and initiated a coup. The text informs the reader that it is because of Zimri's sins and the evil he committed in the eyes of the Lord that the people proclaimed a different king and sought to kill Zimri. When Zimri saw that his city was taken, he set the palace on fire and died in the flames, hence, dying by suicide. Importantly, the text states that he died because of sin, "doing evil in the eyes of the Lord and walking in the ways of Jeroboam and in the sin he had perpetrated and had caused Israel to commit."[51] It seems to imply that death came to Zimri because of his iniquity, even though the death was self-inflicted. "Sin, when full grown, gives birth to death."[52] Was it the *way* he died that was the punishment or was the punishment *that* he died? And was the punishment from God or simply said to be so by the people who were explaining events of a sovereign's death through a theological lens?

Should we even use the word "punishment" since "In the Old Testament, death is not ubiquitously seen as a curse or a punishment for sin."[53] In particular, can God not only assist a suicide, as in the case of Samson, but will or even be the cause of the suicide? The difficulty of the question resides in how one understands the nature of God, humanity, and the nature of death. These are questions for theological inquiry and homiletical exploration.[54] Zimri as recorded in the Bible, was the sixth person to die by suicide.

A well-seasoned pastor of twenty-four years attempted to correct me regarding these first six suicides in the Bible when he said, "You can't compare those suicides with the type of suicides we currently have in our culture. Unlike Bible times, today people kill themselves because they are crazy, not because of politics. Therefore, preaching on those texts with suicide in mind has no current application to today's listeners. Judas is

---

51. See 1 Kgs 16:15–20.

52. Jas 1:15. Keep in mind that sin is not the only thing that gives birth to death. Repentance also births a death of the self which in turn gives birth to life. Repentance is a death of a carcass that fertilizes the soil.

53. Behr, *The Mystery of Christ*, 81.

54. Difficult questions are the "itch" that Eugene Lowery speaks about regarding how one approaches preaching a narrative sermon. Narrative preaching could be seen as a tool for preachers seeking to preach on difficult passages. See Lowry, *The Homiletical Plot*, 29.

the only one relevant." My response was one of keeping-the-peace in silence. But I wonder—has the human somehow changed or evolved to such a degree that we are so very different from Samson or Saul? Do their deaths have nothing to teach us? And what about the silence on female suicides in the Bible?[55] Can we learn nothing from the silence? Have cultural changes over the millennia so drastically altered what it means to be human that an ancient suicide cannot illuminate the predicament of speaking to modern suicide? As already noted, the honor-shame cultural dynamics of antiquity bear more than just a passing resemblance to some modern communal contexts such as the military (although modern individualism certainly complicates the issues).

All six of these suicides mentioned in the Bible are carried out by males and all are civic leaders or associated with civic leaders. The most famous biblical suicide, which is now from the New Testament, fits this schema. Judas was no doubt associated with someone who was a leader now known as the King of Kings. There are some subtle differences between the Judas story and the previous accounts of suicide. For one, there is no textual notification that Judas received a proper burial like Samson or Saul. In contrast, the text explicitly speaks poorly about Judas and even has words of contempt for Judas.[56] Despite Judas's apparent change of heart, remorse, and confession,[57] some within the early Christian community condemned Judas. But the Scriptures do not speak kindly about Abimelech or Zimri either.

Judas is the seventh suicide recorded in the Scriptures. Seven is often considered by many as the number of completion.[58] Yet, the influence of Judas's suicide was far from complete in the first century and has had an enduring impact. Certain theological interpretations of the story of Judas and later attitudes about him would change how future Christian audiences came to view suicide.

---

55. A possible exception might be Jephthah's daughter, who willingly and voluntarily returned from a girls' retreat to face execution at her father's hands. Jephthah's daughter could be seen as a type of Christ, dying as an honor-suicide at the hands of her father.

56. Acts 1:20, 25.

57. Matt 27:3–4.

58. Stookey, *Calendar*, 55.

JUDAS

Like many before him, Judas is not the central figure in this story, but rather, God is the main character. "In the metaphysical realm, the controversies that erupt around Jesus are shown to be manifestations of the cosmic conflict between the Son of God and Satan."[59] It would seem that Judas is not autonomous in the choice to betray his King. He was not an individual acting alone. Matthew 27:8–9 reminds the reader that Judas's actions were to fulfill what the prophet Jeremiah had spoken long ago. Jesus is well aware of the part Judas plays when he says, "The one who has dipped his hand into the bowl with me will betray me. The Son of Man will go just as it is written about him. But woe to that man who betrays the Son of Man! It would be better for him if he had not been born."[60] Judas immediately learns that it is him. In the Matthew text it would seem that either Jesus is condemning Judas or Jesus laments for Judas and in a way encourages Judas to the unhappy task of fulfilling the prophecy. An alternative reading could present Judas as faithfully and obediently fulfilling Jesus's bidding to do this work of betrayal.[61]

Judas can be seen in a less negative light, as one who was fulfilling—even if unwittingly—the specific calling to betray Jesus: "this is to fulfill the Scripture. . . . "[62] And "Jesus answered, 'It is the one to whom I will give this piece of bread when I have dipped it in the dish.' Then, dipping the piece of bread, he gave it to Judas Iscariot, son of Simon. As soon as Judas took the bread, Satan entered into him. 'What you are about to do, do quickly.'"[63] From this perspective, treachery resulted from the leading of God in his life. Because Jesus tells Judas to go and do what needs to be done and because Jesus is the one who administers the bread, it would seem that Jesus shares in the culpability of his own betrayal.

Unfortunately, the church has viewed this episode as depicting Judas to be a lone betrayer, a vindictive and greedy money-grabber, seeking either to push the Messiah into a bloody revolution to overthrow the Romans or simply to perpetrate an act of evil. The latter is the most commonly held view since in John 13:27 it states that when "Judas took

---

59. Robertson, *The Death of Judas*, 84.

60. Matt 26:23–24.

61. This is consistent with God's character as seen in 1 Sam 16:14, 1 Kgs 22:22, or John 9:3.

62. John 13:18b.

63. John 13:21–30.

the bread, Satan entered into him." Hence, Satan enters in as yet another character. With Jesus's prompting, Satan's entering, and Jeremiah's predicting, can we really say that Judas was a lone player, free in volition, and totally independent.[64] In fact, the loss of his volition[65] when Satan enters him could be similar to an individual's loss of volition in some cases due to illness or drug influence.[66] The great reformer Martin Luther wrote, "It is very certain that, as to all persons who have hanged themselves, or killed themselves in any other way, 'tis the devil who has put the cords around their necks, or the knife to their throats."[67]

While this alternative approach cannot exclude consideration of elements in the text that have undergirded the traditional interpretation, it should be sufficient, at least to moderate the traditional interpretation.[68] The beauty of the Bible is that it suggests a variety of interpretations of the event of betrayal through the gospels. This allows for the reader's deeper engagement through a hermeneutic of suspicion, interpreting Scripture by Scripture, and hopefully the realization that suicide is much more complex and messier than one first imagined.

Even with the complexities of multiple actors and forces, God is clearly working out God's plan in Judas's story, the same way God was working God's power and strength through Samson for the liberation of Israel. This might be further seen in the ambiguities of the Greek verb *paradidomi*. It is commonly translated as "betrayed" but can also be translated as "delivered up" as found in Romans 8:32 stating, "God

---

64. Even if there are other characters in play, Judas certainly becomes the scapegoat as reflected in the depiction of his corpse. "The gruesome trauma to the body and the scattering of his bowels and blood indicate violent retribution and divine justice." See Robertson, *The Death of Judas*, 108. This is drawing upon Psalm 69 and 109. The concept of "divine justice" should cause the preacher to pause and consider the ramifications for using such language.

65. Mark on the other hand appears to highlight Judas's volition. See Mark 14:10.

66. The recognition of God's providential interaction in human activity is a central theme throughout the entire Scriptures. From Naomi's sense of providence when she said, "the Lord has afflicted me" (Ruth 1:21) to Jesus having to pray to the Father on behalf of Simon Peter when Satan had asked permission to "sift him as wheat" (Luke 22:31), in a manner similar to Job (Job 1:12). Interestingly, Jesus does not ask for God's intervention in the same way for Judas.

67. Luther, *Table Talk*, 589.

68. And moderation is surely needed in light of the ways that "Judas sermons" could be used to foster division in the church by labelling one's opponents within the church as betrayers who would be better dead (as in the Donatist controversy in the fourth and fifth centuries). See Shaw, *Sacred Violence*, 84, 96–102.

who did not spare his own Son, but delivered him up (*paradidomi*) for us all." Donald Macleod in his book *Christ Crucified: Understanding the Atonement* points out that, "The night of the Last Supper was both the night on which Jesus was 'betrayed' by Judas and the night on which he was 'delivered up' by God the Father."[69] In other words, simultaneously, "Judas's traitorous act is God the Father's priestly act."[70]

The authors of these biblical passages are describing God as very active and present in the stories of suicide. Even in those instances where humans seem (and even try) to take control of life and death, God's activity can be described as "totally in control," or better yet, "sovereign." God has a plan and is working out the plan through the lives, actions, and deaths of God's people. Suicide, therefore, in this context, cannot be seen as simple, but volitionally ambiguous and theologically complex.

While a preacher may not preach directly on these texts (indeed, they are seldom or never included in the lectionary) they are essential for understanding the larger fabric of Scripture and its vision of God, human life, and death. They provide a necessary background for the preacher seeking to help listeners hear the fullness of the biblical narrative on suffering and loss. Thus, preaching a theology of suicide requires interpreting Scripture by Scripture.

The fact that everyone will eventually die was not the issue for the Christian church, but rather how one died and how one was cared for in death. If someone was to die in North America in the twenty-first century, whether they were a pauper or a president, they would not be allowed to have their corpse waste in the open air.[71] They would be buried. It is simply civil to bury the dead.[72] Contemporary culture has implied that Judas was left out in the open to rot.[73] But the Scriptures do not tell us whether Judas eventually received a burial or not. To assume that there was no burial is to believe that the first-century believers and the disciples were grotesquely uncivil, lacking all sense of humanity. It imagines the disciples as people who were so caught up in their own bitterness that they forgot to love their enemy who used to be

---

69. MacLeod, *Christ Crucified*, 25.

70. MacLeod, *Christ Crucified*, 31.

71. To not bury the dead has often been an issue of whether the community sees the deceased as human or not. For an episode in the modern US in which the dead almost did not receive burial, see Chidester, *Salvation and Suicide*, 160–69.

72. Rizpa expresses this by beating away the birds. See 2 Sam 21:10.

73. Acts 1:18.

their brother (and because of his repentance in Matthew 27 was still their brother).[74] Because the Scriptures are silent on the final burial status of Judas's body, we should be careful about a preconceived assumption that the disciples demonstrated vindictive behavior towards Judas's family by not extending hospitality. To neglect a human being after death is not acceptable.[75] To imagine this uncouth behavior from the disciples might force one to reflect on the gaps and spaces within the Scriptures. Arthur Droge and James Tabor state that, "Judas was condemned for betraying the Messiah, not for killing himself."[76]

The "effort to write (record) and right (rectify) wrong" pertaining to how Scripture has been interpreted pertaining to suicide "involves both fear and ferocity" because to write about wrong reminds me that I could be wrong myself.[77] It is very humbling to engage suicide from a biblical, historical, and cultural lens. There are many gaps or spaces within Scripture: gaps where the author apparently did not feel it necessary to explain more of the text or spaces where the author does not elaborate for rhetorical reasons or as a literary device. The presence of gaps or spaces in the Scriptures allows the reader the freedom to imagine something different for the first century Christians who walked with Christ and witnessed the resurrection. The preacher might begin to imagine not barbaric behavior from the disciples, but respectable and humane kindness (especially considering that the act and concept of suicide was not yet at that time vilified). For in the Jewish Scriptures, suicide could be described honorably and heroically if the interpreting community viewed the circumstances and choices of the character with approval. An example of this might be the community providing honorable burial or even giving someone hero status such as Samson, detailed in Hebrews 11:32. This is a process of reading within those gaps and spaces. And as the century moved forward, suicide took on the guise of Christian martyrdom following in the same fashion as Jesus who was willing to

---

74. The confession and remorse of Judas is no small issue. It is translated most often as "I have sinned" (Matt 27:4). The confession, however, is directed to the Jewish leaders rather than to Jesus in hopes that somehow Judas can change the outcome of his actions. See Morris, *The Gospel According to Matthew*, 694.

75. See Sophocles's *Antigone* for a very early account of the unwritten "laws of heaven" and the necessity of burying the dead in Meineck and Woodruff, *Sophocles*, 450–60.

76. Droge and Tabor. *A Noble Death*, 125.

77. Gilbert, *Death's Door*, 87, 94.

lay down his life.[78] Martyrdom could even offer a reward of heavenly assurance.[79]

Even though the actions of those that surround the death of Judas are fraught with difficulties because of gaps and spaces within the text, there is a very beautiful outcome for the future of deceased Gentiles. The field that was purchased with the blood money became a burial ground for Gentiles, and thus became a sacred ground of inclusion for the nations, an inclusion that is symbolized through spiritual death and a place for physical death.[80] Do not be too quick to dismiss the land—for land is a significant motif in Scripture and Potter's Field is fertile ground for homiletical investigation.

Judas was the seventh suicide. An eighth suicide, however, was on the horizon, one that would bring redemption for all suicides, but one that would also add an extra level of complexity to the topic of suicide in preaching.

JESUS AS THE EIGHTH SUICIDE

Eight is a special number in the Judeo-Christian tradition. There were eight people delivered through the flood waters in Genesis.[81] Jewish sons were circumcised on the eighth day of life[82] (later coming to represent baptism among Christians[83]—in fact in Europe many baptistery fonts are eight-sided for this reason).[84] Obed, the one who "renewed Naomi's

---

78. Early martyrs took Mark 8:34–35 literally when it states, "If any man would come after me, let him deny himself and take up his cross and follow me. For whoever would save his life will lose it; and whoever loses his life for my sake and the gospel's will save it." The word "martyr" stems from the Greek word for "witness." See Liddell, Scott, and Jones, *A Greek-English Lexicon*, entry for *martys*, I.

79. Chadwick, *The Early Church*, 30.

80. Matthew 27:7. Once again, the purchase of Potter's Field was a fulfillment of prophecy pointing to Zechariah 11:13 and Jeremiah 18:2–3; 19:1–13; 32:6–15. Morris states, "The prophecy cited ends with the words, 'as the Lord directed me.' These are important for Matthew. He is recording the fulfillment of the Lord's purposes" (Morris, *The Gospel According To Matthew*, 697–98).

81. 1 Pet 3:20.

82. Interestingly, vitamin K (an essential blood clotting agent), I have been told, does not develop in a newborn until the eighth day.

83. Col 2:11–12.

84. The Baptistery of St. John in Florence being the most famous.

life,"[85] the son of the Kinsman-Redeemer, is the eighth name in the gene-alogy of King David. Likewise, David was the eighth child of Jesse. There are seven signs plus one in the book of John.[86] Jesus reveals himself eight times after the resurrection. These may seem mere coincidences to the untrained reader, but when one is instructed in the ancient art of exegesis one learns that the authors of the Scriptures never haphazardly include or omit information. Patterns, chiasms, parallelism, word plays, and even numbers matter a great deal. This is not an exaggeration.

The liturgical calendar reflects this care in detail. For example, after the seven weeks of the spring harvest, the next day, the fiftieth day, is Pentecost. This day is the eighth day of the seventh week (that is, it is seven times seven, plus one). This eighth day and the fiftieth day contin-ues a pattern set from the beginning of creation. God began creating on the first day of the week by saying "Let there be light." Of course, the Sun, the Moon, and the Stars are not created until the fourth day notifying the reader that this light created on the first day is something altogether different than what is created on the fourth day.[87] God rested on the seventh day. But there is an eighth day. The eighth day represents that which goes beyond completeness, a creation of heavenly proportions, a restoration, and final perfection.

Eight is that day beyond what is natural: it is a "new creation." Eight represents miracles and is why the menorah has eight branches. When Jesus resurrected, he had a "new creation" for a body. The body still had the same form and the body even had the scars of his crucifixion, but it was a body that could ascend to heaven. It was a body that could pop in and pop out of locked spaces. Jesus's resurrected body was a new type of creation, never created before, and Christians call the new day of resur-rection the eighth day—the day that Light (remember the first day of creation) defeats darkness through victory over death—Easter.

85. Ruth 4:15.

86. Conservatively speaking, the seven signs include: changing water into wine at Cana in John 2:1–11, healing the royal official's son in Capernaum in John 4:46–54, healing the paralytic at Bethesda in John 5:1–15, feeding the 5,000 in John 6:5–14, Jesus walking on water in John 6:16–24, healing the man blind from birth in John 9:1–7, and the raising of Lazarus in John 11. I like to consider the resurrection of Jesus as the eighth sign (even though John does not explicitly name it a sign, as he does in the case of the others).

87. It also notifies the reader that the creation account is not a scientific record since we humans measure time (24-hour periods) based on the Sun, but the Sun is not created until the fourth day.

Like the first and eighth notes on a musical scale, so the first and eighth day are reflected in the fiftieth day (7x7+1). Pentecost is the birthday of the church, a new creation caused by light, or flames of fire, representing the indwelling of the Holy Spirit. The first, eighth, and the fiftieth day all land on the first day of the week—Sunday, the Lord's Day. The Sabbath is a day of rest, a day when Jews go to Synagogue. Sunday, however, became a day for those early Jewish Christians where the walls crumbled and where Jews and Gentiles could gather as a new people, a new creation to worship the one true God—together. For Christians, Easter or Resurrection Day is considered the eighth day of creation.[88] It is a new creation, a creation like no other. And it is the eighth day on which the entirety of the Christian tradition rests. Without the cross there is no salvation, but without Easter there is no hope. And without Pentecost there is no church.

Table 1:

Day:	Work:	Work of:	Numbers:
First Day of Creation	Light (Light in the beginning)	Father	1
Eighth Day of Creation	Easter (Light defeats darkness)	Son	7 + 1
Fiftieth Day of Creation	Church (Light goes throughout the world)	Holy Spirit	7 x 7 + 1

But just as Easter is the eighth day of creation, Jesus has been considered by many to be the eighth suicide recorded in the Scriptures.[89] A suicide that would bring about life and life everlasting. Thinkers such as Ignatius of Antioch,[90] Tertullian,[91] Jerome,[92] Bede,[93] and John Donne,[94] to name a few, believed that Jesus's death was a suicide.[95] Of course they did not use the word "suicide" because the word "suicide"

---

88. Hull Stookey, *Calendar*, 41.

89. The first suicide was by an illegitimate non-anointed king. The eighth suicide was by the King of kings.

90. Droge and Tabor, *A Noble Death*, 130.

91. Droge and Tabor, *A Noble Death*, 145.

92. Fedden, *Suicide*, 10, 31.

93. Fedden, *Suicide*, 31.

94. Donne, *Biathanatos*, 22.

95. Foreshadowing of Jesus's suicide could be noted as John 8:21–22, "This made the Jews ask, 'Will he kill himself? Is that why he says, 'Where I go you cannot come?'"

was not coined until much later.[96] They used the words "self-homicide," "martyrdom," or "voluntary death." In the case of Jesus and many early martyrs to follow, voluntary death was a death that was deliberately provoked. And as I mentioned earlier, "one who provokes persecution with the intent to be martyred or actively seeks or volunteers for martyrdom may be labeled a suicide."[97]

Jesus as a Sacrificial-Suicide

Jesus states in John 10:17–18, "The reason my Father loves me is that I lay down my life—only to take it up again. No one takes it from me, but I lay it down of my own accord." In this statement Jesus presents his authority over his own life, death, and resurrection. Jesus sets his face towards Jerusalem,[98] knowing full well that the crucifixion is before him, and he willfully, of his own volition, goes to the cross. Like Socrates who was given an opportunity to escape death,[99] he drank the capital punishment willfully. The statement, "Father, into your hands I commit my Spirit," is not spoken by a man who is without control over his own destiny.[100]

   In Jesus's case, however, this is not only suicide, but it is also sacrifice. Jesus saw his death as a sacrifice when he said in Luke 22:20, "This cup is the new covenant in my blood, which is poured out for you." Here Jesus is implying that the Passover meal is representing not the old sacrificial law, but a new sacrifice that is Jesus's death.[101] The Apostle Paul also saw Jesus's death as a sacrifice according to Romans 3:25, when he said, "God presented him as a sacrifice of atonement through faith in his blood." Thus, Jesus is a sacrifice; but Jesus is also a suicide for the simple reason that no one forced Jesus to the cross. Rather, Jesus went willingly as an act of obedience to God the Father,[102] not only as an act of obedience,

---

   96. Some state that the origin of the word "suicide" dates to 1642 coined by Sir Thomas Brown in his memoir *Religio Medici* but was not used in common vernacular until the twentieth century. Alexander Murray contests this, stating that Walter of St. Victor used the word "suicide" first around 1178. See Murray, *Suicide in the Middle Ages*, 38–39.

   97. Amundsen, "Suicide and Early Christian Values," 78.

   98. Luke 9:51.

   99. See the Platonic dialogue *Crito*.

   100. Luke 23:46.

   101. Heb 9:12.

   102. Heb 5:8.

but also as an act of love by the One who deliberately provoked the circumstances.[103] Some might delimit Christ's sacrifice as a "martyr-dom" and seek to avoid naming it a "sacrificial-suicide." Yet, suicide and martyrdom both contain broader spectrums of actions and motivations, and because they can partially overlap (as discussed earlier), Christ's passion seems to be closer to a sacrificial-suicide. This is because God chose to act in Christ as the lamb of sacrifice.

Self-harm is often seen as being violent. Violence is part of the story of the crucifixion, but violence is not what brings atonement; on the contrary, love produced atonement. Violence is not required for salvation, even though it is a part of the crucifixion story. This simply highlights the love of God even more when Jesus says, "Father forgive them."[104] Thus, if we describe it as a suicide, we must note that Jesus's death is unique in comparison to other biblical suicides.

A major difference between King Saul, for instance, and Jesus is that King Saul participated in self-harm to *escape the enemy* (with honor), but Jesus participated in self-harm *to love the enemy* (in humiliation). Another biblical figure whose death needs to be differentiated from that of Christ is Stephen. Stephen's death is a martyrdom, in the most conser-vative sense, and not a sacrificial-suicide because the biblical text gives no evidence that he sought death or that he passed up an opportunity to avoid death. While parts of his sermon were provocative, the surround-ing narrative context gives no hint that he had any choice in being stoned. Unlike Stephen, Jesus set his face to Jerusalem and willfully laid down his life: Stephen only willingly (out of conviction), not willfully (with intention), laid down his life. Jesus, on the other hand, not only willingly but also willfully handed himself over.[105] Some martyrdoms are sacrifi-cial, but not all martyrdoms should be considered under the category of sacrificial-suicide. Thus, as I stated earlier, martyrdom falls along a spectrum only part of which overlaps with the spectrum of suicide.

Since Jesus's suicide was the eighth and, thus, the final suicide of Scripture, one can conclude that this death represents a mending and even a resolving act of the nature of suicide in particular and death in

103. Both the concept of obedience ("not my will . . . ," Luke 22:42) and free voli-tion ("No one takes my life from me . . . ," John 10:18) should be held in a truthful tension acknowledging the mystery of the Trinitarian God.

104. Luke 23:34.

105. Jesus's prayer, "Father, take this cup from me," is often cited as an example of Jesus's desire not to die. See Luke 22:42.

general. Death is experienced by Christ and because of the resurrection death is also defeated by Christ. Christ's death and resurrection speak to a hope amid such suffering; not only a hope of future redemption, but a hope for those who have experienced death in its multifaceted and varied occurrences and circumstances. It is a hope and a reassurance that we humans are not alone in our valley of death, but that God also suffered, that God knows what it is like to die. And God the Father knows what it is like to lose someone to death. It is, however, also a lesson that God prefers life over death because God does not stay dead.

The most common question to me during lectures on biblical suicides has been: "If Jesus's death is a suicide and people want to be like Jesus then isn't telling people that Jesus committed suicide just going to make people want to kill themselves? How is this information *prevention*?" I have always responded, "That's a good question." But in actuality, I do not think it is a good question. Augustine once reported the view that Hell was created for people who ask stupid questions.[106] That is pretty harsh and Augustine remarked that people who give such a response to a questioner are only trying to evade the point at issue. Augustine's critique of that answer is probably correct for the most part. And yet, many of our questions often deserve critique as well; especially when they are asked as a knee-jerk reaction rather than out of actual thoughtfulness. In all fairness, students do not often have a lot of time to think about their questions in a lecture setting and many students are young and biblically illiterate. I have often asked the students in response, "Do you know someone who has given all that they had away to the poor in order to achieve eternal life (Mark 10:21)? Have you ever heard of anybody or known someone who had gouged out their eye or cut off their hand to flee from temptation (Matthew 18:9)?" Then I follow up the questions with, "Why don't people do these things?" There are many people who have a God-complex and some people have even undergone crucifixion,[107] but it is not to save the world. People do many things in the name of Jesus, many terrible things, and yet some wonderful things too.

The original question implies that suicide is somehow "just" suicide. But suicide is not just suicide. Suicide is on a spectrum. Jesus's death is not like a suicide bomber; Jesus's death is nothing like an escape. As

---

106. Augustine, *Confessions*, 11.xii.14 (at Chadwick, 229).

107. For instance, some people in the Philippines undergo a cultural expression of crucifying themselves around Easter in the San Pedro Cutud Lenten Rites as an act of mortification or thanksgiving, but do not actually die from the crucifixion.

noted above (but it is worth reiterating), the difference between Jesus's death and Saul's is that Saul died to escape his enemies; Jesus died to love his enemies. When talking about Jesus's death as a suicide it is vital to remember the spectrum. Jesus's death is not just any suicide, but rather it is a sacrificial-suicide. If someone wants to die by suicide, simply because they are told that Jesus died by suicide, one needs to ask if their suicide is being planned in love . . . for the whole world. Jesus's suicide is elevated. John 3:14–15 states that Christ in his humility is at the same time exalted.[108]

It is well known in scholarship however, that in the first and second centuries people literally took up their cross and followed Christ, seeking that same exalted-humility.[109] And even today, in cultures outside of the Western world people regard martyrdom as an honorable and desirable way to die. Of course, the attentive homiletician will be preaching regularly about the call to die daily to self. This is what a baptized life looks like: drowning daily.

Recognizing Christ's death as a suicide can provide a new way of thinking for the person struggling with suicidal ideation. As they begin to reimagine Christ's motivations and emotions leading up to his death, a more self-reflective awareness of their own motivations and emotions can be opened up. In a more detailed manner, we can begin to imagine our own story, not as disconnected from Christ's story, but rather from within the narratives of Scripture. It is my conviction that to live within the world of the Bible is always a good thing—a life-affirming thing (even if in complex ways). After all, the preacher (or the friend) should always be open to the possibilities of prompting those with suicidal ideation to begin talking, reflecting, and giving renewed attention to the details of Christ's death and life. Without Christ's life, death, and resurrection our life and death do not make sense.

A good response to the previous question could be, "How do you define suicide? How do you understand taking up your cross and following Jesus? What does it mean to die to self? How do you understand baptism as drowning? What does the broken bread on the Table mean to you?" For the thoughtful Christians, suicide is not a black and white issue, but rather it is a deeply rich spiritual and theological issue, one that is at the core of our faith.

108. John 3:14–15 states, "Just as Moses lifted up the snake in the desert, so the Son of Man must be lifted up."

109. See Moss, *The Other Christs*.

Jesus and the Good Death

The fact remains that everyone will die. But not everyone will die *in* Christ. Jesus's death transforms our death, so much so that our calling is to die *with* Christ. But how does one understand and even apply this concept in a culture that has vilified voluntary death?

A better question to consider is, "What is a good death?" When it comes to palliative care in the hospital setting this question should be paramount. We should also ask this question to our congregations, to our parents and to our children. What does it mean to die well? Is death always bad? Can death be good?

Among the proof-texts often cited to condemn suicide are the many references in Revelation used to encourage the persecuted Christians to stay strong (Rev 3:5, 12, 21:7). Others include "no man ever hates his own flesh, but nourishes it and cherishes it" (Eph 5:28), or "the Lord gave, and the Lord has taken away" (Job 1:21), or "choose life, that you and your descendants may live" (Deut 30:19). The most cited text is the Sixth Commandment, "you shall not kill" (Exod 20:13, Deut 5:17). But for me, as a child, it was 1 Corinthians 6:19 that I heard the most regarding suicide. Even though the context is sexual immorality, my youth pastor would quote this text in regard to suicide, "Do you not know that your body is a temple of the Holy Spirit, who is in you," and then he would blend it with 1 Corinthians 3:16–17, "Do you not know that you yourselves are God's temple and that God's Spirit lives in you? If anyone destroys God's temple, God will destroy him for God's temple is sacred, and you are that temple." This text has also been used in sermons denouncing tattoos, smoking, and I even heard it used once for the evils of ear piercing. As a young child, I knew early on that to harm the physical body was to unleash the destruction of God. The fear of hell has been a deterrent to suicide for many people. There is no doubt about that. And I have been instructed that if playing the hell-card prevents suicide, by all means, play the hell-card. But as I have grown, I have wondered, has the culturally accepted suicide prevention monologues weakened Christian theology, debilitated faithful Scripture reading, and ultimately compromised the Gospel? It is so easy to proof-text, but it is so much more rewarding to interpret Scripture by Scripture and to interpret our lives by Scripture.

Contextual readings of Scripture should be used instead of proof-texting when it comes to arguing for the complexity of the topic of biblical suicide.[110] For those who take the Bible seriously, one will recognize that reading Scripture contextually actually shows that nowhere in Scripture (and specifically in the contextual narratives) is suicide defined *explicitly* as a sin or a crime. In order for suicide to be interpreted as a sin the interpreter has to make certain assumptions and sometimes even interpretive interpolations—not the literal meaning of interpolation, but the interpreter's conjecture of the *intended* meaning.[111]

Some say that Augustine does this very thing. As Droge and Tabor state, "Augustine's case against voluntary death was based on a selective reading of Plato, not the Bible."[112] They say it was selective because Augustine ignores certain exceptions that Plato puts forth in his *Laws* for condoning suicide. These exceptions include if one willingly accepts state capital punishment (such as Socrates experienced), if one has experienced serious misfortune, and if one is faced with terrible shame.[113] Droge and Tabor claim that Augustine's interpretation of the text is based on biased and sloppy exegesis, both of Scripture and of Plato.[114] This points to the greater issue of scriptural interpretation and the collective and individual authority given to the text.[115]

If preaching is theology (words about God) rooted in Scripture, then preaching must reflect the same complexities as Scripture (that is assuming that one recognizes the text as complex). The common interpretive inertia in biblical hermeneutical method and historical context have unfortunately maintained stigmas and stereotypes while keeping people from spectrum thinking. This is why people can call Good Friday good while at the same time asserting that Jesus's death was bad (whether it was murder or suicide). My case is that Jesus's sacrificial-suicide was a good death on Good Friday for the good of all creation. This does not remove suicide from being a sign of the tragic nature of the human

110. The conviction that context is vital for scriptural interpretation (especially for preaching) is shared by both Catholics and Protestants. See the *Constitution on Divine Revelation*, esp. pars. 17 and 21; the Augsburg Confession, ch. 5; the Westminster Confession, 21, 5.

111. Achtemeier, *Inspiration and Authority*, 44.

112. Droge and Tabor, *A Noble Death*, 5.

113. Plato, *Laws* 9. 873 c–d, in Cooper, *Plato*, 1532.

114. For an extensive treatment of Augustine's interpretive hermeneutical methods, see Droge and Tabor, *A Noble Death*, 167–80.

115. For a helpful and well written overview of why Augustine was so opposed to suicide, see Shaw, *Sacred Violence*, 727–70.

condition. But it does show that in human nature, in our universal end, in the dreadful fate of death, we can die well. It isn't how we die, but who we die with. Even in suicide, because of God's undeserved grace, a good death is one that is *in* Christ. In Christ because of God's predestined and providential care.

Some might argue that if someone is *in* Christ they wouldn't die by suicide. I beg to differ. Many people who have been adopted as children of God have died by suicide. And because of Jesus's death, God the Father knows what it is like to lose a son to suicide, albeit, a *sacrificial*-suicide.

8

Suicide Ideation in the Scripture

In CHAPTER 1, I briefly touched on suicide ideation. To help clarify, passive ideation involves the thoughts and even the desire to die. After talking to a variety of people about suicide, I have come to believe that passive ideation is actually quite common, and it even seems part of the norm. People have times in their lives where they wish to die; wishing (yet knowing full-well the lack of probability) that they would fail to wake up in the morning. People of all kinds have moments of exhaustive despair and wish their story to be over; yet they have no actual plans of bringing about their death. Active ideation on the other hand moves from merely wishing to die to actively planning to die. This transports the ideation from normal emotions and thoughts to the need for immediate intervention.

Passive ideation can be problematic and misunderstood. Disturbed by my research, people have said to me, "You shouldn't think about suicide. It is not normal nor is it healthy to think about death." Many suppose that if you tell someone that you are struggling with thoughts of suicide then immediately the corresponding response would be to get the professionals involved. Clinicians instruct that if someone tells you that they are struggling with thoughts of suicide, one should ask the question, "What do you mean by thoughts of suicide? Are you thinking of and even planning to hurt or kill yourself?" But if the return response is "No, I'm just thinking about suicide," the responder can be left feeling, well, unprepared to deal with the simple aspect of mere thoughts. Usually when we hear a person say "thinking" it translates into "doing" (even though thinking about suicide does not equate with being suicidal). There are phone numbers to call and people to contact if it is active ideation. But with true passive ideation in which the person is just thinking about suicide—what should we do with that? The reality is that there really is a very fine line between active and passive ideation. Especially since active ideation depends upon passive ideation for self-realization. It is a thin line, but it is still a line. We can only know if someone is having passive or active ideation, by first asking them, living with them, sharing our life with them, or, in the case of Jonah, studying him. There are a handful of people in the Scriptures who exhibit passive or active ideation and Jonah comes to my mind as one who potentially shows both.

JONAH

"The word of the Lord came to Jonah," but "Jonah ran away from the Lord." I have often wondered, why did he run?[1] Why didn't he just ignore God right where he was at and stay put, avoiding all the troubles that come with traveling? Why is geographical movement on land and sea so important for the story? Could it be that Jonah is following a type-scene echoing Adam's hiding?[2] Could it also be symbolic of what a life looks like when it turns away from God, seeking self-sufficiency and abundance—focused and attached to only the material world alone? Psalm 72:10 indicates that Tarshish would be an ideal place for someone seeking self-gratifying idols, forfeiting "the grace that could be his,"[3] because it was a distant and wealthy place.

At the outset Jonah is actively moving away from the true Life-source of the universe. And when you move away from Life, you inevitably move towards death. John Calvin states, "It was not indeed the design

1. John Calvin answers this question by stating, "All flee away from the presence of God, who do not willingly obey his commandments; not that they can depart farther from him, but they seek, as far as they can, to confine God within narrow limits, and to exempt themselves from being subject to his power." In other words, in the act of rejecting God we seek to diminish God's sovereign power. In a way, this began with Eve, who disobeyed God so that she could have life apart from the Life-giver. See Calvin, *Commentaries on the Twelve Minor Prophets*, 31.

2. The pilgrim life, one of movement correlating both the physical and the spiritual, is a pivotal theme throughout both the Old Testament and the New Testament. The pilgrim life could also be seen as an echo in the Second Person of the Trinity's departure, inaugurating the incarnation.

3. Jonah 3:8.

of Jonah to lay violent hands on himself; but though he abstained from violence, he yet, as to the purpose of his mind, procured death to himself; for he submitted not to God, but was carried away by a blind impulse so that he wished to throw away his life."[4] The Scriptures describe the movement away from God as one of going "down," "down to Joppa," [5] going "below deck" and "laying down."[6] It was the captain of the boat who preached to Jonah (to the one who had originally been called to preach), saying, "Get up" (turn back to the Living One) "and call on your god!" The captain resounded God's original calling, "Arise and go." But Jonah said no to God. Could it be, that the basic act of rejecting God the Source of Life is a form of active suicide ideation? Is rejecting Jesus part of a tacit plan to die?

Some might say that I am spiritualizing suicide. But if we recognize that we humans are both spiritual and physical at the same time, just as we are both made in the image of God[7] and yet by nature objects of wrath,[8] the two cannot be separated just as much as the sun cannot be separated from its heat. To be a Christian is to live the paradoxical life, we are both predestined and free, both a universal people and a local people, both saved by grace and working our salvation out with fear and trembling, and we are both spiritual and physical at the same time. Renouncing Jesus, the giver of Life, is to be suicidal both spiritually and physically.[9] By rejecting God, turning away from God in one's full voli-tion, one is demonstrating active suicide ideation, not passive. In other words, those who voluntarily reject Jesus, voluntarily seek death.

Going a little further, what if, when we reject God's son, our physi-cal cells (which, if we are silent, like the rocks will cry out),[10] begin to self-destruct in the absence of their Creator, our mind becomes dark-ened in understanding, and our physical bodies begin to die, like a plant without water? Ephesians 4:18 says it this way, "They are darkened in

4. Calvin, *Commentaries on the Twelve Minor Prophets*, 140–41.

5. Jonah 1:3.

6. Jonah 1:5. See also Jonah 2:2 and 2:6.

7. The Image of God is Jesus (Col 1:15). We regain the Image through faith (Eph 8:9). What this implies is that we were originally made in the Image, but because of the fall, we no longer retain it apart from Jesus. Thus, only believers reflect God's Image (see discussion in chapter 6).

8. Eph 2:3.

9. John 6:53.

10. Luke 19:40.

their understanding and separated from the life of God because of the ignorance that is in them due to the hardening of their hearts." The King James Version says it like this, "Having the understanding darkened, being alienated from the life of God through the ignorance that is in them, because of the blindness of their heart." The idea of alienation and separation from life is caused by turning away from God. Paul is describing the true origins of active suicide ideation in the initial rejection of God.

By running away from God, Jonah was preparing to be separated from Life and to be in death. Yet, even in Jonah's active ideation, when push comes to shove, he doesn't take the initiative and throw himself overboard. Instead, he asks the sailors to throw him over. Why doesn't Jonah just jump? Why does he have to get the whole crew involved in his death? It may be that suicide is always collective. People never die by suicide in isolation from the community. Just as suicide-by-cop is never an individual issue, neither is accidental suicide by substance abuse. There is always a collective element, a culpability, and responsibility of the whole.[11] Hence, when a person dies by suicide, we participate, in small ways, silent ways, and frequently unnoticed ways. "A suicide is a combination of the individual's issues and the network's responses—joint perpetrators within the community circle."[12] How is passive and active ideation, then, a collective endeavor and how can the preacher speak to this from the pulpit?

Despite Jonah's refusal to proclaim God's word, within God's storm Jonah's voice gave way to testimony and witness, "I am a Hebrew," he said to the sailors, "and I worship the Lord, the God of heaven, who made the sea and the land."[13] By his pronouncement, the text says, "the men greatly feared the Lord and they offered a sacrifice to the Lord and made vows to him." This is precisely what Jonah didn't want to happen—the redemption of the Gentile sinners. By Jonah's voice, the sailors (in the grip of death) turned towards Life. One might say[14] that God loved those sailors, and God had planned all along for them to come and bow before

11. Daniel Timmer states that, "spirituality in the book of Jonah is almost exclusively restricted to individual human beings' relationships with the God who created them" (Timmer, *A Gracious and Compassionate God*, 56). On the contrary, I see a corporate spirituality that saturates the entirety of the story.

12. Selden, *The Suicide Solution*, 40.

13. Jonah 1:9.

14. Calvin, *Commentaries on the Twelve Minor Prophets*, 61.

Him.[15] Even when Jonah had "intended harm, God intended it for good to accomplish what is now being done, the saving of many lives."[16] After all, the casting of lots was rigged by an all-Sovereign God as Proverbs 16:33 states: "The lot is cast into the lap, but its every decision is from the Lord."

Beautifully, just as God provided for Adam, who tasted death in his rebellion, God provides salvation at Jonah's point of death. It is only in the throes of danger that Jonah responds to the captain's call to "Get up and call on your god." It was only when he was thrown, hurled overboard, that he went down, "waves crashing" over him; down, down with seaweed entangling him; down, down, down, the "earth barring him forever," that Jonah "remembered" the Lord. Jonah remembered the one whom he was called to worship while on the boat: "The Lord, the God of heaven, who made the sea and the land."[17]

How is this remembering in the belly of the big fish any different than his memory on the boat? And what does remembering have to do with Life-giving breath? How does remembering help us die a noble death and live a noble life? Why do we remember our Lord's body broken and his blood shed with bread and cup? How is remembering the death of Jesus an act of propelling us towards Life? How is this act of remembering like going through the waters of baptism in the Ark, "in it only a few people, eight in all, were saved through water,"[18] seeking that dry and promised land? We who have memory can live in the moment, but without memory, where could we live? This remembering propelled Jonah in moving towards God not away from God, just as the sailors did in prayer. And it is in the prayer that we recognize God's deeper culpability in Jonah's plunge into the waters of death.

We thought the sailors threw him over, but actually, it was the Lord who threw him into the sea. Jonah asserts: "You hurled me into the depths, into the very heart of the seas and the currents swirled about me; all your waves and breakers swept over me."[19] With God's ultimate control established, can we confidently state that Jonah was alone, individually and personally responsible for his active suicide ideation; or

---

15. 1 Tim 2:4.

16. Gen 50:21.

17. Jonah 1:9.

18. 1 Pet 3:20.

19. Jonah 2:3.

is it passive ideation, or did he have any ideation at all? Similarly, Jesus encouraged Judas to go: "What you are about to do, do quickly." As soon as Judas took the bread, Satan entered into him."[20] There are a lot of players when it comes to suicide. And it seems likewise complicated when it comes to suicide ideation.

The complexity is exacerbated in light of the ambiguities of human volition. Sometimes someone might wish for death without actually articulating it for themselves and sometimes people reject Christ without fully knowing what they are doing. This is the problem with the word "ideation." It is too clinical and does not grasp all the ways in which someone might have unformed, not fully articulated impulses, desires, and self-destructive thoughts.

Jonah's prayer complicates the matter. Jonah must have been entrenched in the biblical texts since his prayer is a patchwork of the Scriptures. One might assume that if Jonah was so familiar with the Scriptures he would have been in the habit of praying to God in the Spirit. True prayer, in the Spirit,[21] is moving towards Life rather than moving away from Life. But as the story of Jonah progresses, communication with God has not transformed his character and does not change Jonah's attitude or his emotional highs and lows. He has no desire to sacrifice his anger or his grudge that he has nursed so long towards the Gentiles.[22] Even after his horrifying episode in the big fish, there on dry land in the midst of praying to God, Jonah speaks about death as better than life. If prayer, as an act of remembering, moves us towards Life then why does Jonah continue to ask for death? Is it that, in order to have true Life, one must first die?[23] Could we say that Jonah is really crying out for God to help him die to his resentments so that he can live anew? Could his plea be crying out not only for eternal salvation, but salvation here and now, a salvation that heals us from our addictions, our self-absorption, our racism, that repairs the broken relationships and dissolves the anger? Could Jonah's prayer be elusively hinting, "Save me from myself?"

That interpretation might be a stance of overly optimistic hermeneutics. The story tells us that Jonah did die, the sign of three days in the

20. John 13:27.

21. Rom 8:26–27.

22. This is a reminder that, if Jonah is suicidal, it is not because of depression. Initially it could have been due to anxiety for escape, but by chapter 4, it is because of anger. The *DSM-5* does not indicate that suicide ideation comes from anger.

23. John 12:24.

tomb, and yet his baptism through the waters did not create in him a new heart.[24] He was obedient to God's calling, but his heart had not changed towards the calling. But can't we pray true prayers without always recognizing their truth? Wouldn't praying for healing from racism be a sign of repentance? But it hardly seems Jonah repents of this, even by the end.

There he is, sitting all alone outside the city, a pathetic picture the author paints. Why is Jonah just sitting there? Why isn't he headed home? Is he waiting for the shock-and-awe to drop after forty days? What a pitiful place to be, sitting in the dirt with a drafty and makeshift shelter only to have the true shelter of the vine wither away. It was hot and lonely. Well, that is, it would be lonely if Jonah was an extrovert.

But the text seems to indicate that Jonah is happiest when he is alone. After all, he wasn't up on deck with the crew or the other passengers; no, he chose to be alone in the belly of the boat. And it is only there, alone under the vine, that the text tells us that for the very first time Jonah was "very happy." First, he is angry, then he is happy, then he is angry again. Oi veh!

God askes the question to Jonah, "Is it right for you to be angry about the plant?" Jonah replied, "It is, and I'm so angry I wish I were dead."[25] Like Jeremiah's own complaint, Jonah struggles with how he thinks God should behave. "Why does the way of the wicked prosper? Why do all the faithless live at ease? You have planted them, and they have taken root; they grow and bear fruit."[26] Is Jonah really suicidal because God doesn't act the way he wants God to act? Or is Jonah simply representing the generational ongoing behavior of the elder brother when the prodigal son comes home? Does grace rub us the wrong way because, it just isn't fair? Praying to God in this moment, is Jonah really suicidal?

What does it feel like to go down, down towards death? I suppose it might feel like moving from passive to active ideation. Thinking about suicide might stay at the thinking stage. But sometimes thinking moves downward . . . towards planning. Some might protest and say Jonah was never planning to die; the circumstances of the storm forced him to die. Yet, as was suggested above, turning away from God involves turning towards death and provides an impulse (at the least) towards suicidal ideation in some form.

24. Ps 51:10.

25. Jonah 4:9.

26. Jer 12:1–2.

Regardless, by his watery death, one would hope that Jonah had the opportunity to experience empathy, knowing what it is like to be dead, dead in one's transgressions,[27] in spirit and in body. There in the gut of the big fish, going deeper into the grave, Jonah felt what it was like to be a Gentile, dead in trespasses, "separated from Christ, excluded from citizenship in Israel and foreigners to the covenants of the promise, without hope and without God in the world."[28]

The big fish was not only the means of judgment, but it was also the means of grace; "an agent of death, is also the means of rescue."[29] To be born again, requires one to die first.[30] Surely his own death and new life would provide Jonah with compassion towards those distanced from God, trapped in a life of death. One would think the most empathetic message would be, "Hey, come on guys, God loves you." And they may ask back, "How has he loved us?"[31] But that was not Jonah's method for the message. Rather, Jonah's words, in obedience to God's word, warned of death: "Forty more days and Nineveh will be overturned." In other words, Nineveh is dust! God's message to Nineveh was God's wrath, doom, and destruction, not: "God loves you just how you are." Jonah was called to preach against them. Yet, he intuitively knew that doing so would bring repentance. This seems counter-intuitive to me. People push back when they are pushed. How did Jonah know that they would repent? Once again, the story of Jonah is not really about Jonah but about the miracles of a sovereign God. This should encourage preachers to preach God's word because by God's word people are changed.

Yet, how many preachers run from God's call to preach what God wants us to preach? How often do we preach what *we* want to preach? Preach what I am interested in, what I think matters? Really, who wants to "preach against" wickedness?[32] Not wickedness in general, but the wickedness in us. Nineveh is described as those who have idols, "who plot evil against the Lord," and "are vile."[33] Do we fail to preach repentance because we do not think our people (including ourselves) have

---

27. Eph 2:1.

28. Eph 2:11.

29. Perry, *The Honeymoon Is Over*, 7.

30. 1 Pet 1:23.

31. Mal 1:2.

32. Jonah 1:2.

33. Nah 1:1–14.

anything to repent of? Or is it a cultural issue: being politically correct, or being admired? Deep down inside we just want a nice day where everyone can leave church feeling good. We do not want people leaving feeling depressed and depraved. Why, what would that do to their mental state? Or, I wonder, do we not preach the message of repentance because we know that God is "gracious and compassionate?" That was Jonah's reason.

Ultimately, the reason he ran from his calling to preach was because of God's character. God is "gracious," "compassionate," "slow to anger," "abounding in love," and he "relents from sending calamity."[34] In other words, God is life-giving. When people accept this Life—"the Way, and the Truth, and the Life"[35]—they become part of the faithful collective. They become part of those "born not of blood nor of the will of the flesh nor of the will of man, but of God."[36] And, "The Spirit himself testifies with our spirit that we are God's children."[37]

God's nature of relenting from sending calamity becomes a personal calamity for Jonah. It is precisely this collective nature of the Kingdom of God that Jonah rejects. The following conversation between God and Jonah revolves around why God should "not be concerned about that great city" and their animals. Jonah responds with, "Lord, take away my life. . . ."[38] To have to be connected to the collective, to share life with others, for Jonah, it would have been better to die than to live. Is this passive or active ideation? Or is this just a sulking introvert? Is Jonah suicidal, or is he simply an angry racist who is brooding? Moses seems just as melodramatic in Exodus, passively aggressive and deceptively persuasive when he says to God, "Oh, what a great sin these people have committed! They have made themselves gods of gold. But now, please forgive their sin—but if not, then blot me out of the book you have written."[39] By throwing the threat of death in the face of True Life, can Jonah persuade True Life to bring death to the Gentiles?

Regardless, if Jonah was suicidal, why does he, once again, involve the assistance of another? Why doesn't he just kill himself? As Job's wife

---

34. Jonah 4:2.
35. John 14:6.
36. John 1:13.
37. Rom 8:15–16.
38. Jonah 4:3.
39. Exod 32:31–32.

said, "Curse God and die already!"[40] Jonah is upset about the inclusion of the Gentile community, yet he depends on the Other for his death, and his life. The One who provided the captain, the sailors, the big fish, repentance, forgiveness, and the vine to protect from the sun's heat is the One who controls life and death.[41] Maybe Jonah recognizes his ultimate dependence on God. "If we live, we live for the Lord; and if we die, we die for the Lord. So, whether we live or die, we belong to the Lord."[42] Because Jonah recognized from the very beginning that God is the one who gives life and takes it away, it must be that Jonah has passive ideation and not active, since only God can act on his behalf. But can we be too confident? Jonah could be blinded to his ultimate dependence because his eyes are downcast towards the dust in which he sits.[43] How does preaching lift the eye from the self to God, that God is Sovereign of life and death? How does the illumination of God's revelation lift our eyes away from self to salvation?

> I will lift up my eyes to the hills—
> From whence comes my help?
> My help comes from the Lord,
> Who made heaven and earth.[44]

But Jonah had no compassion on the vine that withered and died; he only cared that he lost his shade. This self-centered focus is what some would call "selfish." The word "selfish" is a loaded word for those who study suicide. Some say that suicide is "the most selfish act" one could do. Yet, suicide often seems anti-self in its nature. Jonah never physically died by suicide. Yet, many have been persuaded that Jonah is suicidal, or that at least he exhibits ideation.[45]

By the way, I should note that suicide is hard to do. It is actually very difficult to die. Researchers agree, that "If you attempt suicide, odds are

---

40. Job 2:9.

41. Job 1:21.

42. Rom 14:8.

43. Self-saturation can be noticed by all the personal pronouns Jonah uses in his prayer in chapter 4.

44. Ps 121.

45. Just as suicide is complicated, so is the very nature of theology. Jonah embodies "the precarious nature of human existence which it metaphorically represents as a haunting biblical witness to a theology that defies easy expression or analysis" (Bolin, *Freedom Beyond Forgiveness*, 178).

you will not succeed."[46] Even with all our modern tools, you might simply be left maimed and handicapped, left completely dependent on someone to bathe you. If someone is depressed because they are a "failure in life," why would they think that they could then succeed at suicide? Many who attempt suicide may only be in despair, but half-hearted towards active ideation (which again raises the issue of one's will, motivations, or intentions in self-harm). Maybe Jonah knew that he couldn't even get death right, so he talked like he was suicidal when he wasn't really. He had passive but not active ideation.

Some have compared Elijah to Jonah. This is primarily because God's character as sovereign over all creation is exhibited—wind, earthquakes, even fire.[47] But also, it is because at one point, after Elijah had been running a great distance, with utter exhaustion he sat under a broom tree and prayed to God, "Take my life." Some might say that by merely requesting death Elijah was suicidal. The reason, however, that he had been running in the first place was to preserve his life. This highlights the fact that verbalized words do not always describe the reality of one's true motivations or intentions.

While examining Jonah, one student in my homiletics class asked if Daniel and Lot's wife could be considered as displaying ideation. Just the question alone indicated to me that some students are engaging in spectrum thinking—which is good. The idea that Daniel's free decision not to submit to the government in idolatrous acts might seem to some as a political protest with death as a possible consequence. Lot's wife is interesting to consider because her story indicates that acts that lead to death could be categorized a suicide if the person has been warned or has prior knowledge of the consequence (even if they otherwise were not intending death but only intending to test death). By putting these passages together, we find more tantalizing hints at how suicide and ideation might show themselves in the breadth of the Bible and in the messiness of our lives.

46. Selden, *The Suicide Solution*, 31. Also see http://lostallhope.com/suicide-statistics or http://www.suicide.org/attempted-suicide-horrors.html.

47. See 1 Kgs 19.

SAUL

I have already discussed Saul at length in the previous chapter. But regarding suicide ideation, let us pause for a moment and consider the power of suggestion.[48] The fear of the amassing Philistine army was already a reality in the mind of Saul at the close of 1 Samuel. All he needed was someone to confirm his worst fears. Erik Vance in his book *Suggestible You*, states that the power of suggestion comes most readily from story. Franz Mesmer states, "Suggestibility relies partially on belief and good story-telling but receives a boost from the power of social pressure."[49] In fact, "any placebo or hypnotic induction is nothing more than a device for storytelling."[50] Weaving a future story into the present story is equipping the present to shape the future. And in Saul's case, the power of suggestion was regarding death, his death. Ross Ellis, a cyberbullying/child abuse expert states that the power of suggestion is so powerful that to suggest suicide to someone today can be enough to send you to jail.[51]

The idea of death was planted in Saul's mind by the woman commonly known as the Witch of Endor. Suicide ideation often works in tandem with suggestion. This is why people often do not want to talk about suicide or even say the word "suicide," because they do not want to put any ideas in someone's mind. Studies have now shown that talking about suicide in general does not elicit suicide ideation. But talking about suicide in personal, detailed, or persuasive ways can elicit harmful ideas. This is why the media must take careful precautions when describing how people died by suicide and in no way portray the death visually, in photography, or in film. The power of suggestion is real. In 1 Samuel, the Witch suggested Saul's death (and this mixed with his devoted belief in the scenario that she presented him –i.e. Samuel's words spoken from the grave) solidified his fate.

Saul was a man of the sword. David was a man of the sword, too. David, however, was also a man of three stones and the words, "You come against me with sword and spear and javelin, but I come against you in

---

48. There was a 65 percent increase in reported alien abduction cases following the release of Whitley Strieber's book *Communion*. He believed that he had been abducted for extraterrestrial experimentation and suggested to others that unusual dreams are an indication of abduction. See Yapko, *Suggestions of Abuse*, 93.

49. Quoted in Vance, *Suggestible You*, 35.

50. Vance, *Suggestible You*, 231.

51. Ellis, "Tell Someone to 'Kill themselves.'"

the name of the Lord Almighty, the God of the armies of Israel, whom you have defied. This day the Lord will deliver you into my hands. . . . "[52] Three stones were enough for David because God was his warrior. But Saul always had a sword. He knew how to use his sword and exactly where to plunge the sword into his foes. Without his sword, how would he defeat his adversaries?

But in the case of Saul's death, the sword would be turned against himself. Had Saul now become his own worst enemy? Those who are familiar with popping pills, choose pills as the method of suicide. Those who are familiar with guns, choose a gun as the method of suicide. Those that are frightfully afraid of heights, do not choose to leap from a high place as a method of suicide. Saul was a man of the sword, so he would die by the sword. Suicide gains courage through practice while in the stages of ideation.

But where was God for Saul? Isn't that what a Christian mother might ask of her child's suicide? The text states that the Witch informed Saul that the Lord had departed from him and had become his enemy. Lest we forget, the Witch was not a truth-teller. Her profession was in lying. As the preacher, I am obligated to ask questions. Questions that my parishioners might also be asking. When Saul took up the sword against God's anointed was God with him? Or, was God really Saul's enemy? Had God departed from Saul like a father who abandons his child? If God was Saul's enemy, even when Saul "inquired of the Lord," prayed, sought, asked, knocked, how is God then, in God's absence, responsible for inciting fear and thoughts of death in the mind of Saul? Can God, who "brings death and makes alive; he brings down to the grave and raises up,"[53] announce the time to die by prompting death ideation within an individual? We do not die early, and we do not die late. We die right on time, under God's sovereign will. David Hume wrote in his brief essay *On Suicide*, "When I fall upon my own sword, therefore, I receive my death equally from the hands of the Deity as if it has proceeded from a lion, a precipice, or a fever."[54] Is this the case for Saul?

---

52. 1 Sam 17:45–46.

53. 1 Sam 2:6.

54. Hume, *Essays On Suicide*, 12.

9

Prayer and Suicide

WHEN JONAH RAGED AGAINST LIFE to Life, he did so in conversation. When Elijah came to the broom tree so that "he might die," it was to God that he pleaded for death.[1] With his hands braced against the pillars of the temple Samson prayed, "Let me die with the Philistines."[2] And "out of the whirlwind" God spoke to Job's supplications of defiance by humbling Job to repentance—to die to self, "in dust and ashes."[3]

Like our ancestors before us, when Christians face death, we pray. Conversing with God is communion with Life. But if prayer is connecting to Life, how could prayer be an active participant in death? Or better stated, how is prayer a way to Life through death? And how then does our preaching guide the church to pray so that we can die in order to live?

In my personal experiences, prayer has sometimes triggered tunnel-vision despondency. The oft-stated quip to, "just take it to Lord in prayer," can cause moments of self-concentrated focus (rather than other-focused thinking) that keeps the depressed person's mind locked in to present time and tuned on to the self without any reflection on what could be in the future. Prayer without service is like faith without works—dead. Likewise, the all too frequent advice to "just ask and it shall be given" can often leave those drowning in self-pity to wonder if they just don't have enough faith and that is why they can't pull themselves out of the

1. 1 Kgs 19:4.
2. Judg 16:30.
3. Job 42:3, 6.

mind-numbing mud pit of melancholy, shackling the self to ever deeper isolation.

Shortly before his suicide, Jarrid Wilson, a pastor at Harvest Christian Fellowship Church, wrote, "Loving Jesus doesn't always cure suicidal thoughts. Loving Jesus doesn't always cure depression."[4] Samson prayed for God's assistance in self-death. And God answered Samson's request with mighty strength. The way we pray determines how we die while we live and paradoxically, how we can find life in the midst of death.

Prayer is commonly prescribed as that first battle cry for the Christian struggling with suicide. It is also understood as that first place of preparation for preaching. If you are suicidal, you should pray. And if you are about to preach, you should pray. Like dying, prayer is required for the entire preparation process of preaching. Maybe this is because, in preaching, we die.[5]

All words are socially constructed, "the theology expressed by prayer is always and everywhere culturally embedded and embodied."[6] We are taught how and why we pray. And if we are honest, most of us have been taught to think that the role of prayer is to get something. Get healthy, get promoted, get married, get better at and get our hands on whatever it is that we want. However, in this chapter, I claim that prayer, by its very nature, is not about retrieving, but it is about release. In other words, prayer is a form of dying. And, when understood in this way, prayer may actually avoid the self-focused isolation that so many experience.

GOOD WORKS, RIGHT WORDS

The Edict of Thessalonica (380 CE) established an "imperial church," which was part of a longer process that inadvertently gave birth to a movement of desert fathers and mothers exemplifying a transformation from martyrdom to monasticism.[7] Instead of physically dying under persecution, monastic Christians would die to the world by the way they lived. Death would be a companion during the everyday habits of self-denial.[8] During my senior year in college I spent four days at a Roman

---

4. See "Jarrid Wilson, Pastor and Mental Health Advocate, Kills Himself."

5. Rom 12:1–2.

6. Edwards, *A History of Preaching*, 377.

7. Edwards, *A History of Preaching*, 124.

8. Since death is an everyday companion, Christians are called to be companions

Catholic community in Snowmass, Colorado. When I arrived, my host said to me, "If you need anything, please let us know and we will help you live without it." The help would come in the form of prayer. Because prayer was the means by which I would let things go.

Unfortunately, a four-day retreat was not long enough to combat years of indoctrination that prayer is about manipulating God in order to get what I want. I was taught that sin hindered my prayers like a chasm too wide for my voice to cross, that prayer depended upon my good works, because after all "the prayer of a righteous man availeth much."[9] The right way to pray was with good credit to my name along with the right words in my mouth. There was a formula to prayer. A formula that crossed over historical, denominational boundaries.

For instance, Origen,[10] Clement of Alexandria[11] and Gregory of Nyssa[12] all agreed that good deeds gave you a special pass to talk to the King. After all, Romans 10:9 states, "That if you confess with your mouth, Jesus is Lord, and believe in your heart that God raised him from the dead, you will be saved." This seems straightforward, that if only we *do* something (i.e. believe) God will hear us and save us. On closer examination however, one verse earlier, Paul states that the ability to confess comes to us from God, "The word is near you; it is in your mouth and in your heart, that is the word of faith we are proclaiming."[13] First Corinthians 13:13 states that faith is a gift, a gift that does not originate with us but rather comes to us from outside of us. Galatians 3:23 states it this way, "Before this faith came, we were held prisoners by the law, locked

---

with those who are dying. Mary Magdalene, Mary the mother of Jesus, and James were companions with Christ at his death. The Father had not forsaken Christ but was present through the life of God's people. They were life for the Giver of Life who was dying for our life.

9. Jas 5:16 (KJV). I believe that Elijah's prayer was a snapshot and a reflection of the wandering in the wilderness, desperate for the living water of the promise land. Elijah's prayer for famine then for rain is a foreshadow of the Christian life within those moments of sanctification reflecting Christ on the via Delarosa. A righteous man is one whose life reflects the death and the resurrected life of Christ.

10. Origen states, "It is, then, neither in our power to make progress apart from the knowledge of God, nor does the knowledge of God compel us to do so unless we ourselves contribute something towards the good result." See Origen. *On First Principles*, 3.1 (in Butterworth, 210).

11. See Hammerling "Introduction," 11.

12. Brown "Piety and Proclamation," 108–13. See also, Gregory of Nyssa, *The Lord's Prayer*, 21.

13. Rom 10:8.

up until faith should be revealed." Thus, those who pray in Spirit and Truth, only pray because God first equipped them to pray. God equipped Jonah to pray in the belly of the whale for God's ultimate glory. And God prompted Samson to pray to die by self-death. Jonah's prayer *in* death and Samson's prayer *for* death—prayer was not what they did, but what God did through them. But this is not what we are taught.

Augustine instructed that to pray the Lord's Prayer was to make satisfaction for daily sins. This was especially helpful for those Christians who sinned after they had been baptized. Since Christians were only baptized once, they needed another way of returning to the font, and that passage was opened through the recitation of the Lord's Prayer.[14] Augustine was a defender of teaching the recitation of the Lord's Prayer to those being prepared for Baptism. But the problem with teaching the Lord's Prayer to unbaptized catechumens is that by their saying, "Our Father," they are verbally acknowledging the present spiritual adoption before water baptism. Their words actually create the reality of a spiritual adoption before their actual baptism. Ambrose of Milan, a contemporary preacher of the fourth century, argued for keeping the Lord's Prayer away from unbaptized ears.[15] The consequences of prayer are thus dependent on what we do and the words we say.

In the thirteenth century, Rogation was celebrated as a series of three holy days preceding the ascension of Christ that focused its attention on the theme of prayer.[16] It is said that the ritual originated when a man named Mamertus, who, fearing an impending disaster to hit Vienne, introduced prayer and fasting to save the city.[17] *Rogat* in Latin literally means "to ask." These days were influenced by the passage in James 4:3, "You do not get because you do not ask," and the words of Christ in Matthew 21:22, "Ask and you shall receive." Rogation included parades with dragons (that represented evil), litanies, and sermons.[18] The dragon acted as a visual aid paralleling the excerpt of the Lord's Prayer that states, "But deliver us from evil."[19]

14. Brown "Piety and Proclamation," 187.

15. Hammerling "The Lord's Prayer," 180.

16. Ember Days are also days dedicated to prayer, specifically for agriculture and/ or ordination commemorations. See Connelly, "Rogation Days," in Davies, *The New Westminster Dictionary of Liturgy and Worship*, 222.

17. Robinson, "The Lord's Prayer and Rogation Days."

18. Robinson, "The Lord's Prayer and Rogation Days," 450.

19. Matt 6:9–13.

Thus, prayer, from the earliest centuries, through the Middle Ages continued to be propagated as a kind of powerful incantation when performed in the right way. This influenced the participants to see prayer as control of one's situation, a way to manipulate God and the outcome through one's words. Thus, after much prayer, if one persisted in suicide ideation, the consensus was that the person didn't pray in the right way. If Judas would have simply prayed the way Jesus taught his disciples to pray by saying, "lead me not into temptation [testing]," could he have avoided the prophetic curse that lay heavily upon him? If only he had prayed with the right words in the right way?

Proclaimers of the Prosperity Gospel of the twentieth century, like many in preceding centuries, emphasized that prayer is a formula. If you say the right formula, you will get the desired results. The formula requires faith. If one has enough faith and prays in faith and then thanks God that what was asked for will be done, then the person will get what they asked for.[20] Casey Treat, the founder of the Christian Faith Center of Seattle, has preached and written about prayer extensively over his thirty years of ministry.[21] In his most-watched sermon on prayer, Casey Treat illustrates prayer with a rope. He swings the rope and lassos the pulpit. This illustrates how we should claim, grab, lasso what we want. Then we are to pull in our desires the way we would pull in cattle. The rope is faith. For Treat, prayer is believing (doing something) and then speaking what you want into reality. Treat highlights James 5:15–16 as evidence that prayer will not "work" if we do not "keep our faith working." He then asks the congregation, "What kind of prayer do you pray? Do you pray whiny, sissified prayers?" Or do you pray prayers with a voice of authority and claim what you want?[22]

Prayers as magical incantations are well attested in pagan literature and lend themselves to a purpose founded in the human desire for control and power. To say a prayer and to preach prayerfully, with the mindset that the words in the prayer themselves have power to control the outcome of salvation, the circumstances of atonement, and even control God, should cause the preacher to pause and discern. Is that the Christian way to talk about prayer?

20. Two foundational passages that Casey Treat uses to support his argument are Mark 11:24 and Matt 7:8.

21. See "Casey Treat."

22. Casey Treat, *Your Unlimited Life.*

I believe, this type of theology hijacks the human hope for health in times of depression and suicidal ideation because prayer ultimately depends on the perceived sovereignty and control of the self. This type of preaching relies fundamentally upon self, thereby turning people towards death. It is suicide promotion under the ruse of prevention in the most inappropriate way. But isn't that what suicide prevention too often is: helping people help themselves through self-confidence, boosting self-esteem, and self-promotion by proclaiming that we are worthy? Indeed, a clinical psychotherapist once told me that the way to prevent suicide is to persuade the suicidal person into thinking about how great they are.

PRAYER AS HELPING THE SELF

Harry Emerson Fosdick was the king of the self-help preachers. With the onslaught of new ideas within science and Biblical Studies in the early twentieth century, Fosdick had two spiritual and mental break-downs as a young college student.[23] These mental challenges were in a way deconstructing his "foundational" belief systems which he would reconstruct with a posture of self-defense.[24] Fosdick's sermons were, as he would say, "personal counseling on a group scale," with Scripture sprinkled in to give it weight.[25] His sermons were often polemical, focusing on hot button issues and even at times creating division within the church.[26]

For Fosdick, prayer, (in opposition to Gregory of Nyssa), is not based on good works nor is it a good work.[27] Prayer is something we do because we are human. It is a universal anthropological endeavor.[28] Fosdick states that "in the lowest form, among the most savage peoples, prayer and magic were indistinguishable."[29]

23. Edwards, *A History of Preaching*, 665.

24. Fosdick helped set the stage for a liberal Christianity that gained the freedom to question foundational ideas of the viability of the Apostles' Creed, the Virgin Birth, and the inspiration of Scripture. See "Harry Emerson Fosdick, Liberalism's Popularizer."

25. Moats Miller, *Harry Emerson Fosdick*, 251.

26. His sermon "Will the Fundamentalist Win?" is a good example of divisive rhetoric.

27. Fosdick, *The Meaning of Prayer*, 44.

28. Fosdick, *The Meaning of Prayer*, 1.

29. Fosdick, *The Meaning of Prayer*, 28.

For Fosdick, the purpose of prayer is to help God release his power. Prayer puts us in an attitude to help God.[30] Fosdick states, "Prayer cannot change God's purpose, but prayer can release it." And, "some things God never can do until he finds a man who prays."[31] Fosdick appealed to Meister Eckhart who said, "God can as little do without us, as we without Him."[32] Prayer then, is mutual cooperation and dependency.[33] No doubt this concept of prayer is connected to Process Theology which holds to the belief that human actions determine God's actions.[34] Fosdick's most concrete views on prayer can be found in his book, *The Meaning of Prayer*. In his sermons however, prayer becomes merely a subtopic that is subtly implied in how we should deal with an array of issues. But when prayer became a minor player, separate from preaching, the sovereign economy of God wanes in power. Think of this in light of self-help preaching. Self-help does not lend itself to God's sovereign reign. If the unleashing of God's power depends on my prayers, then God is not sovereign.[35] Self-help preaching is a message of me saving me by getting God to do my will.

If prayer is an issue of self-help, then prayer's purpose is to help suicidal persons to help themselves. Does prayer as self-help assist the suicidal person to die by suicide like Samson or does it aid the person not to die by suicide? Some might propose that the ultimate purpose of prayer is to secure one's desires. But if we pray and ask God to change our hearts, to heal our addictions, to dispel depression, (and for the preacher) to give us words to speak, are we not essentially asking God to take away our own free-will including our desires? And if we ask God, "not my will but Your will," are we not essentially asking to die?

PRAYER AS LOVE

Not everyone has viewed prayer as a means of acquiring our wishes. Gregory of Nazianzus (a friend of Gregory of Nyssa) approached prayer

30. Fosdick, *The Meaning of Prayer*, 59.

31. Fosdick, *The Meaning of Prayer*, 64.

32. Fosdick, *The Meaning of Prayer*, 64.

33. Fosdick, *The Meaning of Prayer*, 65.

34. See Epperly, *Process Theology*.

35. It is an understatement to claim that how one understands prayer will directly influence how one preaches.

from the perspective of Trinitarian Perichoresis Theology, that is: an appreciation of the loving relationship between the Father, the Son, and the Holy Spirit. Prayer not only is a social praxis, but it is also a theology of knowing because "perfect knowledge of God is identified with the summit of prayer."[36] And knowing God is to know that perfect love of mutuality between the members of the Godhead. Therefore, to pray is essentially to be in love. A love that reflects the love between a bride and her groom. One that is sacrificial, based not on getting but giving.

For the reformer John Calvin, true prayer is a relationship between reason and love. "The tongue, indeed, is not always necessary, but true prayer can never be without understanding and affection,"[37] and to hear God's voice from our very mouth directed by the Holy Spirit through his Scriptures in the moment of proclamation is an event of love. Preaching is prayer in a loving relationship with God and with others.[38] For Calvin, prayer is like two lovers intimately knowing each other. It is the "sweetness of love."[39] No doubt Calvin was influenced by the Cappadocian Father's theology of perichoresis. I pray for my enemies not because of my love, but because of God's love for me, and God's love for my enemy. For the one who is suicidal, true prayer comes to their lips not because they love themselves (like Narcissus) but because God loves them. Prayer is dependent on the sovereignty of God, who is Love.

Calvin calls prayer, "the chief exercise of faith." This is a faith that is first a gift from God. Hence, God enables one to seek God in prayer.[40] We have the ability to call God, but not without God calling us first.

36. Brown, "Piety and Proclamation," 113.

37. Calvin, *Catechism of the Church of Geneva*, III. Of Prayer, S. 240.

38. Augustine begins his *Confessions* by beseeching God in a supplication for knowledge, "Grant me Lord to know and understand, which comes first—to call upon you or to praise, and whether knowing you precedes calling upon you. But who calls upon you when he does not know you?" Augustine, *Confessions*, 1.i.1 (at Chadwick, 3).Knowing the Other effects knowledge of the self, (like a gemologist who recognizes a fake immediately only because he knew what a real diamond looked like originally). In prayer we see our flaws more starkly: our depression, our ideation, our temptations, our jealousy of others. Prayer reveals our unworthiness. Like Adam and Eve who eat the fruit of the Tree of Knowledge, prayer unwraps our wrongs, sins, and our ugliness. How then could prayer be life-affirming for those who are suicidal? How does confession lead to restoration? One does not come to know oneself by looking in, but rather by looking out. You can only know who you are by knowing the other. Hence, prayer is not only knowledge of God, but it is an avenue for knowledge of self.

39. Calvin, *Catechism of the Church of Geneva*, III. Of Prayer, S. 240.

40. Calvin, *Institutes*, III.20.1.

God equips us to call upon God.[41] Calvin's understanding of prayer is consistent with his understanding of preaching: "a sermon is the work of the Holy Spirit."[42] God, the giver of faith, the origin of prayer, and the birth-place of preaching is also the source of the active response to the preaching. After all, faith comes through hearing.[43] And hearing is an act of prayerful communion. Answered prayer is accomplished by God through God's servants who love God by loving others.[44] Outside of direct miracles, God manifests his will through the obedience of his servant's voice and hands—this is how God works in the world.[45] "Whom shall I send, and who will go for us?" God asks. Isaiah's encounter with God is a visualized prayer. Isaiah first recognizes who he is in light of who God is and he feels the weight of his brokenness in the presence of Perfection. Isaiah's sins are forgiven and in gratitude Isaiah responds to God's voice by way of prophetic preaching. The listeners were (like all listeners are) dependent upon God opening up of their ears to God's voice. The listener is dependent on hearing for communing. We are dependent on prayer in order to respond to the voice of God through Isaiah's preaching. Preaching is not simply God's call for active response by his administration, but it is an intimate communion with God who is "wholly present to

41. Calvin, *Institutes*, III.20.5.

42. Leith "Calvin, John," 61.

43. Rom 10:17.

44. Calvin preaches, "We must not wish to bind God to certain circumstances. Because in this very prayer we are taught not to put on him any law, nor to impose upon him any condition." This is in direct opposition to prayer as incantation. Calvin states, "The Lord's Prayer does not bind us to its form of words but to its content." Prayer then, should not be used to control or coerce God. And this is then, therefore, the same for preaching. Preaching as an act of prayerful communion with God is first the call to humility. We cannot somehow persuade God's people to fix people any more than we can persuade God to fix people. See Calvin, *Institutes*, III.20.49.

45. Calvin states, "For, before making any prayer for ourselves, before all things, we ask that his will be done; if having the heart formed in this obedience, we permit ourselves to be governed according to the good pleasure of the divine providence. . . . "With the collaboration of both wills, Calvin then gives comfort to those who still find themselves in want by saying, "And even if at the end, after long waiting, our mind cannot understand the profit of our praying and our senses feel no fruit thereof, nevertheless our faith will certify unto us what our mind and sense will not . . . and [God] alone will be sufficient unto us for all things. . . . " Calvin allows for prayer to reside in mystery. For Calvin, it is not as if "prayer works" but rather that God works God's sovereign will regardless of how, when, or why we pray. Should this not also be the case for preaching? See Calvin "Instruction in Faith," 230–31.

us."[46] Without prayer there is no preaching. And without love there is no prayer. This is why gospel preaching is paramount. No life can exist apart from the one who so loved this world that he gave his Life. Prayer is an exchange from our old selves to the new (or rather, a return to our original imago Dei selves) by the power of God's forgiveness.[47] Repentance through prayer, for the Reformers, is actually repentance to regeneration in the process of hearing God's voice.[48] Praying is dying, so that we can be born again. Born again into a new communion, as a new people.[49]

Consider the paralyzed man—loved by his friends, he was lowered down from a hole in a roof to see Jesus.[50] The prayer of the friends was love manifested in active faith, just as all of creation groans in her labor pains.[51] Preaching is like a friend, who drawn by God, goes to God in the assembly, to plead with God, and in the end, gives birth to healing, from God.

PRAYER AS THE STARTING POINT FOR THEOLOGY

It is impossible to exhaust the diversity of preachers in the twentieth century who pray as preaching and preach as prayer. When Fosdick reduced prayer to self-help, he turned inwards towards the self. When Spirit-filled preaching is an act of prayer, dependent on God's sovereign economy, the preacher inevitably turns towards God. If this is the case, then preaching on death must always turn towards Life since preaching as prayer is turning towards Life in communion. Thus, a Christian understanding of suicide has its ultimate goal, not in self-preservation, but in God glorification.[52] The goal is not to stop people from dying. The goal is to help people die in the appropriate manner. Turning to God is the only right way to die. Prayerful preaching turns the listener to God in prayer. From Jonah to Jesus, this is how it is done: in the belly of the whale or hanging from a tree, we turn to God in praise and obedience.

---

46. Calvin, *Institutes*, I.18.1; III.20.2.

47. Redding, *Prayer and the Priesthood of Christ*, 106.

48. Calvin "Instruction in Faith," 227.

49. 1 Pet 2:10.

50. Luke 5:17–39.

51. Rom 8:19–21.

52. Phil 1:21.

We comprehend prayer based on our understanding of God—as absolute sovereign or sitting at the edge of human's free-will eagerly awaiting the humans' every beck-and-call. Inversely, we comprehend God based on our understanding of prayer. We have come to know prayer through the lenses of changing scientific or biblical discoveries or through the barter system of good deeds and formulas. Some have identified prayer as a way of changing God, pressuring God and controlling future outcomes, while others have seen prayer as a means, not only to understand God, but to understand ourselves. For the preacher who seeks to engage suicide from the pulpit, the question is: are we preaching as a way of praying? And is our praying reflected in our preaching? Because what we really believe about God comes out by how we pray to God.

I will be honest. The idea that prayer somehow can change God or that prayer can manipulate God seems blasphemous to me. Blasphemous to the very truth of God's sovereign economy. The idea that my human, fallen, sin-stained words have the potency to pressure the all-knowing, holy God is absurd! Those who adhere to this position, which is fundamentally human but not necessarily Christian, point to verses such as Abraham's plea to God for Sodom in Genesis 18 or King Hezekiah's prayer for a longer life in 2 Kings 20. This position on prayer insists that Abraham and Hezekiah's prayers actually *changed* God.

While driving home one evening I noticed that this position had insidiously and subtly crept even into the Reformed mindset when I saw a Presbyterian church post on their outside sign, "God is faithful if you trust in Him." The "if" implies that God's faithfulness depends on me. Yet, it is theologically reckless to purport that we can access God in our own time and on our own terms.[53] To do so is simply arrogant and ignorant. The idea that prayer has power in its own right, apart from God, is well rehearsed and repeated among Christians through their idolatrous, capitalistic enterprises with pithy unorthodox statements plastered on pens, cards, stationery, blankets, dishes, placards, bumper stickers, t-shirts, gardening stones, and all wrapped up with "Christian" wrapping paper. People, sloppy with their words, will often say that there is power in prayer ignoring the distinguishing markers of Christian prayer in contrast to non-Christian prayer, namely Jesus. Muslims pray. Jews Pray. Hindus pray. The power for the Christian is rooted in the true God, not

---

53. See the prologue of Augustine's *Confessions* at 1.i.1—1. v.6 (at Chadwick, 3–6) for the problems of involving God on our own terms.

in the act of prayer itself. Telling someone who is suicidal to "just pray" is deeply human but it fails to grasp the distinctive mysteries of Trinitarian petition—the power rests with God, not us. This is why gospel preaching is paramount.

I recently came across a broken and dusty book published in 1885, titled, *The Wonders of Prayer*. The entirety of the book consists of stories of prayer answered in the affirmative. There is a story about *Prayers for a Hat*, or *Prayers for Rain*, or *Prayers for the Locomotive Train*. The most interesting one for our purpose is the story entitled *Insanity Cured and Suicide Prevented*. Apparently, there was a young lady who had been raised in luxury which caused her to be "delicate" and "ill-fitted for calamity." In due time her mother died, and she lost her inheritance which caused her to become "insane." Under the watchful eye of her friends, she tried to die by suicide. But the text tells us that her friends decided to pray for her. "No immediate result appeared; but the friends persevered." Even though the women felt "forsaken by God" she attended a prayer meeting, which "immediately" had a "good effect upon her" and her health returned to her.[54]

I believe that God can heal our physical worlds. I too, have had physical healings which I attribute to God's power through the prayers and laying on of hands by the Elders. My challenge is not with God's care, but in how the preacher shapes the listener's view of God's nature through prayer. The author of the story *Insanity Cured and Suicide Prevented* reveals the author's own theology that persistence and perseverance is the key to coax God to respond. Once again, this is a self-help approach to prayer.

In the parable of the persistent widow, the text states that God will be quick, not slow when God's chosen ones pray day and night, which, by the way requires faith. "When the Son of Man comes, will he find faith on the earth?"[55] We are reminded that faith is a gift,[56] and a fruit of the Spirit.[57] Faith is that pipe (so to speak) through which grace flows— through faith and not of ourselves.[58] Keeping this in mind, I wonder, what if I looked at persistence in prayer not as a way to bend God's ear,

---

54. Whittle, *The Wonders of Prayer*, 103–4.

55. Luke 18:18.

56. 1 Cor 13:13.

57. Gal 5:22.

58. Eph 2:8.

but rather as a way to bend my ear, to mold my mind, to sculpt my sight, shape my heart, and whittle my will just as regular sit-ups whittle away at my waist-line.

In the process of guarding our understanding of the nature of the all-encompassing and sustaining God, prayer should not be seen as a way to change God, but rather: when we encounter the unchangeable God, we are the ones changed. Prayer is not for God. God does not need us to pray to God. Prayer is for us, to transform us, given as a gift to equip us to holiness. If this is true, can a life that is in the daily, without ceasing, in and out, up and down, addictive habit of prayer be a life that at the same time seeks death? Notice I did not say desires death as passive ideation, but rather a life that actively seeks death through preparing, planning, and plotting. This would be a good time to ask the question, "What do we mean by death?"

Prayer is no doubt a signal notifying the devil to attack with temptations, distractions, and doubt to the one on their knees. Our battle is not "one of flesh and blood . . . but against the powers of this dark world and against the spiritual forces of evil in the heavenly realms."[59] This is evident in Jesus's desert prayers. But here is the rub—it was the Spirit that "led Jesus into the wilderness" to be enticed. Jesus in his desert temptation had the whispers of self-annihilation, "throw yourself down."[60] The devil wanted Jesus to die. Yet, this was the Father's plan all along! For what the devil desired for evil, God planned for good.[61] What is scarier, to face the devil or to face God? For when we go out to pray, we encounter them both. And even more terrifying, we encounter ourselves. This is what happens when you go out to be with God. It is a wrestling match such as Jacob's prayer was, "face to face" with God.[62] When we seek God's face in prayer, when we seek the True Life, are we not essentially seeking death? For according to Exodus 33:20, no one can see God's face and live. Even the Seraphim covered their faces in the presence of the Presence.[63] Isaiah knew this to be a problem when he cried, "Woe am I . . . my eyes have seen the King, the Lord Almighty."[64] We hold this in tension with

59. Eph 6:12.

60. Matt 4:6.

61. An allusion to Gen 50:20.

62. Gen 32:30.

63. Isa 6:2.

64. Isa 6:5.

Jonah who turned towards death by turning away from God's presence. Yet prayer is moving towards death while seeking Life. Prayer is not only profoundly mysterious; it is perilous (to our old selves) as we teeter out to that precipitous place of reverence and holiness.

Jesus's prayer in the garden on the night of his arrest holds the resistance to death and the acceptance of death in partnership. Prayer, true prayer, encountering "the King, the Lord Almighty," drives us to die to self, in many ways, in order to live holy. Galatians 2:20 says it like this, "I have been crucified with Christ, and I no longer live. . . . " Prayer, best understood, requires examining Jesus and how he prayed. "Teach us," the disciples ask, "Teach us to pray." God who prayed to God. The Lord who said to the Lord, "Sit at my right hand. . . . "[65] Prayer, true prayer, is prayer only and always in the Spirit. Prayer is God talking to God in our hearts and with our mouths. When the preacher realizes this, the three-point sermon on prayer just doesn't cut it anymore.

The humbled preacher recognizes that prayer is a profound mystery reflected in God's marriage with the church.[66] Within this relationship prayer is not considered a sacrament, but it is sacramental. Where two or three are gathered together, there God's body also dwells.[67] Communal prayer is where *the body* of Christ, in prayers of supplication and intercession, are *broken* for each other through petitions and thanksgiving. True prayer is spoken in reverence by God's grace through faith, transforming the one praying into a person who seeks Life by accepting death, daily death, self-death, and even physical death. Prayer, in its very nature reflects the narrative and story of Christ—first to Calvary then to Easter; prayer is death as an avenue to Life. In prayer we die. Thus, the only way to combat suicide is suicide. And Christians do this every day.

---

65. Ps 110:1; and see Prov 8:30.

66. Ezek 16:8–14.

67. Matt 18:20.

10

Preaching and Suicide

"A human is earth that suffers."[1]

"In Christ, we become fully human in solidarity with the dying."[2]

My DEFINITION[3] OF PREACHING is simple at first glance: *The mystery of preaching is the proclamation of the good news of Jesus based upon the biblical revelation for the cultivation of the church.* Of course, that seems simple, but anybody who dives daily into theology (words about God) knows that my definition is not simple and is not shared by all preachers. The challenge arises when someone asks, "What do you mean by proclamation?" Or, "What do you mean by good news?" Or, "What do you mean by Jesus?" Or, "What do you mean by biblical revelation?" Fine then, let me explain.

Proclamation is the act of speaking as a herald—"hear ye, hear ye." It can be narrative, inductive, deductive, prescriptive, expository, rhetorical, manuscript-delivered, or extemporaneous. The diversity of how one

1. *Epistle of Barnabas* 6.9 (in Ehrman, *Apostolic Fathers*, II.33).

2. Levering, *Dying and the Virtues*, 118.

3. I understand that the definition of preaching has always been a collective activity. I do not propose a definition of preaching "as if I were the first on whom the responsibility of proclaiming the word of God has fallen" (Lischer, *The Company of Preachers*, xiii).

might deliver words is extensive and lovely. There is something radically different about hearing a sermon from just reading a sermon—since "Faith comes through hearing"—but surely the Holy Spirit can use the re-printed copies. Of course, what does one mean by "hearing"? True hearing requires the Holy Spirit. It is God who allows us to hear, but a hearing that is deeper than just the physical functions of the ear. The deaf can hear God by the power of God's Spirit. This type of hearing is true hearing. The dead man Lazarus heard Jesus's voice to "come out" of the tomb not based on his physical ear function, but by the power of the Holy Spirit. Hearing at its core is a *mystery*. "Very truly I tell you, a time is coming and has now come when the dead will hear the voice of the Son of God and those who hear will live."[4]

The *good news of Jesus* derives its meaning from Paul in his letter to the Galatians. The good news is that "freedom in which Christ has set us free."[5] This good news is the message that salvation is dependent on Jesus and Jesus alone. The gospel is this—Jesus saves us. In fact, he "rescues us from this present evil age."[6] It isn't that Jesus saves us *if* we believe in him or *if* we pray or *if* we do missions. Salvation is not Jesus plus church, plus tithes, plus good works as if it is a mathematical equation—no, "the proof of God's amazing love is this—Christ died for us while we were still sinners."[7] The salvation of Jesus did not come to us because of us, but because of God's character of love. Salvation is a free gift. This may seem like a no-brainer for the cradle Christians until they say something like, "That's right, all you have to *do* is believe." No, not even belief provides salvation. Even the demons believe.[8] The good news is that there is nothing we can do and nothing we have done to receive salvation. Salvation is dependent on what God has done through Jesus Christ. Only Christianity has this good news to offer. Islam and Judaism cannot say this. They do not say this. This definition of Gospel or good news can fit with topical preaching but not so much with self-help messages. In fact, self-help seems antithetical to the good news. Really, even self-control for the Christian is not an issue of the self but of the

---

4. John 5:25.

5. Gal 5:1.

6. Gal 1:4.

7. Rom 5:8.

8. Jas 2:19.

Spirit, who, in sovereign economy equips us to crucify our sinful nature. This is how we know that we actually "belong to Christ."[9]

What I mean when I say *Jesus* is the incarnate Second Person of the Trinity echoing the words of the Nicene Creed, "Light of Light, very God of very God, begotten, not made, being of one substance with the Father." [10] Jesus is fully God and currently stands at the helm of creation in a redeemed human body. Jesus is not only Creator, but Jesus is also Intercessor and Judge because Jesus is fully "God of God." Jesus is the Priest and at the very same time the sacrifice. A sermon without Jesus the living Messiah at its center relegates the act of speaking to an unchristian talk by someone who is otherwise a Christian. In other words, for a sermon to be a Christian sermon it must be Christocentric—whether it is dedicated to an Old Testament passage or a New Testament passage, whether it includes recent events or contemporary issues. For the good news to be proclaimed it must be Christocentric (there is no good news apart from Christ).

This is difficult for those preachers who insist that Old Testament preaching should not bring Jesus into the sermon since Jesus was not born until New Testament times. But Jesus was begotten, not made: the Son is the Wisdom of Proverbs 8 and the glory of Psalm 8. The Son was one of the visitors who dined with Abraham near the great tree of Mamre.[11] The Son provided presence in Nebuchadnezzar's fiery furnace[12] and the Son wrestled with Jacob/Israel till daybreak.[13] All the Scriptures concern him.[14] Jesus is established as the reason and the hope for which all of creation groans.[15] The Second Person of the Trinity is eternally being begotten in a way that transcends the boundaries of time and space. How does one put the Son, who is incarnate as Jesus, into words when Jesus is God, beyond human words—and yet Jesus is fully human, speaking words, words spoken by the Word? The Father revealed Godself through Jesus and the Holy Spirit points to Jesus as the only way to the Father. Yes, I know, this is a *mystery* at its core! Nonetheless, I am of the opinion,

---

9. Gal 5:24.

10. See *The Nicene Creed*.

11. Gen 18:1.

12. Dan 3:25.

13. Gen 32:25.

14. Luke 24:27.

15. Rom 8:19–23.

despite some homiletical experts, that a sermon without Jesus is not a Christian sermon. Likewise, a proclamation that does not arise from the biblical record is not a Christian sermon.

I believe that the Bible is authoritative as a true record of the Revelation, who is Jesus the Word. The Bible may be the record of the Word but the Bible is not the Word properly speaking (but only by extension). Being that it is the record of the Word makes it very special. And that is an understatement. I believe that the Bible has been preserved by God's will for our hearing, to hear the words of our ancestors in the faith who encountered the Word in a personal and life-changing way. And this hearing arises by the power of God's breath, softening our hearts, opening our ears, to hear the Spirit speak through this word pointing to the Word.

A speech can be based on anything, but a Christian sermon derives from the biblical witness. Scripture must be foundational to a sermon. A Christian sermon is not a Christian sermon without the Jesus of Scripture.[16] After all, there are many Christs of our own making. There are many who say, "Look, there he is, or here he is."[17] But we are told not to listen to those voices, but to the Scriptures that testify about him. Therefore, Scripture is not a preference for the Christian preacher, it is a requirement.[18] In the case of many "sermons," Scripture is only read at the beginning, or Scripture is sprinkled throughout (proof-texted) only as a way to prove the speaker's ideas rather than illuminate and magnify Jesus, the way Mary sings, "My soul glorifies the Lord, and my spirit rejoices in God my Savior."[19]

The Bible does proclaim a social justice message and speaks about moral issues of our own day, but these are only properly understood in light of God's power. Often, the Christocentric dominion of true justice is removed or at least reduced in the contemporary self-help, activist, politically driven, health-wealth, and me-centered sermons which are only

16. John 20:31.

17. Luke 17:23.

18. Natural Revelation tells us that there is a God. But Special Revelation shows us who this God is. And according to Barth, Special Revelation is Jesus in the theology of the threefold form of the Word in which preaching or "Real proclamation, then, means the Word of God preached and the Word of God preached means—man's talk about God on the basis of God's own direction, which fundamentally transcends all human causation, which cannot, then, be put on a human basis, but which simply takes place, and has to be acknowledged, as a fact" (Barth, *Church Dogmatics*, I.90).

19. Luke 1:46.

a cheap counterfeit of authentic justice. Without God in Christ, social justice is just a humanistic venture to make us feel good about ourselves as we make "our mark" on history. Both brothers Abel and Cain, brought service and gifts to God. But only one of the brothers' gifts was received. Because "without faith, it is impossible to please God."[20] Giving a cup of water to the least of these requires a Christ-centered faith in order for it to be a justice that resembles the biblical witness and points to Jesus as its true source.[21] As Ignatius of Loyola once said, "Charity and kindness unwedded to truth are not charity and kindness but deceit and vanity."[22]

Of course, biblical revelation should not be understood in a simplistic way that ignores the complexity of interpretation and hermeneutics. I do not discount the discussion of hermeneutics, especially the hermeneutics of suspicion of oneself,[23] not for one moment. Hermeneutics (that is, recognizing those forces, assumptions and interpretive practices that shape the ways we seek to make sense of the Scripture) is a vital aspect of preaching. And defining my terms is a major element of hermeneutical exploration. This is especially true since I am attempting to shape my definitions to those passed down through Christian tradition and the biblical witness while at the same time humbly submitting to the biblical awareness of human sinfulness and acknowledging my inevitable handicap of only seeing through a glass darkly.[24]

Thus, defining preaching is like describing in minute detail how authentic preaching is really submitting to God's words—written, preserved, proclaimed, in the moment, transformative and life-preserving—equipped and empowered by the One who is outside of us, yet, at the same time has called us to be "in" Christ.[25] Preaching is both physical and spiritual. Like all the other areas of the Christian life, it is a paradox—approaching with childlike faith,[26] yet at the same time called to Christian

20. Heb 11:6.

21. In spite of my deep respect for Dr. Anna Carter Florence and her insights into homiletics, her sermon entitled "The Girls in the Reeds" on Exod 1:8–14, 22, 2:1–10, was sadly void of Jesus.

22. See Hevenesi, *Thoughts of St. Ignatius Loyola*, 17.

23. By this phrase I mean the attempt to unveil the ways in which certain paradigms of interpretation are unhealthy or otherwise misleading. See Westphal, *Suspicion and Faith*.

24. 1 Cor 13:12.

25. Eph 1:12.

26. Matt 18:2–4.

maturity;[27] given free will,[28] yet at the same time being predestined;[29] redeemed and justified, yet[30] living in a fallen and broken world with a dying body.[31] Preaching is a mystery because God is the author and the ultimate definer of preaching. Thus, *mystery* is a fundamental and necessary component of my definition even though mysteries are by definition undefinable. It is the effortless *mystery* that makes preaching worth the laborious effort. And what is it all for? Certainly, for the glory of God.

> "Oh, the depth of the riches of the wisdom and knowledge of God! How unsearchable his judgments, and his paths beyond tracing out! Who has known the mind of the Lord? Or who has been his counselor? Who has ever given to God, that God should repay them? For from him and through him and for him are all things. To him be the glory forever! Amen."[32]

This glory is seen in God's son Jesus who by the power of the Holy Spirit incarnates the church, his body.[33] I love what Bishop Robert Barron once said, "Jesus is the Son of God, and his purpose is not primarily to construct a smooth-functioning human society; it is to establish the kingdom of God—that is to say, a body formed by those who participate in him, who share his relationship with the Father."[34] Our purpose is not only to glorify God and enjoy him forever,[35] but it is to "not stop meeting together as some are in the habit of doing."[36] This life "in" Christ is one of reaching out to the unsaved, but also to reach towards the saved. Paul's letters were written to Christians, to the churches, reminding them of what being born again looks like.[37] Being born from above[38] involves

27. Heb 6:1.

28. Rom 10:13.

29. John 6:44.

30. Heb 2:8 states, "God left nothing that is not subject to him. Yet at present we do not see everything subject to him."

31. Rom 8:10–11.

32. Rom 11:33–36.

33. 1 Cor 12:27.

34. Barron, "Begotten Not Made."

35. *Westminster Shorter Catechism*, Sess. 19, Question 1.

36. Heb 10:25.

37. John 3:14.

38. Eph 2:6.

becoming new citizens[39] and literally, even ethnically a new people.[40] And as a new people, "if anyone does not provide for his own, and especially for those of his household, he has denied the faith and is worse than an unbeliever."[41]

The first epistle of John provides words that some have critically labeled as a separatist theology, a theology claiming special privilege for those who are in the family. First John 2:15 states "Do not love the world or anything in the world," which differentiates between the love for those who are in the family of God, while 1 John 4:21b states, "Whoever loves God must love his brother." This love then is shown specifically to the children of God, or those who belong to God by faith. Galatians 6:10 sums this up when it says, "Therefore, as we have opportunity, let us do good to all people, especially to those who belong to the family of believers."

I will not argue that Christians should be unconcerned for non-believers who experience suicidal ideation or loss to suicide—but only that there is no solution apart from Christ and the people whom he is redeeming for himself. My claim is that Christianity does not offer just one solution among many, but that it is the only solution. There is no salvation apart from the church (*extra ecclesiam nulla salus*).[42]

Furthermore, there is no generic human understanding of suicide—there are only Christian, Hindu, Muslim, evolutionary-materialist, and other frameworks of understanding the taking of one's own life. When Christians speak of suicide as though it is a commonly understood phenomenon, they inadvertently relinquish a distinctively Christian understanding of suicide for an American secularized, human-centered set of assumptions.

In my definition of preaching, I chose to use the word *cultivation*. It is an agricultural term that fits beautifully with the agrarian nature of the Scriptures in the reality of how the church is born, nurtured, pruned,[43] and sown by the Farmer[44] who scooped us up in his calloused mighty

---

39. Phil 3:20.

40. 1 Pet 2:9. For discussion, see Johnson, "Ethnicity: Greeks, Jews, and Christians."

41. 1 Tim 5:8.

42. Cyprian, *Letter* 72, (in Wallis, 384).

43. John 15:2.

44. Matt 13:3–23.

hands and blew. "Dust we are and to dust we shalt return."[45] Like Lazarus, we play no part in our resurrection. We do not give God a hand in rescuing us from the grave, just as we do not contribute to our salvation in any way. Our good deeds come only as a response to what God has done. God is the Sower and the first mover . . . always.

PREACHING SUICIDE

It should be obvious by now that I believe that the sermon is an appropriate place to address the topic of suicide. Of course, there are other places for addressing suicide. But the weekly sermon is the best place because it more adequately gets into the world of the biblical narratives and engages the imagination of the congregation's personal narratives within the space of worship.

Before Ted died, he wrote a note to his wife Pat. But she failed to see the note when she came across his bloodied body from a self-inflicted gunshot wound. When the police came and taped off the house, they retrieved the note. Placing it in a plastic bag they kept it for evidence per protocol. No one told Pat that there was a note. It wasn't until four months later when she went to the police station to retrieve a few personal items. Only then did she see the note. On a small crumpled piece of paper, Ted had written a bank account number and then simply said, "I hope this is all you will need." That is all he said. Pat held the paper in her hand and said out loud in disbelief, "All I will *need?*"

Some preachers believe that all one needs to preach on suicide is a suicide, and of course, a few Scripture passages that will support and comfort the family in their time of grief. I have learned that most lay leaders and preachers falsely assume that preaching on suicide is limited to the funeral homily alone.[46] Bryan Chapell admits to this when he comments on Jerram Barr's sermon, *The Greatness of God's Mercy,* saying, "This sermon is unusual, not only because the circumstances are scandalous [a suicide], but also because the comfort offered is directed to an entire congregation rather than to a specific family."[47] He rightly recog-

---

45. Gen 3:19.

46. See, for instance, the majority of sermons (though there are notable exceptions) included in Clemons, *Sermons on Suicide*; the five sermons included in Chapell, *The Hardest Sermons*, 227–75; and Gibson and Mason, *Preaching Hope in Darkness*.

47. Chapell, *The Hardest Sermons*, 261.

nizes the unique significance of the communal orientation; but such preaching should not wait for "scandalous" circumstances.

When I taught a college homiletics class, the assumption that the topic of suicide should be relegated to the funeral homily was deeply held among the students. It was a novel concept to the students when I informed them that preaching on suicide should not be limited to the funeral. One student balked at the idea saying, "There is only so much that can be said about Judas." But in light of Jesus, there is never enough that can be said about Judas, or the other biblical suicides for that matter. As I will show later, there are a number of ways that a weekly sermon can address suicide without waiting for the funeral of someone who has died by suicide. Some of these sermons will adopt a "direct" approach which explicitly names suicide and deals with one or more of the biblical suicides. But others can adopt an "indirect" approach which helps listeners think in more healthy ways about death (including self-death) and God's presence in our suffering. But before we turn to homiletical modes of addressing suicide from the pulpit, we must address the risks involved.

RISK

Preaching suicide is risky. Risk is "the possibility of loss or injury."[48] The word *possibility* acknowledges that risk is very subjective. What one person thinks is a risk might have more to do with their perception and not actually be a real risk. There is always a perceived risk by the preacher and by the congregation regarding the sermon. The perceived risk may seem like a real risk to the preacher or to the congregation, but just because the preacher perceives the risk to him or herself does not mean that the congregation share their assumptions. The perceived risk is always dependent on the context, whether personal, communal, or more broadly cultural.[49]

For many preachers, they find themselves in a context that has been inundated with myths about suicide.[50] And myths contribute to the sense of risk. Some of the more dominate myths include:

48. See "Risk," in *Webster Ninth New Collegiate Dictionary*, 1018.

49. See Dale Martin's discussion on Richard Hays's and Stanley Fish's theory of hermeneutical meaning: essentially that all interpretation is based on "social context" and "social agreement," in Martin, *Pedagogy of the Bible*, 31–34.

50. Thomas Joiner provides a comprehensive study on the vast variety of myths associated with suicide. See Joiner, *Myths About Suicide*.

1. To talk about suicide is to create the idea in someone's head and thus increase the likelihood of somebody acting out their suicidal ideation.

2. The Bible says that suicide is a sin. It is risky to talk about sin.

3. People who attempt or commit suicide are totally selfish.

4. Only those who are crazy kill themselves.

These myths have been known to paralyze a pastor regarding preaching suicide since they provide a basis for their perception of risks. Other risks may be much more personal. For example, the preacher might perceive that preaching on suicide will cause him or her to be:

1. Ashamed of the self (if the preacher has experienced suicidal ideation) or of events within the congregation (that might seem embarrassing to outside judgment).

2. Uncomfortable about the listener's perception, since suicide is so taboo and may fall under the norm of "those things we just do not talk about."

3. Worried that talking about suicide might cause some parishioners to become sad or even consider suicide (which is one of the myths already listed above).

4. Uncertain about the validity of their words and the lack of certification as a professional suicidologist or therapist.

5. Fear or unwillingness to deal with follow-up pastoral concerns.

I have watched with my own eyes the transformation within homiletics students when risks were articulated and acknowledged. Unveiling the elephant in the room is empowering. Taking time to verbalize perceived versus real risks is an essential conversation because the line between perceived and real risk can be very blurry. Perceived risks feel very real to the one who is perceiving them. It is precisely this type of conversation that is lacking in suicide awareness programs. This conversation can and should be implemented in theological studies. In fact, I would go as far as to say that every seminary should provide a suicide unit in their theological curriculum.

Keep in mind that risks are not isolated events. It can help the preacher to know that risks always give birth to other risks. Risks are like dominoes. For example, one very real risk is for the preacher to be overcome by perceived risks to the point that the preacher avoids the topic and remains silent regarding suicide. The silence around suicide, however, becomes another real risk, a risk that would keep the congregation from growing and engaging in hope-filled and life-empowering tasks. By avoiding one risk the preacher actually risks keeping the congregation at risk.

Sometimes, the preacher is not willing to take the risk because of the perceived risk to one's self. It may seem an insurmountable risk for the preacher to have to deal with his or her own mental health. This risk can be multiplied when parishioners have questions (or resistance) and want to talk with the pastor after the sermon, which may lead to pastoral care concerns. Having to talk with a parishioner about suicide when the preacher knows that they themselves struggle with ideation is risky and will no doubt involve a lot of discomfort. What if the parishioner found out that the preacher herself struggles with thoughts of self-harm?

An obvious risk for preaching on the topic of suicide includes the preacher's carelessness about the subject of suicide; the lack of care will play out through the sermon. It is revealed in a biblically and conceptually incoherent manuscript thoughtlessly thrown together the night before. This risk to the sensitive nature of the subject and effectiveness of preaching arises when the preacher is sloppy with their words, overly confident and arrogant about their preaching ability, and ignorant of the sensitivity needed for the topic. When the sermon preparation has not received sufficient thoroughness, the preacher may rely on talking about themselves for most of the sermon, causing a self-centered narcissistic presentation or anecdotes that allow for misleading inferences. Or the preacher may repeat inappropriate or unhealthy ideas about suicide, thus perpetuating misguided patterns of thinking or acting by members of the congregation. If the preacher does not care or just has insufficient time and does not do the work of sermon preparation the preacher should not attempt to preach a topical sermon on suicide. I would hope that most preachers know that careless words can be damaging.[51] As already argued, both preaching and praying involve dying to oneself in order to gain life. We must continually "take captive" and die to our commonsense

---

51. Because of the Werther Effect much has been discussed regarding proper reporting for the media regarding suicide. Guidelines such as not describing the actual process someone uses to die should be taken seriously by homileticians. See, Reporting on Suicide.org.

ideas or taken for granted assumptions, our interpretive inertia or homiletical laziness.

EVALUATING PREACHING

For the preacher, evaluating and assessing homilies is a challenging task. Homilies are designed for a particular moment and a particular setting with particular people and particular issues. Homilies are at their essence events in time while encountering the God who is beyond time. Michael Pasquarello states it like this, "Ultimately the Holy Spirit is the one who teaches the art of preaching, granting not only human eloquence but a 'divinely attractive word.' Only God is able to call, equip, and send preachers to speak a living word to a dying world."[52] In other words, "Speaking of God cannot be reduced to saying things about God; rather, speaking of God will draw us into a relationship with God, in union with Christ, so that prayer and preaching are inseparable."[53] Effective preaching can only come about when the Holy Spirit is engaging the congregation through the engagement of the preacher. Preaching is an event of encountering God. Humbly, we must recognize that spiritual growth comes from God and thus to measure that growth would be futile because one cannot measure God.

Preaching, as popularly defined by Phillips Brooks, is "truth through personality."[54] Each preacher will have his or her own unique way, led by the Holy Spirit, to proclaim the good news. I am tempted to advise to start off with "indirect" sermons first and work up to more "direct." But I have found that this advice is a poor replacement for the leading and calling of the Holy Spirit. Because after all, if the Holy Spirit is the one hardening or softening hearts, opening or closing ears, even an "indirect" sermon can seem very direct and a "direct" sermon can fall on deaf ears. The very reality of our total dependency on the Holy Spirit as preachers makes this entire book of preaching suicide seem so worthless. God is sovereign. Yet, he seeks our participation. God does not need me to preach. God wants me to preach. And when we preach with excellence,

---

52. Pasquarello, *We Speak*, 68.

53. Pasquarello, *We Speak*, 148.

54. Brooks, *Lectures on Preaching*, 5.

we experience joy and God is glorified. Surely, this is a reflection of the chief end of a human.[55]

Preaching with excellence, however, requires humility. It actually may take God placing one in a headlock to "make" her lay down in green pastures. To humble a cherished and beloved preacher who has been held in honor for so long by so many can only be the work of the Holy Spirit. I dare to say that it is almost impossible to change the mind of a preacher who has preached suicide as murder because that would mean that the preacher would have to acknowledge being wrong and that is a rare happening. Evaluating preaching usually requires an outside perspective and one who has some authority with the preacher. Evaluations feel like pruning, with sharp, pointy scissors. As painful as it is, every preacher should have someone who is honest with them about their preaching and forthright about the temperature of the congregation.

Wilson Benton once admitted in one of his sermons "I am not a psychologist, but in layman's language it [suicide] happens when one focuses on the problems rather than on the solutions."[56] What Benton fails to understand is that, for the contemplating person, suicide isn't the problem, it is the solution. For many, the problem is the collective, it is the church. But what preacher would admit to that? Because doesn't the church reflect the preacher? Then a few moments later Benton stated, "We are not to take matters into our own hands."[57] But didn't he just preach to focus on solutions? Benton's language is stuck in the boxes of interpretive inertia regarding notions like "sin" and "murder" so that he actually missed out on an opportunity to speak to the profound mystery of life and death. Instead, he presented suicide as a textbook science in eight "obvious questions" or eight points.[58] The only reason I am able to evaluate sermons in this way is because at many points along the way I have had my interpretive inertia interrupted and I was forced to re-evaluate my position.

Unlike Benton, who emphatically preached that suicide is exclusively an individual act, Bryan Chapell, preached that everyone is held accountable for acts of suicide. He said, "'Of course we did not do enough and of course we expected too much. We live in a fallen world and our

55. *Westminster Shorter Catechism*, Sess. 19, Question 1.

56. Benton, "Thinking Biblically About the Tragedy of Suicide," 245.

57. Benton, "Thinking Biblically About the Tragedy of Suicide," 246.

58. Benton, "Thinking Biblically About the Tragedy of Suicide," 242.

entire nature has been so corrupted that each of us who is responsible
for one another in the body of Christ has in some measure failed to be
all that we should be."[59] This is a truthful word. But then Chapell calls
the death of the person who died by suicide "evil" thus fortifying harmful
taboos.[60] Too often, sermons reflect society's taboos and biases rather
than breaking them.

Why do preachers do this? Maybe interpretive inertia, lack of reflection, a sense of superiority, arrogance, a deficiency of humility, and an
absence of awe in the God who is revealed in Jesus's voluntary death. This
book has been an attempt to break up such interpretive inertia and resist
glibly tying suicide to murder or the unreflective assumption that it is
faithless preaching to "imply that suicide is no sin."[61]

Like the Roman Catholic Church, many Protestant denominations
have demonstrated that they too have been influenced by their past and
the present discoveries in the social sciences about suicide. But this has
not always been in positive and life-affirming ways. Charles Stanley, a
popular Baptist preacher from Atlanta, gave a lengthy "sermon" entitled
Suicide: The Impact on Believers,[62] in which he exhaustively provides
statistic after statistic, littering the manuscript with numbers and providing high platitudes about God's character. But he barely touches the biblical text. While he reads from the twenty-seventh chapter of Matthew,
he doesn't open up the text. It is like someone showing you a Tennessee
Moon Pie but never opening up the wrapper so you could actually taste
it. There was no opportunity to chew on the word, to ingest the scroll.

When I hear a sermon, I always ask the question, *Did the preacher
show me Jesus?* Just as the Greeks asked Philip the disciple, "Sir," they said,
"we would like to see Jesus,"[63] I did not hear Jesus proclaimed in Charles
Stanley's sermon on suicide. Instead, I heard him says things like, "yet
here you still are because you trusted Jesus Christ as your Savior," which
implies that if you are not still here it's because you didn't trust in Jesus.
He stated that suicide is a sin, "a pardonable sin"—because murder is
not the unpardonable sin. He spent a chunk of time paralleling abortion
with suicide because abortion is murder, which moved the listener off

59. Bryan Chapell, "Funeral Message for Pastor Petros Roukas" in Chapell, *The
Hardest Sermons,* 234.

60. Chapell, *The Hardest Sermons,* 238.

61. Chapell, *The Hardest Sermons,* 229.

62. Stanley, "Suicide."

63. John 12:20–21.

the topic of suicide onto the topic of abortion and this leads the listener to think that the topic of the talk really was murder. Furthermore, he uses fear as a tactic of prevention when he says, "You've been given that privilege [of life] and so what do you do? You commit suicide, you short-circuit, listen, your life here on earth, God's purpose and plan for your life; and you lose the reward which God would have had for you had you lived it out in obedience to him. It is an expression of pure ingratitude toward God."[64]

What does that statement say to those who are grieving the loss of a loved one who died by suicide? This is not sensitive language either to those who mourn the loss or to the intricacy of suicide. On top of that he has no qualms in calling suicide a "selfish act." But even more problematic is when he asks the questions, "What's happening to our country?"[65] erroneously purporting that this is a concern for Americans rather than the church universal. There is so little thoughtfulness and exploration of the complexity of the topic of suicide in Charles Stanley's talk. There is no room for wonder. There is no room for mystery. The message is really a Christian speech using Christian lingo on suicide, it is not a Christian sermon. Speaking about suicide from the pulpit should be much more than a talk strewn with 'the 'Deadly Be's' that sting listeners with unqualified moralism"[66] or placate listeners to utter zombified stupor because they have heard this all before.

The preacher Bryan Chapell reminds us that " . . . the 'be like' messages are not wrong in themselves; they are wrong by themselves."[67] Without underscoring Jesus as the source of the power to change one's life, the message becomes simply a self-help motivational talk that someone can buy into with enough effort and without immersion in the world of the Bible. I am not seeking to shame anyone. No, I am simply stating that we can do better.

Preaching should always be an exploration of the biblical world and a reminder that, for all its strangeness, it is a world worth inhabiting. Preaching should be an art, and the preacher an artist—painting on a canvas of floating words; unique to their personality and simultaneously rooted in the ancient words; showing rather than telling. Lectures are for

64. Stanley, "Suicide."
65. Stanley, "Suicide."
66. Chapell, *Christ-Centered Sermons*, 110.
67. Chapell, *Christ-Centered Sermons*, 110.

the classroom and self-help talks are for other venues. Preaching is for the pulpit.

THE FUNERAL HOMILY

The funeral sermon is a unique breed of homily which requires additional preparation (meeting with a funeral director and with the family). Some bereaved families may deliberately request that no mention of suicide take place within the homily or during any part of the funeral service. Likewise, some bereaved families prefer to use the words "passed on" rather than "dead" or "died." In contrast, some bereaved families may be adamant and emphatic that suicide be mentioned. In all cases, the preacher should take the time to be pastoral and talk with the family regarding their desires and expectations for the homily.

Personally, I avoid the topic of suicide completely during a funeral unless specifically requested by the family. There is no need to talk about the way or reasons why someone died during a funeral homily. Some preachers might think that they have to say something in hopes of preventing copycat suicides. But I firmly believe that funerals are the wrong time for suicide awareness. Funeral homilies typically do not dwell on the specific way someone died, whether reckless driving or addiction or cancer or heart failure, so why bring up suicide? The funeral should rather be focused on giving witness to the resurrection. It is a time to focus our attention on the hope that we have in Christ. Our focus should not be on how a person died but rather on the central fact that Christ died so that we can live.

Yet, preachers still feel the need to mention how someone died *if* that person died by suicide. A striking example is the story of Fr. Don LaCuesta, a Roman Catholic priest in the Archdiocese of Detroit serving at Our Lady of Mt. Carmel Parish in Michigan.[68] Apparently, an 18-year-old parishioner, died by suicide. The family had a set of expectations for the service. "We wanted it to be about family. We wanted him to talk about loving one another, lifting one another up, and being kind to one another. That's what we wanted the homily to be about."[69] Reading between the lines there is a sense that the homily was seen as

---

68. For the manuscript of Rev. Don LaCuesta's homily for this funeral, see LaCuesta, "Homily."

69. Yan and Bowman, "A Priest Condemned Suicide."

a consumeristic commodity. It seems that they assumed a homily could be made to order and, when they did not hear what they wanted to hear, they sued.

Unfortunately, the family also carried with them a bag of taboos regarding suicide. Suicide brought a pall of shame. It was so shameful that they could not even come to grips with the very word "suicide." The mother said, "He basically called our son a sinner in front of everyone." His father stated that, "After the first few times that he said that word (suicide), I approached the pulpit and I told him, "Father, please stop." The priest failed to recognize the risks perceived by the family, thus exposing himself and his diocese to the real risk of a lawsuit. There were misunderstandings on all sides.

How many preachers have experienced their homilies as a consumeristic product, depicted and defined as valuable or worthless, truthful or invalid, by the customer? While the preacher ought to exegete their audience, the homily should never be treated as an object of economic exchange. People often come to church to get. Getting what we deserve is a different mindset then receiving what we are not worthy of. The latter mindset instills gratitude and gratitude blossoms into thankful service.

Unfortunately, so often people confuse a Christian funeral homily with the eulogy. I was once scolded by the grieving because I failed to mention the musical talent of the deceased in the homily. The bereaved sister said to me, "You talked about Jesus too much. Jesus wasn't the one being buried today!" How many preachers have been maligned because of what was said in their homilies for causing "pain and suffering"?[70] LaCuesta and the Diocese were sued for compensatory and punitive damages to "help prevent such 'outrageous conduct' from happening again."[71] The archdiocese "apologized to the family" and assured them that LaCuesta would be "getting help from professionals."[72] Nowhere does the news article mention how long LaCuesta had been at the parish, nor does it mention that North America was not his native culture. Nowhere in the article does it mention the collective responsibility of the church for and to the preacher and the family.[73] And nowhere does it

---

70. Yan and Bowman, "A Priest Condemned Suicide."

71. Yan and Bowman, "A Priest Condemned Suicide."

72. Yan and Bowman, "A Priest Condemned Suicide."

73. Known as the "Priesthood of All Believers" (both ministerial and universal).

mention that lawsuits among believers are morally disgraceful according to Scripture.[74]

Regardless, LaCuesta's primary failure was ultimately an issue of timing. As theologically and liturgically rich funerals might be, they are not the right time to mention how someone died. The weekly worship service is the right time to talk about death. As ironic as it may be, funerals are the right time to talk about life. Keeping suicide for a Sunday morning homily directs the attention to the biblical characters, not particular people sitting or no longer sitting in the pews. Long story short—funerals are not the right place to speak on suicide. Save suicide for Sunday.

LITURGY AND SUICIDE

Thankfully, preaching as verbal theology is not an isolated event but rather it is supported by its family of non-verbal theology through what is known as "liturgy"—the hard "work of the people." Because, after all, preaching is part of the liturgy, not somehow separate. Pope Francis said, "The church evangelizes and is herself evangelized through the beauty of the liturgy."[75] Long before Augustine (generations before the criminalization of suicide), the early Christian church of the second and third centuries displayed, or better yet, re-enacted a sense of hope through their work. This hope was visible by the wearing of white vestments, carrying forth the deceased during the day rather than night, and singing the alleluia.[76] This living liturgy reflected their theology about death, a revelation not based on the judgment of sin, but based on a living hope. One might wonder what our contemporary living liturgy might say about our current theology. The American Christian behavior is often dependent, not on the liturgy or the work of the corporate church (to wash, prepare, and bury the body), but on a secular mortuary littered with legal documents and high price tags. Douglas Davies suggests that "the more decorated and individualized the coffin the less likely it is that people will want it 'presented to the cross.'"[77]

The hope built into the liturgy of the church should resemble mortar connecting the living stones of God's temple. A primary tool for

---

74. Matt 18:15–20 and 1 Cor 6:1–8.

75. Pope Francis, *The Joy of the Gospel*, no. 24.

76. White, *Introduction to Christian Worship*, 296.

77. Davies, *Theology of Death*, 25.

the preacher can be liturgy, the hard and deliberate work of the people, equipped and empowered by the Holy Spirit. Liturgy supports the sermon as a living, active, and embodied theology of worship. Liturgy has been designed to reflect the life-and-death tension in which we humans exist.[78] Through the entire calendar, moment by moment, step by step through the worship service, the liturgy of life and death are proclaimed as the center beams to the Temple. Baptism is the work of going down into the watery grave, dying with Christ in order to be raised up with Christ.[79] Eucharist is the painstaking sign of remembering the body of Christ broken for God's people as a Passover or a "passing over" from death to life.

In many Protestant churches baptism and Eucharist are the extent of the sacramental expression. But even in Protestant churches, the living rituals of life and death continue through all the aspects of liturgy. The Call to Confession is the act of penance, and a dying to self: it moves to the Assurance of Pardon, a life-affirming act of reassurance.[80] The Lord's Prayer is a mainstay in most Christian traditions with a constant eschatological reminder of "thy kingdom come." Weddings remind us that marriage is the most sublime metaphor of Christ and his church, "until death do us part." Flowers are a symbol of the bride of Christ not only to garland the wedding, but to adorn the sanctuary Sunday after Sunday. Acolytes bring in the light and take the light back out. From music to prayers to the benediction of good words that "God goes with us," liturgy is the flow, the work, the tools, the support, and the garland for the people as the preacher inhales the Holy Spirit, and exhales words of life while preaching the cross.[81] God's breath is the essence of labor within the mouths of a proclaimer. As the Persian poet Hafiz (c. 1320–1389) said:

78. For one example of how liturgy might reflect on suicide in particular, see Gibson and Mason, *Preaching Hope in Darkness*, 185–96.

79. See Rom 6:4. Origen stressed the obligation of martyrdom in the context of baptism when he implies that sins committed after the baptism of water can only be forgiven by the baptism of blood. See Origen, *Exhortation to Martyrdom* 30. In his *Homilies on Leviticus* 2.4, Origen saw baptism and voluntary death (martyrdom) as a way of attaining forgiveness.

80. The value of the Call to Confession and the Assurance of Pardon in the liturgy cannot be underestimated here. Herbert Hendin states, "When I think of myself as a recovering patient, I am more patient with myself and more willing to change things. When I compare myself to my potential, I mourn." See Hendin, *Suicide in America*, 24.

81. The sermon is not somehow separate from liturgy but rather, it is part of the liturgy, a labor of the people to listen and engage God's voice through the obedience of

I am
a hole in a flute,
that Christ's breath moves through,
listen to this music.[82]

Liturgy is the past and present shaping the future. It is the visible church of today shaped by the invisible church of yesterday. Liturgy or the work of the people in worship is the best way to understand the history of suicide. And preaching is part of the liturgy. Keeping this mind, consider the Tenebrae Service. It is often a service held on Good Friday in which a candle is extinguished for every one of the last seven statements of Christ. As the service progresses the room gets darker. On the last reading the last candle is blown out. The presider walks out of the service. No benediction, no final prayer, no announcements. Just darkness and confusion for the congregation as they experience what the disciples might have felt, "What now?" It is a somber, contemplative service. I have always loved the Tenebrae service. It provides a feeling of finality. That's it, he is dead. It is finished![83] Certainly, this is how the disciples walking on the road to Emmaus felt. There was no reason to stay in Jerusalem anymore. As much as I love this service, however, it fails to give a well-rounded theology of Good Friday. For Good Friday was not somber and dark for everyone. There was darkness, indeed, but there was also an earthquake, rocks split open, and the bodies of many dead people were resurrected.[84] By Jesus's death the dead had life. Good Friday became Easter for these risen ones. The voluntary death of Jesus not only shook the earth, it rattled time and transformed history.

DIRECT AND INDIRECT RISK: A TAXONOMY OF PREACHING METHODS

It seems clear that, like our ideas about suicide itself, perceptions of risk are likewise on a spectrum. How might the possibilities of preaching about suicide reflect and adapt to this risk spectrum? Because perceived

---

the preacher. Preaching and listening to preaching is hard work.

82. Hafiz, "The Christ's Breath," 153.

83. This is not the case with the Roman Catholic Triduum liturgy, which begins with a processional before the Mass of the Lord's Supper on Thursday and is one continuous liturgy that doesn't conclude until the recessional at the Easter Vigil Mass.

84. Matt 27:51–55.

risk varies by person or by community, modes of preaching can and should vary as well. I have labeled the two ends of the homiletic spectrum as the Direct and Indirect approaches, depending on the degree to which the sermon explicitly addresses the issue of suicide (and thus faces more directly or indirectly the perceived risks of talking about suicide). I believe that, even if the perceived risks might be high, a careful employment of a Direct form of preaching about suicide can have clear benefits of helping the congregation overcome taboos and think in healthy and more distinctively Christian ways about suicide. This taxonomy is very versatile.[85]

The preacher must be aware of different perspectives and different hermeneutics involved, whether arising within the text or within the congregation. And for many preachers there will be a blending, a moving back and forth on the spectrum depending on the seasons of the congregation.

Direct A and Direct B (or Perceived High-Risk)

These forms of preaching about suicide encompass one category of approaching suicide from the pulpit in which suicide as an issue is named and explored.

Direct A: This method produces a homily that explicitly focuses on a scripture text that directly deals with suicide (like Samson) or suicide ideation (like Jonah). As such, it will of course be biblically based; but the preacher must aim always to present suicide (whether in the Old Testament or New Testament) in light of Christ. For instance, a sermon on Saul might seek to draw out the similarities between his condition and PTSD, his feelings of hopelessness or betrayal/abandonment, or the Witch of Endor's role in implanting suicide ideation through the power of suggestion (all of which were discussed in earlier chapters). Explicit attention to such details in the biblical narratives would function to

---

85. Like suicide, the high and low-risk evaluation can be applied to a broad range of topics. For example, environmentalism is a sensitive topic today, riddled with politically loaded taboo terms such as "tree-huggers" or "climate-coo-coos." How shall the preacher approach environmental stewardship from the pulpit? Only on April 22nd (Earth Day)? Other taboo topics could include marriage and sexuality, racism and justice, nationalism, the immigration crisis, or even personal finances and the growing disparity between the rich and the poor. How shall the preacher incorporate Christ as the central message for all these issues?

increase awareness and sensitivity regarding suicide in the congregation. If it stops there, however, the sermon is not a Christian sermon by
my definition earlier. As noted in my previous discussions on Saul and
Christ, there are ways in which Saul's suicide can highlight the unique
difference of Christ's willful sacrifice. The terrible beauty of Christ's death
can stand in stark relief against the rich background of the Saul narrative. Because there are multiple aspects to suicide as an issue, multiple
biblical narratives of suicide or suicide ideation, multiple sets of details
(or gaps and spaces in those details), and multiple angles of approaching
and reimagining Christ's death, the number of sermons that could be
produced in the Direct A method are quite expansive.

Direct B: This type of homily does not specifically engage a text that
directly deals with suicide but does explicitly mention the issue or simply
the word "suicide" as the sermon progresses. In Direct B, the text deals
primarily with the topic of death or the broad range of topics covered by
thanatology. This could include topics such as death with dignity, palliative care, hospice ministry, etc. The Direct B sermon might be especially
appropriate for Ash Wednesday or All Saints Day. But keep in mind that
because of such a liturgical context, the homily may actually be considered as low-risk. The congregation might expect a homily on such a day
to deal with death and thus the preacher's perception of risk would be
relatively low. An example of a Direct B homily that would not be on a
specially designated day might be one dedicated to a verse such as Proverbs 14:12, "There is a way that seems right to man, but in the end it leads
to death," in which the sermon explicitly includes examples of suicide as
an extension of a possible meaning of this verse. Because the verse itself
is not explicitly about suicide, but the sermon directly addressed the topic
of suicide, such a sermon would belong to a Direct B (rather than Direct
A) method.

Both Direct A and B methods of preaching on suicide can be
beneficial because all people need a direct message sometimes (whether
it is comfortable or not). As expected, the Direct A and B type methods
might be perceived as a higher risk because they may seem to be too
forward, and bluntness may seem insensitive to social norms and taboos
that exist within the community. The "preacher as ethnographer"[86] must
be sympathetic to the congregation's context. The preacher must take the
time to build trust within the community so that when the preacher does

---

86. Tubbs Tisdale, *Preaching as Local Theology*, 59.

preach, the congregation will listen with the recognition that their pastor is speaking from a place of wisdom, is trustworthy, and genuinely cares for them. With that said, however, lest we are tempted to boast, it is good to remember that it is the Holy Spirit that softens hearts and opens ears, not the pastor's respectability. This is good news for the preacher who is a guest speaker or the one who stands on the street corner with strangers. We do not preach to convert. Only God saves. We preach out of gratitude for the gift of salvation; we preach in order to be faithful to God's calling and we seek to do it with excellence.

Indirect A and Indirect B (or Perceived Low-Risk)

These methods lie on the other end of the spectrum and will probably be considered as lower risk forms of preaching.

Indirect A: This method of preaching could be deductive or inductive and might even use the word "suicide" explicitly; but the focus, the function, and the Scripture text would not be directly dealing with death or suicide. Suicide is not central to the homily even if indirectly suicide awareness is one of the objectives of the sermon. While it need not mention the word "suicide" even in passing, it should not shy away from such a possibility; a passing allusion to suicide helps remove the taboo on talking about suicide and could help some members of the congregation begin to talk or think in healthy ways about their own or other's experiences.

For instance, a sermon that broached the topic of loneliness and then commented on the statistical relation of loneliness to suicide would be an example of an Indirect A sermon. This is because neither the text nor the focus and function were directly dealing with the issue of suicide and the comment on suicide might only be limited to a single sentence. To repeat: even when the word "suicide" is said in passing, it is still very significant because it is part of the preacher's broadening or revising of the congregation's vision of suicide. Just saying the word can go a substantial distance towards breaking the taboo.

Indirect B: This method involves the perception of a very low risk. Indirect B does not name or even mention suicide or death. But rather it intentionally focuses (deductively or inductively) on the preventative groundwork of suicide awareness by discussing subjects such as hope, community, collective responsibility, or life-empowering behavior.

Indirect B homilies are ones that build the groundwork for Christian living. For example, a sermon on 1 Cor. 1:10b–11a which states, "On him we have set our hope that he will continue to deliver us, as you help us by your prayers," could focus on the faithfulness of God and the importance of the prayers of fellow believers, without naming death or suicide. Because it focuses upon principles that are fundamentally relevant to having a healthy vision of life and death, it still remains the case that an Indirect B sermon is highly significant in providing essential context for suicide awareness. Preachers must recognize that grappling with the issue of suicide in their congregations is not merely an issue of explicitly naming suicide but requires an entire framework of thinking truthfully about life and death, as well as relating truthfully to God and others.

Both Indirect A and Indirect B methods of preaching as a means of suicide awareness can be beneficial for all listeners, just in different ways. All listeners need to have both specific and general approaches in order to have a better grounding in understanding suicide. Indirect A and Indirect B methods can be considered low-risk because, while they are targeting suicide awareness, they are not making that target explicit, but are essentially laying the broader groundwork or coming at the topic with a higher sense of caution. Indirect A or B may have a lower risk of seeming insensitive to others but may have an unintended high-risk of not being forward enough regarding the importance of the subject. Indirect A or B sermons may cause the perception by the congregation that the preacher is uncertain, uncomfortable, and unwilling to be more forthright (they may think, "He always avoids tough topics," for instance).

It should be noted that preaching for a Christian understanding of suicide should not be limited to a sermon series dedicated to a few brief weeks every few years. Preaching suicide awareness should be an ongoing, consistent practice within the life cycles of the church, especially since many sermons a preacher preaches can function as Indirect B sermons and especially since the heart of the Gospel involves a God who willingly died and called us to follow his example. Laying the groundwork with life-empowering (and self-dying) sermons is vital. The agenda for every homily could be Indirect B, but preaching directly and openly about suicide is also crucial for clear directional growth and helps the congregation think and speak truthfully about suicide and suffering. In a nut-shell, the preacher should focus on three objectives (which should permeate the spectrum of Direct or Indirect methods):

- The wrath and mercy of God (the crucifixion and resurrection of Jesus).

- Biblical literacy (living in the Scriptural texts).

- Ecclesiology (individual dependency on the Holy Spirit in community).

Applying the Taxonomy

For those preachers who are limited to preaching only the Lectionary, one suicide (namely that of Judas) may be the only biblical suicide that is actually mentioned within the Scripture texts read from the pulpit.[87] Lectionary preachers may not have the option to engage in these biblical preaching methods as freely as others. Hence, these preachers may feel limited to primarily Indirect A or B sermons with only the rare instance for a Direct A or B sermon during passion week on Palm Sunday, Year A (Matthew 27 or Acts 1), which is the only mention of suicide in the daily or Sunday Roman Catholic lectionary and the Revised Common Lectionary adopted by Presbyterians, Lutherans, and others. Matthew 26:14–27:66 (a very large pericope) is included as one gospel choice for Palm Sunday. This is the only reading for the three-year cycle that offers a narrative of Judas and his suicide. Sadly, in Year B, the seventh Sunday of Easter only includes Acts 1:15–17, 21–26, obviously cutting out any mention of Judas. As a friend of mine, who serves the Diocese of Charlotte, North Carolina, related, "While we [the priests] are supposed to attend to the scriptural texts, the liturgical texts can be the basis of the homily, or, a preacher can choose to preach on some need within the community on occasion if needed."[88] Even while it might at first glance seem there is less freedom for the lectionary preacher in contrast to other biblical preachers, there is, in fact, much freedom to creatively bring to bear all of Scripture upon the particular passage of the daily lectionary.[89]

Obviously, in order to preach suicide as a topic, the preacher needs to do some preparatory education on that topic. Topical preaching

---

87. Preachers, of course, could mention others even if they are not read as part of the lectionary.

88. Fr. Benjamin Roberts, e-mail message to author, April 21, 2018.

89. Biblical preaching is defined as that method of choosing Scripture texts that are not ecclesiastically bound to the prescribed lectionary texts. Vincie, "Liturgy and Preaching."

requires one to engage in the academic disciplines of the day.[90] The Bible does not supplant the statistical platform that science has established when it comes to suicide; it merely places that data in its proper theological framework. The preacher does not have to agree with the social or behavioral sciences in order to engage well with those disciplines; rather, it simply means being informed about the common ideas and language used, the pitfalls to avoid, and opportunities worth exploring.[91]

90. Keep in mind that to address suicide in a sermon does not require that the sermon be topical. The preacher could use any type of form. Topical sermons are not easier or better than exegetical sermons or forms, they are just different.

91. For example, like the methods put forth for preaching on the topic of suicide, environmentalism is a topic that also requires engagement with the scientific community (global warming, plastic crisis, consumer waste, etc.); study of Scripture (stewardship passages, theology of creation/Creator, wilderness motif, eschatology, and the new creation, etc.); tradition and history (creation, animals and wilderness in monastic literature, the compromise of Christianity and industrialization, etc.), and of course, taking the time to know one's congregation in order to choose how direct or indirect the delivery should be.

11

Final Thoughts

"So, a certain absence, a kind of death—spacing, hiatus, gap—is required for speech to live."[1]

TO TRULY CONFESS ONE'S sins is to die. Confession is a habitual death, dying a little bit every day. It is a turning away from the old self. To say "no more" to that person who once was. As preachers, we stand in front of the assembly, acknowledging, giving testimony on the witness stand, and confessing, "We are guilty and in need of a Savior!" and "Let us die so we may live."

My hope in writing this book was originally to shine a light on an impoverished area in the field of homiletics and encourage preachers to address suicide within a Christocentric framework from the pulpit. It was only while writing that I slowly realized that preaching itself was a kind of suicide. Like Stephen, like Peter, like Paul, who were compelled by the Holy Spirit, to preach is to die.[2] The preacher does not just preach on suicide but rather the act of preaching, in the Spirit,[3] is suicide. Furthermore, the preacher calls others to die with Christ. We die and we call others to die.[4] To do so is the only way to find life.

1. Myers, *Preaching Must Die*, 154.
2. Acts 14:19.
3. Acts 4:29.
4. God will be the one who provides the Life.

True preaching is an act of self-emptying. The preacher has to die to self in order to fully and faithfully preach. To heed the call to proclaim the Truth we take up our cross and we die to self-assured truths and taken for granted assumptions. We die to trusting in self-knowledge and self-effort. We die to our platforms and accolades. And in utter exhaustion, with the adrenaline wearing thin, we die to our posturing as we hear the parishioners, one by one say the same unthinking remark, "Nice talk pastor."

When a well-dressed visitor approached me after the service one day, along with all the others filing out of the sanctuary, he stopped and said, "I liked what you said about Jesus. But I don't like that *you* said it. Women should remain silent." I thanked him for coming to worship with us. But his words lingered long, long after he left. Many years later I am learning that to die to self includes my identity—I must die to what it means to be female, what it means to be Presbyterian, what it means to be Caucasian, what it means to be American, and what it means to be personally offended. Like confession, to forgive is to also die. But how do I die to myself and still be myself? I cannot. That is the point. I must die so that I become God's body, broken for those God loved so much that he gave his very self. To die every day is to confirm that Life is not about my life, but Life is about my death.

> Well might the sun in darkness hide, and shut its glories in,
> When Christ the great Redeemer died for human creatures' sin
> But drops of grief can ne'er repay the debt of love I owe;
> Here, Lord, I give myself away, Tis all that I can do.[5]

---

5. Watts, *Alas! And Did My Savior Bleed.*

Bibliography

Achtemeier, Paul J. *Inspiration and Authority: Nature and Function of Christian Scripture*. Peabody, MA: Hendrickson, 1999.

Ainsworth, Patricia. *Understanding Depression*. Jackson: University Press of Mississippi, 2000.

Alvares, A. "The Background." In *Suicide: The Philosophical Issues*, edited by M. P. Battin and David J. Mayo, 10–11. New York: St. Martin's, 1980.

Alt, Florence May. "The Weaver." *Somerset Herald*. Somerset PA, July 27, 1892.

Ambrose of Milan. *On Virgins*. Translated by H. De Romstin and H. T. F. Duckworth. Nicene and Post-Nicene Fathers 10. Grand Rapids: Eerdmans, rep., 1983.

American Association of Suicidology. http://www.suicidology.org/.

Amundsen, Darrel W. "Suicide and Early Christian Values: The Nature of the Problem and the Scope of This Essay." In *Suicide and Euthanasia: Historical and Contemporary Themes*, edited by Baruch A. Brod, 77–153. London: Kluwer Academic, 1989.

Anderson, A. A. *2 Samuel*. Word Biblical Commentary Series. Nashville: Thomas Nelson, 1989.

Aquinas, Thomas. *Summa Theologiae*. Translated by Fathers of the English Dominican Province. 2nd ed. 1920. Edited online by Kevin Knight, 2017. http://www.newadvent.org/summa/ 3064.htm#article5.

Archives of Suicide Research. https://www.tandfonline.com/loi/usui20.

Aries, Philippe. *The Hour of Our Death*. Oxford: Oxford University Press, 1981.

Arthurs, Jeffrey D., *Preaching as Reminding: Stirring Memory in an Age of Forgetfulness*. Downers Grove: IVP Academic, 2017.

Augustine. *Against Two Letters of the Pelagians*. Translated by Peter Holmes and Robert Ernest Wallis. Nicene and Post-Nicene Fathers 5. Buffalo, NY: Christian Literature, 1887.

———. *City of God*. Translated by Henry Bettenson. London: Penguin, 1984.

———. *On the Trinity*. Translated by Arthur West Haddan. Nicene and Post-Nicene Fathers 3. Grand Rapids: Eerdmans, 1980.

Aviv, Rachel. "What Does it Mean to Die?" Annals of Medicine. *The New Yorker*. February 5, 2019. https://www.newyorker.com/magazine/2018/02/05/what-does-it-mean-to-die.

Baechler, Jean. *Suicides*. Translated by Barry Cooper. New York: Basic, 1975.

Barbour, Scott and Helen Cothran, eds. *Suicide: Opposing Viewpoints*. Farmington Hills, MI: Greenhaven, 2003.

Barr, Alfred H. *Picasso: Fifty Years of His Art by Chapter.* New York: The Museum of Modern Art, 1946.

Barron, Robert. "Begotten Not Made." *Word on Fire Homilies.* June 16, 2019. https://www. wordonfire.org/resources/homily/begotten-not-made/5157/.

Bartlett, Gary. "Betting on the Lord's Prayer." *Learning, Laughing, Loving, and Living for Him.* September 28, 2008. https://garybartlett.wordpress.com/2008/09/28/betting-on-the-lords-prayer/.

Barth, Karl. *Church Dogmatics.* Translated by G.W. Bromiley et al. Edinburgh: T. & T. Clark, 1975.

Beecher, Henry Ward. *Yale Lectures in Preaching.* New York: Howard and Hulbert, 1892.

Befrienders Worldwide Volunteer Action to Prevent Suicide. https://www.befrienders. org/ suicide-statistics.

Begg, Alister. "The Way We Were," *Truth For Life.* https://truthforlife.org/resources/sermon/ the-way-we-were-ephesians/.

Behr, John. "Learning Through Experience: The Pedagogy of Suffering and Death in Irenaeus." In *Suffering and Evil in Early Christian Thought,* edited by Nona Verna Harrison and David G. Hunter, 33–47. Grand Rapids: Baker Academic, 2016.

————. *The Mystery of Christ: Life in Death.* Crestwood, New York: St. Vladimir's Seminary Press, 2006.

Bell, Brad. "Fundamental Attribution Error." *Psychologyandsociety.com.* http://www. psychologyandsociety.com/attributionerror.html.

Bender, David L., and Bruno Leone, eds. *Suicide: Opposing Viewpoints.* San Diego: Greenhaven, 1992.

Benton, Wilson. "Thinking Biblically About the Tragedy of Suicide." In *The Hardest Sermons You'll Ever Have to Preach,* edited by Bryan Chapell, 241–252. Grand Rapids: Baker Academic, 2013.

Bicchieri, Cristina. "Scripts and Schemas." *Coursera - Social Norms, Social Change II.* https:// www.coursera.org/lecture/change/9-5-3m1nZ.

Bolin, Thomas M. *Freedom Beyond Forgiveness: The Book of Jonah Re-Examined.* Sheffield: Sheffield Academic, 1997.

Bolte Taylor, Jill. *My Stroke of Insight: A Brain Scientist's Personal Journey.* New York: Penguin, 2006.

Borgman, Paul. *David, Saul, and God: Rediscovering an Ancient Story.* Oxford: Oxford University Press, 2008.

Bregman, Lucy. *Death in the Midst of Life: Perspectives on Death from Christianity and Depth Psychology.* Grand Rapids: Baker, 1992.

Brooks, Phillip. *Lectures on Preaching: The Yale Lectures on Preaching, 1877.* Grand Rapids: Baker, 1981.

————. "O Little Town of Bethlehem." In *The Presbyterian Hymnal,* 44. Louisville: Westminster John Knox, 1990.

Brown, Michael Joseph. "Piety and Proclamation: Gregory of Nyssa's Sermon on the Lord's Prayer." In *Brill's Companions to the Christian Tradition: A History of Prayer: The First to the Fifteenth Century,* edited by Roy Hammerling, 79–116. Boston: Brill, 2008.

Brown, Thomas. *Religio Medici,* Public Domain, Eugene, Ore: Freebook. http://0-eds.a. ebscohost.com.library.acaweb.org/ehost/detail/detail?vid=0&sid=84ef1aa2-c4f5-43f0-af7c-cb9775b73d45%40sdc-v sessmgr01&bdata=JkF1dGhUeXBlPXNzbw%3d%3d#db=nlebk&AN=2009590.

Brown, Warren S., et. al., eds. *Whatever Happened to the Soul: Scientific and Theological Portraits of Human Nature.* Minneapolis: Fortress, 1998.

Brueggemann, Walter. *Preaching the Old Testament.* Minneapolis: Augsburg, 2019.

Burghardt, Walter, *The Image of God in Man According to Cyril of Alexandria.* Baltimore: Woodstock College, 1957.

Burpo, Todd and Lynn Vincent, *Heaven Is for Real: A Little Boy's Astounding Story of His Trip to Heaven and Back.* Nashville: Thomas Nelson, 2010.

Bushnell, Horace. *The Vicarious Sacrifice, Grounded in Principles of Universal Obligation.* New York: Scribner, 1866.

Butler, Trent. *Judges.* Word Biblical Commentary Series. Nashville: Thomas Nelson, 2009.

Calvin, John. *Catechism of the Church of Geneva.* https://reformed.org/documents/calvin/ geneva_catachism/geneva_catachism.html.

———. *Commentaries on the Twelve Minor Prophets.* Translated by John Owen. Grand Rapids: Eerdmans, 1950.

———. *Institutes of the Christian Religion.* Edited and translated by John T. McNeill. Philadelphia: Westminster, 1960.

———. "Instruction in Faith." In *Great Voices of the Reformation,* edited by Harry Emerson Fosdick, 234–258. New York: Random House, 1952.

———. *The World's Great Sermons,* vol. 1. Compiled by Grenville Kleiser. London: Funk and Wagnalls, 1909.

Capra, Frank. *It's a Wonderful Life.* RKO Radio Pictures, 1946.

Cappell, Bill. "Text Messages Urging Suicide Result in Involuntary Manslaughter Conviction." National Public Radio. Last modified June 15, 2017. http://www.npr. org/sections/thetwo-way/2017/06/16/533220739/text-messages-urging-suicide-result-in-involuntary-manslaughter-conviction.

Carson, D. A. "Sweep of Praise," *Truth For Life.* May 9, 2016. https://www.truthforlife. org/ resources/sermon/sweep-praise/.

Carter, Chris. *Science and the Near-Death Experience: How Consciousness Survives Death.* Rochester, Vermont: Inner Tradition, 2010.

Carter Florence, Anna. "The Girls in the Reeds." *John S. Marten Program in Homiletics and Liturgics.* 2017. https://www.youtube.com/watch?v=bouPBKo1HBo.

———. *Preaching as Testimony.* Louisville: Westminster John Knox, 2007.

Catechism of the Catholic Church, Libreria Editrice Vaticana. Liguori, MO: Liguori,1994.

Centers for Disease Control and Prevention. "Holiday Suicides: Fact or Myth." Last modified December 31, 2013. https://www.cdc.gov/violenceprevention/suicide/ holiday.html.

———. "Suicide Rates Rising Across the U.S., Comprehensive Prevention Goes Beyond a Focus on Mental Health Concerns." June 7, 2018. https://www.cdc.gov/ media/releases/2018/ p0607-suicide-prevention.html.

———. *Web-based Injury Statistics Query and Reporting System (WISQARS).* Last modified May 3, 2018. http://www.cdc.gov/injury/wisqars/index.html.

Chadwick, Henry. *The Early Church: The Story of Emergent Christianity from the Apostolic Age to the Foundation of the Church of Rome.* London: Penguin, 1967.

Chapell, Bryan. *Christ-Centered Sermons: Models of Redemptive Preaching.* Grand Rapids: Baker Academic, 2013.

———, ed. *The Hardest Sermons You'll Ever Have to Preach.* Grand Rapids: Baker Academic, 2013.

Chapman, Stephen B. *1 Samuel as Christian Scripture: A Theological Commentary.* Grand Rapids: Eerdmans, 2016.

Chidester, David. *Salvation and Suicide: An Interpretation of Jim Jones, the Peoples Temple, and Jonestown.* Bloomington: Indiana University Press, 1988.

Christian Reformed Church, *Apostles' Creed.* https://www.crcna.org/welcome/beliefs/creeds/ apostles-creed.

Christianity Today. "Harry Emerson Fosdick, Liberalism's Popularizer." http://www.christianitytoday.com/history/people/pastorsandpreachers/harry-emerson-fosdick.html.

Christo, Gus George. *Martyrdom According to John Chrysostom: To Live is Christ, To Die is Gain.* New York: Edwin Mellen, 1997.

Clement of Alexandria. *Stromata or Miscellanies.* Translated by Rev. William Wilson. Ante-Nicene Fathers 2. New York: Christian Literature, 1885.

Clemons, James T. ed., *Sermons on Suicide.* Louisville: Westminster John Knox, 1989.

"Clinical Depression: Symptoms and Treatments. Bereavement Leading to Suicide: Statistical Analysis." http://depressivedisorder.blogspot.com/2011/03/bereavement-leading-to-suicide.html.

Compassion and Choices. "Information on Medical Aid in Dying for People with Terminal Illness." https://www.compassionandchoices.org/information-on-medical-aid-in-dying-for-people-with-terminal-illness/.

Concordia. *Augsburg Confession.* St. Louis: Concordia, 2013.

Cooper, John, ed., *Plato: Complete Works.* Indianapolis: Hackett, 1997.

Cox Miller, Patricia. *Women in Early Christianity.* Washington DC: CUA Press, 2005.

Craddock, Fred B. *Craddock Stories,* edited by Mike Graves and Richard Ward. St. Louis: Chalice, 2001.

———. "Jesus Saves," July 10, 2011. https://video.search.yahoo.com/search/ video?fr=mcafee&p=fred+craddock+jesus+saves+sermon#id=1&vid=aa0abf86396cfa18 70e58076716b9273&action=click.

Craddock, Fred, Dale Goldsmith and Joy V. Goldsmith. *Speaking of Dying: Recovering the Church's Voice in the Face of Death.* Grand Rapids: Brazos, 2012.

Creamer, Deborah Beth. "John Calvin and Disability." In *Disability in the Christian Tradition: A Reader,* edited by Brian Brock and John Swinton, 216–250. Grand Rapids: Eerdmans, 2012.

Crisp, Thomas M., et al. *Neuroscience and the Soul: The Human Person in Philosophy, Science, and Theology.* Grand Rapids: Eerdmans, 2016.

Cyprian. *Letters.* Translated by Ernest Wallis. Ante-Nicene Fathers 5. New York: Christian Literature, 1890.

D'Ambrosio, Rocco. "The Reform and the Perspective from Below." In *Will Pope Francis Pull It Off? The Challenge of Church Reform.* Translated by Barry Hudock. Collegeville: Liturgical, 2017.

D'Aquili, Eugene and Andrew B. Newberg. *The Mystical Mind: Probing the Biology of Religious Experience.* Minneapolis: Fortress, 1999.

Davies, Douglas. *Theology of Death.* New York: T. & T. Clark, 2008.

Davies, J. G., ed. *New Westminster Dictionary of Liturgy and Worship.* Philadelphia: Westminster, 1986.

De Ste. Croix, G. E. M. *Christian Persecution, Martyrdom, and Orthodoxy.* Edited by Michael Whitby and Joseph Streeter. Oxford: Oxford University Press, 2006.

Death with Dignity. https://www.deathwithdignity.org/.

D'Holbach, Baron. *The System of Nature*. Translated by H. G. Robinson. Boston: Mendum, 1889.

Diagnostic and Statistical Manual of Mental Disorders (DSM-5). "Depressive Disorders." 155–187. 5th ed. Washington, DC: American Psychiatric, 2013.

———. "Suicidal Behavior Disorder: Comorbidity." 801–803. 5th ed. Washington, DC: American Psychiatric, 2013.

Donne, John. *Biathanatos*, edited by William A. Clebsch. Chico CA: Scholars, 1983.

Droge, Arthur J. and James D. Tabor. *A Noble Death: Suicide and Martyrdom Among Christians and Jews in Antiquity*. New York: HarperCollins, 1992.

Dunn, James D. G. *The Theology of the Apostle Paul*. Grand Rapids: Eerdmans, 1998.

Durkheim, Emile. *Suicide: A Study in Sociology*. Translated by John A. Spaulding and George Simpson. New York: Free, 1979.

Edwards, O. C. Jr. *A History of Preaching*. Nashville: Abingdon, 2004.

Eells, Gregory. "Cultivating Resilience," Jan. 16, 2015. https://video.search.yahoo.com/search/ video?fr=mcafee&p=Greg+Eells#id=5&vid=566213of1deaaf862c40df8e5 530a289&action=view.

Ehrenberg, Alain. *The Weariness of the Self: Diagnosing the History of Depression in the Contemporary Age*. Montreal: McGill-Queen's University Press, 2010.

Ehrenreich, Barbara. *Natural Causes: An Epidemic of Wellness, the Certainty of Dying, And Killing Ourselves to Live Longer*. New York: Twelve, 2018.

Ehrman, Bart. *Apostolic Fathers*. Vol. 1. Loeb Classical Library 25. Cambridge, MA: Harvard University Press, 2003.

Ellens, J. Harold. "Inequality or Singularity of Institutionalized Death: Soldiers' Deaths" in *The Unequal Before Death*, edited by Christina Staudt and Marcelline Block, 193–203. Cambridge: Cambridge Scholars, 2012.

Ellis, Ross. "'Tell Someone to 'Kill themselves' and You Could End Up in Jail," Huffington Post, June 17, 2017. https://www.huffpost.com/entry/tell-someone-to-kill-themselves-and-you-could-end_b_5945800ce4b0940f84fe2f19.

Epperly, Bruce G. *Process Theology: A Guide for the Perplexed*. New York: T & T Clark, 2011.

Eriksson, Cynthia. "Suffering With: A Tender Journey of Mutuality in Suffering, Comfort, and Joy." *Fuller* 14 (2019) 38–41.

Eusebius. *The Ecclesiastical History*. Translated by J.E.L Oulton. Vol. 2. Cambridge: Harvard University Press, 1994.

"Euthanasia Terminology," A New Zealand Resource for Life Related Issues. Last modified 2011. http://www.life.org.nz/euthanasia/abouteuthanasia/euthanasia-controversy1/.

Evans, Robert F. *Pelagius: Inquiries and Reappraisals*. New York: Seabury, 1968.

"Facts about Alcohol and Suicide," *MCES Building Better Tomorrows*. http://mces.org/pages/ suicide_fact_alcohol.php.

Fast, Julia and John D. Preston. *Bipolar Disorder: Understanding and Helping Your Partner*. 2nd ed., Oakland: New Harbinger, 2012.

Fedden, H. R. *Suicide: A Social and Historical Study*. London: Peter Davies, 1938.

Flatow, Nicole. "Father Shoots and Kills 14-year-old Daughter, Saying He Mistook Her for Burglar," *Think Progress*, December 24, 2013. https://thinkprogress.org/father-shoots-and-kills-14-year-old-daughter-saying-he-mistook-her-for-burglar-a4bf5e6d3290/.

Fosdick, Harry Emerson. *The Meaning of Prayer*. New York: Association, 1920.

Foucault, Michel. *Madness and Civilization: A History of Insanity in the Age of Reason.* New York: Vintage, 1965.

Fuller Torrey, E. *Surviving Schizophrenia: A Family Manual.* New York: Harper, 2013.

Gibson, Scott M. and Karen Mason, *Preaching Hope in Darkness.* Bellingham, WA: Lexham, 2020.

Gilbert, Sandra M. *Death's Door: Modern Dying and the Ways We Grieve.* New York: W.W. Norton, 2006.

Gore Jr., Ralph J. "Deductive, Inductive. . . And a Third Way." Conference on Sermon Studies, October 20, 2017. https://mds.marshall.edu/cgi/viewcontent. cgi?referer=https://www.google. com/&httpsredir=1&article=1017&context=ser mon_conference.

Greene-McCreight, Karen. *Darkness Is My Only Companion: A Christian Response to Mental Illness.* Grand Rapids: Brazos, 2006.

Gregory of Nyssa, *The Lord's Prayer; The Beatitudes.* Translated by Hilda Graef. Ancient Christian Writers 18. Westminster, MD: Newman, 1954.

Haelle, Tara. "Hospital Sees Growing Number of Kids and Teens at Risk for Suicide," *Shots Health News NPR.* May 16, 2018. https://www.npr.org/sections/health-shots/ 2018/05/16/611407972/hospitals-see-growing-numbers-of-kids-and-teens-at-risk-for-suicide.

Hafiz, Shams-ud-din Muhammad. "The Christ's Breath." In *Love Poems from God: Twelve Sacred Voices from the East and West,* edited by Daniel Ladinsky, 153. New York: Penguin Compass, 2002.

Haiken, Melanie. "More Than 10,000 Suicides Tied to Economic Crisis, Study Says." *Forbes.* Last modified June 12, 2014. https://www.forbes.com/sites/ melaniehaiken/2014/06/12/more-than-10000-suicides-tied-to-economic-crisis-study-says/.

Hamilton, John. "FDA Expected to Approve Esketmine Nasal Spray for Depression," March 4, 2019. https://www.npr.org/sections/health-shots/2019/03/04/700014137/fda-expected-to-approve-esketamine-nasal-spray-for-depression.

Hammerling, Roy. "Introduction: Prayer-A Simply Complicated Scholarly Problem." In *Brill's Companions to the Christian Tradition; A History of Prayer. The First to the Fifteenth Century,* edited by Roy Hammerling, 1–27. Boston: Brill, 2008.

———. "The Lord's Prayer: A Cornerstone of Early Baptismal Education." In *Brill's Companions to the Christian Tradition; A History of Prayer. The First to the Fifteenth Century,* edited by Roy Hammerling, 167–182. Boston: Brill, 2008.

Harvard TH. Chan School of Public Health 2018, "Suicide." https://www.hsph.harvard. edu/ hicrc/firearms-research/gun-ownership-and-use/.

Hauerwas, Stanley. *Suffering Presence: Theological Reflections on Medicine, the Mentally Handicapped, and the Church.* Notre Dame: University of Notre Dame Press, 1986.

———. *Truthfulness and Tragedy: Further Investigations into Christian Ethics.* Notre Dame: University of Notre Dame Press, 1985.

Haynes, Thomas. *The General View of the Holy Scriptures.* London: J. B and S. B., 1640.

Hays, Richard B. "Awaiting the Redemption of Our Bodies." In *Virtues and Practices in the Christian Tradition,* edited by Nancy Murphy, et al, 206–214. Harrisburg: Trinity Press International, 1997.

———. *The Moral Vision of the New Testament: A Contemporary Introduction to New Testament Ethics.* New York: Harper Collins, 1996.

Heard, Matt. *Life with a Capital L: Embracing Your God-Given Humanity.* Colorado Springs: Multnomah, 2014.

Hendin, Herbert. *Suicide in America.* New York: W.W. Norton, 1995.

Hershfield, Jon. *When a Family Member Has OCD: Mindfulness and Cognitive Behavioral Skills to Help Families Affected by Obsessive-Compulsive Disorder.* Oakland: New Harbinger, 2015.

Hevenesi, Gabriel, SJ. *Thoughts of St. Ignatius Loyola; For Every Day of the Year, Scintillae Ignatianae.* Translated and compiled by Alan G. McDougall. New York: Fordham University Press, 2006.

Hilkert, Mary Catherine. *Naming Grace: Preaching and the Sacramental Imagination.* New York: Continuum, 1997.

Hillman, James. *Suicide and the Soul.* New York: Harper and Row, 1964.

Hirshbein, Laura D. *American Melancholy: Constructions of Depression in the Twentieth Century.* New Brunswick: Rutgers University Press, 2009.

Hollenbach, Paul W. "Jesus, Demoniacs, and Public Authorities: A Socio-Historical Study." *Journal of The American Academy of Religion* 49.4 (1981) 567–588.

Horton, Michael. *Cross Way.* "John Calvin on the Role of the Pastor." October 24, 2014. https://www.crossway.org/articles/john-calvin-on-the-role-of-the-pastor/.

———. "Our Redeemer Lives and So Shall We." In *The Hardest Sermons You'll Ever Have to Preach*, edited by Bryan Chapell, 253–260. Grand Rapids: Baker Academic, 2013.

Hovey, Craig. *To Share in the Body.* Grand Rapids: Brazos, 2008.

Hull Stookey, Laurence. *Calendar: Christ's Time for the Church.* Nashville: Abingdon, 1996.

Hume, David. *Essays on Suicide and the Immortality of the Soul.* Basil, U.K.: Collection of English Classics, 1799.

Humphry, Derek. *Final Exit: The Practicalities of Self-Deliverance and Assisted Suicide for the Dying.* Eugene, OR: The Hemlock Society 1991.

"Jarrid Wilson, Pastor and Mental Health Advocate, Kills Himself." BBC News, September 12, 2019. https://www.bbc.com/news/world-us-canada-49667775.

Johnson, A. P. "Ethnicity: Greeks, Jews, and Christians." In *Blackwell Companion to Ethnicity in the Ancient Mediterranean*, edited by Jeremy McInerny, 376–389. Oxford: Wiley- Blackwell, 2014.

Joiner, Thomas. *Myths About Suicide.* Cambridge: Harvard University Press, 2010.

———. *Why People Die by Suicide.* Cambridge: Harvard University Press, 2005.

Kastenbaum, Robert J. *Death, Society, and Human Experience,* 9th ed. London: Routledge, 2016.

Keefe, Rachel A. *The Life Saving Church: Faith Communities and Suicide Prevention.* Saint Louis: Chalice, 2018.

Keller, Tim. *Counterfeit Gods: The Empty Promises of Money, Sex, and Power, and the Only Hope that Matters.* London: Penguin, 2011.

Kim, Jichan. *The Structure of the Samson Cycle.* Kampen, Netherlands: Kok Pharos, 1993.

King Jr., Martin Luther. "Transformed Non-Conformist." In *Strength to Love*, 11-21. New York: Harper and Row, 1968.

Klebold, Sue. *A Mother's Reckoning: Living in the Aftermath of Tragedy.* New York: Crown, 2016.

Kluckhohn, Clyde and Henry Murray. *Personality in Nature, Society, and Culture.* New York: Alfred A. Knopf, 1948.

Knowles, Michael P., and Paul Wilson, *Of Seeds and the People of God: Preaching as Parable, Crucifixion, and Testimony.* Eugene OR: Cascade, 2015.

Kowalski, Robin and Drew Westen. *Psychology.* 4th ed. Hoboken, NJ: John Wiley and Sons, 2005.

Kübler-Ross, Elisabeth. *Death is of Vital Importance: On Life, Death and Life After Death.* New York: Stanton Hill, 1995.

———. *On Life After Death.* Berkeley: Celestial Arts, 1991.

LaCuesta, Don. "Homily." http://cdn.cnn.com/cnn/2018/images/12/16/father.lacuesta.homily. maison.hullibarger.funeral.pdf.

Larson, David B., et al. "The Role of Clergy in Mental Health Care." In *Psychiatry and Religion: The Convergence of Mind and Spirit,* edited by James K. Boehnlein, 125–142. Washington DC: American Psychiatric, 2000.

Leith, John H. "Calvin, John." In *Concise Encyclopedia of Preaching,* edited by William H. Willimon and Richard Lischer, 60–63. Louisville: Westminster John Knox, 1995.

Lester Randall Preaching Fellowship. "Metaphor and Metamorphosis." November 3, 2015. Video, 1:10:44. https://video.search.yahoo.com/search/videofr=mcafee&p=Leonard+sweet+Metaphor+as+metamorphosis+youtube#id=1&vid=d42ebc7428f9efe1845b4c cdc18ebedc&action=click.

Levering, Matthew. *Dying and the Virtues.* Grand Rapids: Eerdmans, 2018.

Liddell, Henry George, Robert Scott, and Henry Stuart Jones. *A Greek-English Lexicon.* 9th ed. Oxford: Clarendon, 1996.

Lischer, Richard, ed. *The Company of Preachers: Wisdom on Preaching, Augustine to the Present.* Grand Rapids: William Be Eerdmans, 2002.

Liu, Steven. "Social Media and Depression." Culture Youth Studies, May, 2015. http://cultureandyouth.org/social-media/research-social-media/social-media-and-depression/.

Logan, William Bryant. *Air: The Restless Shaper of the World.* New York: W.W. Norton, 2012.

London, Jack. *Jack London's Tales of Adventure,* ed. Irving Shepard. Garden City, NY: Hanover House, 1956.

Long, A. A. *Greek Models of Mind and Self.* Cambridge: Harvard University Press, 2015.

Long, Thomas G. and Leonora Tubbs Tisdale, eds. *Teaching Preaching as a Christian Practice: A New Approach to Homiletical Pedagogy.* Louisville: Westminster John Knox, 2008.

Lowry, Eugene L. *The Homiletical Plot: The Sermon as Narrative Art Form.* Louisville: Westminster John Knox, 2001.

Luther, Martin. *Table Talk.* Translated by William Hazlitt. London: H. G. Bohn, 1857.

MacLeod, Donald. *Christ Crucified: Understanding the Atonement.* Downers Grove: IVP Academic, 2014.

Martin, Dale. *Pedagogy of the Bible: An Analysis and Proposal.* Louisville: Westminster John Knox, 2008.

"Martyr." In *Merriam-Webster Dictionary.* Last modified May 15, 2018. https://www.merriam-webster.com/dictionary/martyr.

Mason, Karen. *Preventing Suicide: A Handbook for Pastors, Chaplains and Pastoral Counselors.* Downers Grove: InterVarsity, 2014.

Matthew, Michelle. "Defining Our Terms Sermon Series." April 26, 2019. https://www. youtube. com/watch?v=Q_TT02ds2jc.

McArthur, Nicole, *Not One More Vet*. https://www.nomv.org/story/.

McClure, John. *Preaching Words: 144 Key Terms in Homiletics*. Louisville: Westminster John Knox, 2007.

Meineck, Peter and Paul Woodruff. *Sophocles: Theban Plays*. Indianapolis: Hackett, 2003.

Mental Health Daily. "16 Suicide Warning Signs and Behaviors to Recognize." https:// mentalhealthdaily.com/2014/07/29/16-suicide-warning-signs-behaviors-to-recognize/.

"Mental Illness." In *Merriam-Webster Dictionary*. Last modified May 27, 2018. https:// www.merriam-webster.com/dictionary/mental%20illness.

Metzger, Bruce M., ed. "Wisdom of Solomon." In *The Apocrypha*, 102–127. New York: Oxford University Press, 1977.

Michael Hecht, Jennifer *Stay: A History of Suicide and the Arguments Against It*. New Haven: Yale University, 2013.

Middleton, Paul. *Martyrdom: A Guide for the Perplexed*. New York: T. & T. Clark, 2011.

Moats Miller, Robert. *Harry Emerson Fosdick: Preacher, Pastor, Prophet*. Oxford: Oxford University Press, 1985.

Morris, Leon. *The Gospel According To Matthew*. Leicester: InterVarsity, 1992.

Moodie, Susanna. *Life in the Clearings Versus the Bush*. London: Richard Bentley, 1853.

Morrison, Craig E. *2 Samuel*. Berit Olam: Studies in Hebrew Narrative and Poetry. Collegeville, MT: Liturgical, 2013.

Moss, Candida. *The Other Christs: Imitating Jesus in Ancient Christian Ideologies of Martyrdom*. Oxford: Oxford University Press, 2010.

Motter, Alton M., ed. *Preaching about Death; Sermons dealing with Death and Hope*. Philadelphia: Fortress, 1975.

Murphy, Nancy. *Bodies and Souls, or Spirited Bodies?* Cambridge: Cambridge University Press, 2006.

Murray, Alexander. *Suicide in the Middle Ages: The Violent Against Themselves*. Vol. 1. Oxford: Oxford Press, 1998.

Myers, Jacob D. *Preaching Must Die: Troubling Homiletical Theology*. Minneapolis: Fortress, 2017.

National Institutes of Health, *NIH Human Microbiome Project Defines Normal Bacterial Makeup of the Body*, June 13, 2012. www.nih.gov/news-releases/nih-human-microbiome-project-defines-normal-bactieria-makeup-body.

Navasky, Miri. and Karen O'Connor. "The Suicide Plan." *Frontline*. Aired November 13, 2012. PBS. www.pbs.org/video/frontline-suicide-plan.

"Nearly 7 in 10 Americans Take Prescription Drugs, Mayo Clinic, Omsted Medical Center Find" Mayo Clinic, June 19, 2013. http://newsnetwork.mayoclinic.ord/ discussion/nearly-7-in-10--Americans-take-prescription-drugs-mayo-clinic-omsted-medical-center-find.

Newberg, Andrew. *Principles of Neurotheology*. London: Routledge, 2010.

New Zealand Resource for Life Related Issues. "Euthanasia Terminology." Last modified 2011. http://www.life.org.nz/euthanasia/abouteuthanasia/euthanasia-controversy1/.

The Nicene Creed. https://www.rca.org/resources/nicene-creed.

Niebuhr, Richard. *The Self and the Dramas of History*. London: Faber and Faber, 1956.

Nock, Matthew K., ed. *The Oxford Handbook of Suicide and Self Injury*. Oxford: Oxford University Press, 2014.

Norris, Frederick W. "Suicide." In *Encyclopedia of Early Christianity*, edited by Everett Ferguson. 1094–1095. 2nd ed. New York: Routledge, 1999.

Nuland, Sherwin B. *How We Die: Reflections on Life's Final Chapter*. New York: Alfred A. Knopf, 1994.

Origen. *Contra Celsum*. Translated by Henry Chadwick. Cambridge: Cambridge University Press, 1953.

———. *Exhortation to Martyrdom*. Translated by Hans Urs Von Balthasar. Mahwah, NJ: Paulist, 1979.

———. *Homilies on Leviticus: 1-16*. Translated by Gary Wayne Barkley. The Fathers of the Church 83. Washington DC: CUA Press, 2010.

———, *On First Principles*. Translated by G. W. Butterworth. Gloucester: Peter Smith, 1973.

Orthodox Presbyterian Church. *Westminster Confession*. Sydney: Christian Education, 2007.

Ossa-Richardson, Anthony. "Possession or Insanity? Two Views from the Victorian Lunatic Asylum." *Journal of the History of Ideas* 74.4 (Oct. 2013): 553–575.

Pabst Battin, Margaret, ed. *The Ethics of Suicide*, J. Willard Marriott Library Digital Archive at the University of Utah: Oxford Press. https://ethicsofsuicide.lib.utah.edu/category/author/ clement-of-alexandria/.

Pasquarello III, Michael. *We Speak Because We Have First Been Spoken: A Grammar of the Preaching Life*. Grand Rapids: Eerdmans, 2009.

Patel, Eboo. "Religion is as Important as Ever." *Inside Higher Ed*. January 9, 2019. https://www. insidehighered.com/blogs/conversations-diversity/religion-important-ever.

Pedersen, Traci. "Suicidal Ideation." PsychCentra. Last modified Sept. 26, 2018. https://psychcentral.com/encyclopedia/suicidal-ideation/.

Perry, Theodore Anthony. *The Honeymoon Is Over: Jonah's Argument with God*. Peabody, MA: Hendrickson, 2006.

Peterson, Gregory R. *Minding God: Theology and the Cognitive Sciences*. Minneapolis: Fortress, 2003.

Plantinga Pauw, Amy. *Church in Ordinary Time: A Wisdom Ecclesiology*. Grand Rapids: Eerdmans, 2017.

Platzman Weinstock, Cheryl. "More Religious Leaders Challenge Silence, Isolation Surrounding Suicide." NPR. Last modified Feb. 11, 2018. https://www.npr.org/sections/health-shots/2018/02/11/583432455/more-religious-leaders-challenge-silence-isolation-surrounding-suicide.

Pohl, Christine D. *Making Room: Recovering Hospitality as a Christian Tradition*. Grand Rapids: Eerdmans, 1999.

Poland, Scott. *Suicide Intervention in the Schools*. New York: Guilford, 1989.

Pollan, Michael. *How to Change Your Mind: What the New Science of Psychedelics Teaches Us About Consciousness, Dying, Addiction, Depression, and Transcendence*. New York: Penguin, 2018.

Pope Francis, *The Joy of the Gospel. Evangelii Gaudium*. Erlanger, KY: Dynamic Catholic Institute, 2014.

Pope Paul VI. *Constitution on Divine Revelation*. UK: St. Paul, 1965.

Porter, Roy. *Madness: A Brief History*. Oxford: Oxford University Press, 2002.

Powery, Luke. *Dem Dry Bones: Preaching, Death, and Hope.* Minneapolis: Fortress, 2012.

Putnam, Robert D. *Bowling Alone: The Collapse and Revival of American Community.* New York: Simon and Schuster, 2000.

Quinnett, Paul. *QPRT Suicide Risk Assessment and Management.* https://courses.qprinstitute.   com/index.php?option=com_joomla_lms&Itemid=238&task=show_lpath&course_id=24&id=188.

Rahner, Karl. *On the Theology of Death.* London: SCM, 1972.

Ramachandran, V.S. and Sandra Blakeslee. *Phantoms in the Brain: Probing the Mysteries of the Human Mind.* New York: William Morrow, 1998.

Ray of Hope, Mental Health America of Westmoreland County. http://www.rayofhopewestmoreland.org/faqs.html.

Redding, Graham. *Prayer and the Priesthood of Christ in the Reformed Tradition.* New York: T. & T. Clark, 2003.

R.E.M., "It's the End of the World as We Know It (And I Feel Fine)," 1987 album *Document.* https://genius.com/Rem-its-the-end-of-the-world-as-we-know-it-and-i-feel-fine-lyrics.

Reporting on Suicide.org. Last modified 2015. http://reportingonsuicide.org/.

Reynolds, Thomas E. *Vulnerable Communion: A Theology of Disability and Hospitality.* Grand Rapids: Brazos, 2008.

Rieff, David. *Swimming in a Sea of Death: A Son's Memoir.* New York: Simon and Schuster, 2008.

"Risk." In *Merriam-Webster Dictionary.* Last modified May 27, 2018. https://www.merriam-webster.com/dictionary/risk.

Robertson, Jesse E. *The Death of Judas: The Characterization of Judas Iscariot in Three Early Christian Accounts of his Death.* Yorkshire: Sheffield Phoenix, 2012.

Robinson, Paul. "Sermons on the Lord's Prayer and the Rogation Days." In *Brill's Companions to the Christian Tradition: A History of Prayer: The First to the Fifteenth Century,* edited by Roy Hammerling, 441–62. Boston: Brill, 2008.

Rogers, Jack. *Jesus, the Bible and Homosexuality; Explode the Myths, Heal the Church.* Louisville: Westminster John Knox, 2006.

Salters-Pedneault, Kristalyn. *Suicidality in Borderline Personality Disorder: Why It's So Common and How to Help.* Last modified March 15, 2017. https://www.verywell.com/ suicidality-in-borderline-personality-disorder-425485.

Schlafer, David J., *Playing with Fire: Preaching Work as Kindling Art.* Cambridge, MA: Cowley, 2004.

Schneider, Tammi J. *Judges.* Collegeville: Liturgical, 2000.

Seder, Lloyd. "Adverse Childhood Experience." *Psychology Today.* Last modified November 30, 2013. https://www.psychologytoday.com/us/blog/therapy-it-s-more-just-talk/201311/ adverse-childhood-experiences-aces.

Selden, Frank. *The Suicide Solution: Understanding and Dealing with Suicide from Inside the Mind of Someone Who's Been There.* Bloomington, IN: Archway, 2016.

Seligman, Katherine. "Hastening the End." Last modified June 8, 2008. https://www.sfgate.com/ magazine/article/Hastening-the-End-3281002.php.

Sensing, Tim. *Qualitative Researcher: A Multi-Methods Approach to Projects for Doctor of Ministry Theses.* Eugene, Oregon: Wipf and Stock, 2011.

Shaw, Brent D. *Sacred Violence: African Christians and Sectarian Hatred in the Age of Augustine.* Cambridge: Cambridge University Press, 2011.

Shneidman, Edwin. *Definition of Suicide*. New York: John Wiley and Sons, 1985.

————. *The Suicidal Mind*. New York: Brace and World, 1938.

Siegel, Michele, Judith Brisman and Margot Weinshel, *Surviving an Eating Disorder: Strategies for Family and Friends*. 3rd ed. New York: HarperCollins, 2009.

Smith, Charles Ryder. *The Bible Doctrine of Sin and of the Ways of God with Sinners*. London: Epworth, 1953.

Snider, Phil, ed., *Preaching as Resistance: Voices of Hope, Justice, Solidarity*. St. Louis: Chalice, 2018.

Sproul, R. C. *What We Believe: Understanding and Confessing the Apostles' Creed*. Grand Rapids: Baker, 2015.

Stanley, Charles. "Suicide: The Impact on Believers." https://sermons.love/charles-stanley/3916-charles-stanley-suicide-the-impact-on-believers.html.

Staudt, Christina and Marcelline Block, eds. *Unequal Before Death*. Cambridge: Cambridge Scholars, 2012.

Sternberg, Eliezer J. *My Brain Made Me Do It: The Rise of Neuroscience and the Threat to Moral Responsibility*. New York: Prometheus, 2010.

Stetzer, Ed. "The Epidemic of Biblical Illiteracy in Our Churches." The American Bible Society Barna Group. Last modified July 6, 2015. https://AmericanBible.org/uploads/content/state-of-the-Bible-data-analysis-american-Bible-society-2014.pdf.

Stoevesandt, Hinrich. "Barth, Karl." *Concise Encyclopedia of Preaching*, edited by William H. Willimon and Richard Lischer, 26–27. Louisville: Westminster John Knox, 1995.

"Suicidal." In *Merriam-Webster Dictionary*. Last modified May 12, 2018. https://www.merriam-webster.com/dictionary/suicidal.

"Suicide." In *Merriam-Webster Dictionary*. Last modified May 12, 2018. https://www.merriam-webster.com/dictionary/suicide.

Suicide Prevention Online Training "Medical Examiners and Coroners." https://www.sprc.org/ sites/default/files/migrate/library/Medical%20Examiners%20and%20Coroners.pdf.

Suicide Prevention Resource Center. "Suicide by Age." http://www.sprc.org/scope/age.

Suicidology.org, "U.S.A. Suicide: 2015 Official Final Data." http://www.suicidology.org/ Portals/14/docs/Resources/FactSheets/2015/2015datapgsv1.pdf?ver=2017-01-02-220151-870.

Tertullian. "Apology." In *The Writings of Tertullian*. Translated by S. Thelwall. Ante-Nicene Fathers 3, 17–60. New York: Christian Literature, 1890.

Thieda, Kate N. *Loving Someone with Anxiety: Understanding and Helping Your Partner*. Oakland: New Harbinger, 2013.

Thomas, Dylan. *Do Not Go Gentle into That Good Night*, Academy of American Poets. www.Poets.org.

Thomas, Frank A. *Preaching as Celebration. Digital Lecture Series and Workbook*. Rhode Island: Hope for Life International, 2014.

Thompson, Lisa L. *Ingenuity: Preaching as an Outsider*. Nashville: Abingdon, 2018.

Thornton, John F. and Katharine Washburn, eds. *Tongues of Angels, Tongues of Men*. New York: Doubleday, 1999.

Timmer, Daniel. *A Gracious and Compassionate God: Mission, Salvation and Spirituality in the Book of Jonah*. Downers Grove, IL: InterVarsity, 2011.

Tolkien, J. R. R. *The Monsters and the Critics and Other Essays*. London: HarperCollins, 1990.

Tollefson, Lindsey. "Letters." In *Coloradan*, 62. Summer 2019.

Tomkins, Michael A. and Tamara L. Hartl. *Digging Out: Helping Your Loved One Manage Clutter, Hoarding and Compulsive Acquiring*. Oakland: New Harbinger, 2009.

Treat, Casey. *Your Unlimited Life – Praying with Purpose*. https://www.youtube.com/watch?v=077VmGR65Ds.

Tubbs Tisdale, Leonora. *Preaching as Local Theology and Folk Art*. Minneapolis: Fortress, 1997.

"Uniform Determination of Death Act." http://lchc.ucsd.edu/cogn_150/Readings/death_act.pdf.

Vance, Erik. *Suggestible You: The Curious Science of Your Brain's Ability to Deceive, Transform, and Heal*. Washington D.C.: National Geographic, 2016.

Vincie, Catherine. "Liturgy and Preaching." Unpublished lecture, Aquinas Theological Institute, St. Louis, MO, October 4, 2016.

"Volcano Suicides." *Providentia: A Biased Look at Psychology in the World*. July 22, 2016. https://drvitelli.typepad.com/providentia/2016/07/the-volcano-suicide-craze.html.

Walsh, Chad. "Pilgrimage to the Perennial Philosophy: The Case of Aldous Huxley." *Journal of Bible and Religion* 16.1 (1948) 3–12.

Watts, Isaac. "Alas! And Did My Savior Bleed." In *The Presbyterian Hymnal*, no. 78. Louisville: Westminster John Knox, 1990.

Westphal, Merold. *Suspicion and Faith*. New York: Fordham University Press, 1998.

Westminster Shorter Catechism. Assembly at Edinburgh, July 28, 1648. Sess. 19. https://prts. edu/wp-content/uploads/2013/09/Shorter_Catechism.pdf.

"What is Mental Illness?" American Psychiatric Association. Last updated 2018. https://www. psychiatry.org/patients-families/what-is-mental-illness.

White, Carolinne. *Early Christian Lives*. London: Penguin, 1998.

White, James F. *Introduction to Christian Worship*. Nashville: Abingdon, 2000.

Whittle, D. W., ed. *The Wonders of Prayer*. Chicago: Evangelical Literature, 1886.

Wilkie, Brian and James Hurt, eds. *Literature of the Western World: Vol 1, The Ancient World Through the Renaissance*. New York: MacMillan, 1984.

Williams, Paul. "Thankful Heart." The Muppets Christmas Carol, 1992. https://genius.com/The-muppets-thankful-heart-lyrics.

Wilson, Reid. *Accelerator Treatment for Anxiety: Core Concepts*. Psycotherapy.net Streaming Video. http://0-www.psychotherapy.net.library.acaweb.org/stream/leeuniversity/video?vid=289.

Wolterstorff, Nicholas, *Lament for A Son*. Grand Rapids: Eerdmans, 1987.

World Health Organization, "Suicide." http://www.who.int/mediacentre/factsheets/fs398/en/.

Yan, Holly and Rachel Bowman, "A Priest Condemned Suicide While Speaking at a Teen's Funeral. Now a Grieving Mother is Suing Him." CNN. November 20, 2019. https://www.cnn. com/2019/11/20/us/michigan-mom-sues-priest-for-condemning-suicide-at-funeral/index.html.

Yapko, Michael D. *Suggestions of Abuse: True and False Memories of Childhood Sexual Trauma*. New York: Simon and Schuster, 1994.

Ylvisaker, John. "They Can't Kill Me." On the album, *Do Not Cut the Baby in Half*. Moorhead, MN, 1964.

Yoder, John C. *Power and Politics in the Book of Judges: Men and Women of Valor*. Minneapolis: Fortress, 2015.

Zimmer, Carl. *Soul Made Flesh: The Discovery of the Brain and How it Changed the World*. New York: Free, 2004.